All Change
British Railway
Privatisation

All Change British Railway Privatisation

Edited by

Roger Freeman

PricewaterhouseCoopers

Jon Shaw

University of Aberdeen

THE McGRAW-HILL COMPANIES

London · Burr Ridge IL · New York · St Louis · San Francisco · Auckland
Bogotá · Caracas · Lisbon · Madrid · Mexico · Milan · Montreal
New Delhi · Panama · Paris · San Juan · São Paulo
Singapore · Sydney · Tokyo · Toronto

Published by
Mcgraw-Hill Publishing Company
SHOPPENHANGERS ROAD, MAIDENHEAD, BERKSHIRE SL6 2QL, ENGLAND
Telephone +44 (0) 1628 502500
Fax: +44 (0) 1628 770224   Web site: http://www.mcgraw-hill.co.uk

---

British Library Cataloguing in Publication Data
A catalogue record for this book is available from the British Library

ISBN 007 709679 7

Library of Congress Cataloguing-in-Publication Data
The LOC data for this book has been applied for and may be obtained from the
Library of Congress, Washington, D.C.

Publisher	Alfred Waller
Sponsoring Editor	Elizabeth Robinson
Produced by	Steven Gardiner Ltd
Cover by	Simon Levy
Cover photograph by	Milepost $92\frac{1}{2}$

Mcgraw-Hill
A Division of The **Mcgraw·Hill** Companies

1 2 3 4 5 CUP 4 3 2 1 0
Printed and bound in Great Britain at the University Press, Cambridge

Contents

Preface

The main purpose of this book is to set down a record of the reasons for, and what happened during, the privatisation of British Rail (BR) and to publish that record before the freshness of the memories of those most involved begins to fade. I hope it will be an appropriate, permanent contribution. The book also provides an assessment, as at Spring 2000, of rail privatisation and offers some thoughts as to the future of the rail industry. The text is not intended to be definitive but instead seeks to draw out the key events and indicate the circumstances which surrounded them.

The book contains essays from a number of authors on different aspects of the privatisation. Chapters draw upon documentary research and a series of detailed interviews with a wide range of key people – from ministers to railway-industry personnel – who took part in railway privatisation. A few of the quotations presented are anonymous at the request of those interviewed. As far as possible, fact and opinion have been separated so that a record of the events can be identified by the reader who may also appreciate studying the views of those involved as they add texture and depth to an understanding of the process. It is apparent that there are many varying recollections of British railway privatisation – each interviewee described events differently – but the individual authors have constructed what seemed to them the most plausible account.

BR was completely privatised – as over 100 separate businesses – in a manner compliant with European Union Directives within a single parliament between 1992 and 1997. The government, with strong direction from the then Prime Minister, John Major, was determined to fulfil a key manifesto commitment of 1992. Despite a reducing working majority in the House of Commons, the government met the election pledge. The significance of this relatively rapid timescale is considered in the book from a number of perspectives.

The structure of the book is as follows. Sir Christopher Foster (erstwhile adviser to John MacGregor, who was the cabinet minister responsible for rail privatisation during its legislative phase) writes the foreword. Dr Jon Shaw and Clive Charlton (both academics) deal with the history and creation of the new privatised railway. John Edmonds (former Chief Executive of Railtrack) records the setting up of the infrastructure body in the new vertically separated railway up to 1997, and Arthur Leathley (transport correspondent for *The Times*) comments on Railtrack's recent performance. Dr John Prideaux (former Chairman of Angel Train Contracts) discusses the rolling-stock leasing companies. Christian Wolmar (a railway journalist), together with Roger Ford (Editor of *Rail Business Intelligence*), cover the creation of the franchised train-operating companies, and Julia Clarke (former Director of the Rail Freight Group) details the privatisation of the rail freight businesses. John Swift QC (the first Rail Regulator) comments on the role of his Office and, finally, Lord Bradshaw (a member of the Commission for Integrated Transport) outlines his view of the way forward for improving the new railway.

The present government, elected in 1997, has set about reshaping and refining some of the structural features of privatisation, but the basic privatised structure, described in this book, remains unaltered. The government seeks ways of enhancing co-ordination between the disparate parts of the railway, providing additional funds for removing bottlenecks on the infrastructure, considering greater powers for the public sector in controlling both the level and content of the investment programmes and increasing the penalties for slack punctuality and reliability. There is also the commencement of re-franchising, which may offer a lengthening in return for higher investment and improvements in the quality of service. At the time of going to press, a Transport Bill, providing for the creation of a Strategic Rail Authority and other measures, is before Parliament.

There are many acknowledgements due to those who have assisted in the completion of this book. First and foremost, I should like to thank all the authors and my colleagues on the editorial team, particularly Jon Shaw, who has been responsible for some of the detailed research and indeed is one of the main contributors to the text. David Campbell Bannerman's input has been very helpful, especially through his initial work with the Association of Train Operating Companies, which provided support for the project. Greg Selkirk, Peter Smith, Robert Pettigrew, Jonathan Stevens and Steve Bennett have also been of invaluable assistance.

This book does not seek to represent the views of the various Secretaries of State for Transport who had responsibility for developing and implementing rail privatisation policy. The book is a collection of chapters written by a number of authors whose views are their own.

The editorial team owes a sincere debt of gratitude to PricewaterhouseCoopers for supporting the publication of this book.

Outstanding secretarial support has come from Miranda Aldeburgh, Kate Hopewell and Sally Bishop; Gerard Farrelly and Terry Armsby of PricewaterhouseCoopers have expertly provided the artwork. Finally, the project could not have been undertaken without the co-operation of the many interviewees who have generously given their time and expertise to the authors over the past year. I thank them all.

Responsibility for the contents of, and arguments advanced within, each individual chapter rests with its author(s). The editors have sought to ensure consistency of style and clarity of expression but the reader's judgement of the entire text will inevitably rest upon a tapestry of different contributions. The final verdict on the value of rail privatisation should, in all fairness, await the fuller benefits of substantially increased private-sector investment to service the 25 per cent increase in passengers and freight since 1997. I firmly believe that the quality and quantity of rail services will continue to improve and that this verdict will be positive.

Roger Freeman
London, March 2000

Foreword

Railway privatisation was the last, but far from the least important or interesting, of the major privatisations in Britain. The essays in this volume reflect on its many aspects and are written from many standpoints across the industry. Like every other privatisation of a complicated industry, it was impossible to plan or predict in advance exactly how it would develop, just as no one could have forecast in advance how slowly mainstream competition would develop in telecommunications or that it would develop as fast as it did in gas. Or that property would provide such a handsome dowry to the National Freight Company or the use of its grid for telecommunications purposes to the National Grid. Or that except in water, costs and therefore prices would fall as fast as they did. Similarly, since trends in rail traffic had declined from the mid-1950s, no one foresaw, or could have been expected to foresee, the degree of increase in rail traffic since privatisation which nevertheless has led to over-crowded trains, posed problems for reliability and has necessitated a huge increase in planned investment as well as being an extra challenge for the railway regulators.

My own role in this was as an adviser to John MacGregor from when he became Secretary of State for Transport in 1992 until 1994. As it seemed to ministers, the need for change was as great on the railways as it had been for the other nationalised industries. Like them, it suffered from poor standards of service, consumer relations and image, being widely regarded as dear, often dirty, overcrowded and unreliable. Like British Telecommunications, the British Airports Authority, electricity and water it required massive investment, in this case to replace old rolling stock and restore an ancient, decayed infrastructure which had been undermaintained for decades; but the Treasury was not prepared to find the billions of public funds needed by these industries, given their adverse effect on the economy through the public-sector borrowing requirement.

A fundamental transformation of the railways was needed if they were to realise their potential as well as to help relieve congestion and pollution on the roads. Hence there was another fundamental reason for privatisation, even if public funds had been abundant. It had proved impossible for many years to motivate public monopolies to improve their efficiency.[1] Again like BT and the other large public monopolies, British Rail had no incentive to know the costs of its different services or the cost of expanding and contracting them as a commercial business would have been forced by competition to know such incremental costs. For example, the 1968 Transport Act was based on the belief that rail passenger and freight traffic should be encouraged where relief of road congestion and other social benefits justified maintaining or even improving rail services. But within a few weeks of the passing of that act, British Rail told the Ministry of Transport that it was an accounting impossibility to produce such information. The Ministry could do nothing to counter that refusal. Given the power which those public monopolies had then and their lack of motivation to understand their costs in detail, only privatisation, introducing the pressures of competition and economic regulation, could change their intransigence. Already since privatisation, cost analysis is developing to the point where what was once held impossible is on its way to becoming normal business practice within the railways, though there is still further to go. This outcome makes it easier to justify rail development as an important instrument of an integrated transport policy.

While the details of privatisation were being finalised in 1992, there were already three reasons for believing costs would be identified and fall. Every other privatisation had shown the incentive it gives to reduce costs and pass them on in falling prices – of course, rail efficiencies are currently passed on to HM Treasury through subsidy levels falling rather than wholly to consumers, an important difference from unsubsidised, but regulated, industries – though there was another forerunner, water, which suggested another possibility: that the additional cost of investment will be great enough to keep costs and prices up for a time for more social and environmental enhancement. Secondly, even as long ago as 1993 many ideas were already coming forward on how railway working practices could be improved. Again like the other industries, the railways had inherited old established working practices, which raise costs and needed to be got rid of so employees could enable the railways to fulfil its true potential. Thirdly, the structure of the industry which was adopted was designed to reduce costs and improve quality through incentivising the various parties to do so. Moreover, in a wide range of applications, from the scheduling of maintenance, registering the condition of assets and investigating the causes of unreliability, to timetabling and the scheduling of staff, computers can and are being used to transform working arrangements and yield greater efficiency.

While the case for rail privatisation had from the beginning been as strong as for the others, there were understandable reasons why the then government delayed it until after the rest. With all its shortcomings there had always been strong public support and affection for the railways. Attempts to rationalise them, as by Dr Beeching, had proved the graveyard of reputations. Ministers knew they cut services at their peril. Mostly because of this, the railways were heavily

---

[1] The best evidence is in R. Pryke, *Public Enterprise in Practice*, McGibbon and Kee, 1971; and *The Nationalised Industries: Policies and Performance Since 1968*, Martin Rotherham, 1980. In the first he noted the improvement in efficiency after nationalisation. The second found the impetus had mainly petered out.

subsidised as the other nationalised industries were not. Privatising an industry which would continue to need large subsidies itself raised major problems. Given the long-lasting resistance to any railway closures, ministers felt it right to maintain the existing railway system not merely in terms of the routes to be kept open but more exactly in terms of the timetables of the services to be run on them. The criteria for timetable changes needed to be stringent ones: they must leave users better off than before. Moreover, the early privatisations had shown the supreme importance of introducing as much competition as possible while privatising. As Jon Shaw points out in Chapter 1 of this book, before 1992 there had been several Secretaries of State in succession and lengthy debate over the options for rail privatisation which were, however, more at the level of ideas than of practical proposals before John MacGregor, ideas which had not been fully thought through and had only been agreed by being kept at the level of generality. Because the structure of the industry was very complicated, the need was for a new structure which would strike a balance between maximising competition and practicality.

Before a bill could be drafted MacGregor had several fundamental decisions to make. One was to confirm there would be vertical separation between the train-operating companies and the track. This issue was often discussed as if operators could only feel secure if they control the track and that to do so it must belong to them. But that was too simple a conclusion. Most businesses do not try to own their own suppliers' intermediate processes or retail outlets. Modern methods of communication and management mean ever more firms demerge or outsource as many activities as they can. By contrast, the old command and control relationships on the railways had been long established, largely unanalysed, bureaucratic, inefficient and often relied on masses of paper which were seldom read. Instead it was decided the time had come for train-operating companies to contract for the use of track of a stated reliability and capacity at stated times with, as far as possible, well defined responsibilities for achieving that reliability, for dealing with emergencies and with predetermined access charges, as well as, most important of all, improving rail safety. The second fundamental decision was that while there should be a number of train companies, there should only be one infrastructure provider, Railtrack. The argument for this would not have been as strong in countries whose railway systems are in clearly separated geographical regions, but in Britain, with its high-density network of often overlapping routes, however one drew regional boundaries there would be many cases where passenger and freight trains crossed boundaries, causing operational problems if the infrastructure were under separate regional control but without increasing competition since such regions would remain local monopolies and would still have to be regulated.

The third strategic decision John MacGregor had to make was on the extent of competition. There were many ways in which it seemed straightforward to secure the benefits of competition by setting up a number of rolling-stock companies, train-operating companies and maintenance companies; but as Shaw shows there had been strong support for so-called open-access competition by which different train companies were to be allowed to compete with each other throughout the network. For the reasons which Shaw discusses, John MacGregor agreed early on this solution would not work because of the density of the network and the fullness and complexity of the timetable, though there were political reasons why this could not be announced for some time. Instead it was decided to rely here on competitive franchising to achieve a measure of competition.

Another important decision MacGregor had to make was how to distinguish between the roles of OPRAF and ORR. The principle was clear. OPRAF was the guardian of public money put into the rail system through subsidies. As such it awarded and monitored franchises. To ensure value for public money it had to specify at least a minimum level, quantity and quality of service to be provided, the contribution the fare-box would make to the financing of these services and any investment in or for them to be made by the franchisees and Railtrack. ORR was to regulate Railtrack's natural monopoly in the interests of those who used it and supplied it as well as to ensure that the operations of the whole system were as competitive as possible, which included ensuring the structure of fares was not discriminatory or predatory. But, as Chapters 6 and 9 indicate, the detail of making this distinction was full of problems.

Thereafter the need was to hammer out workable proposals and then agreements for every aspect of these changes, which required heroic efforts from all concerned throughout the railways, in the Department of Transport, and among the various advisers. To get difficult issues resolved within the timetable inevitably meant there were compromises and a few misjudgements, but the structure chosen is standing the test of time and allowing the development of the railways as a safe and more reliable form of transport in the face of unexpected growth in demand for it. Already there have been improvements in reliability though they levelled off for a time after the initial improvements. Fares have fallen in real terms. While the growth of traffic on some routes has led to more overcrowded trains, there are more trains on the timetable. Freight traffic has also grown, though it levelled off during 1999, while passenger traffic went on growing. More new trains are being ordered though not enough to replace all the old stock. Investment in infrastructure has more than doubled. The backlog of investment which had not been made in the past has been found to be far greater even than was previously supposed. The unexpected growth of traffic already referred to both created capacity problems on many routes and taxed the railway system with the problem of joint investment planning to overcome bottlenecks.

Both the last and this government have attached a high priority to increasing the capacity of the rail system to siphon traffic off the roads. Aside from improving reliability, raising service quality and increasing the frequency of trains where there is capacity, the main policy issue for the immediate future is to decide how most effectively capacity bottlenecks on the system can be relieved and where this can be done at a price which the nation is prepared to pay. It would not have been possible to achieve these objectives without the incentive for change, the clearer focus, the greater efficiency, and the ability to commit adequate resources for investment which the privatisation programme has made possible. The European Union's drive to achieve interconnection between European railways is forcing them to think about the contractual and performance arrangements needed.

Lessons are being drawn from UK experience. Already other overseas railways have analysed our experience and learned from it while, of course, allowing for the fact that every railway's circumstances are different.

This book is a timely and very welcome contribution to our understanding of the development and initial outcomes of British railway privatisation policy.

Sir Christopher Foster

Notes on Contributors

Bill Bradshaw joined BR in 1959 and went on to hold numerous senior posts including Chief Operations Manager, Director of the Policy Unit and General Manager of the Western Region. After leaving the railway industry in 1985, he became a Professor of Transport Management at Salford University, the Chairman of Ulsterbus and was elected a Fellow of Wolfson College, Oxford. Lord Bradshaw was a specialist adviser to the Transport Select Committee of the House of Commons throughout the process of rail privatisation and recently became a member of the Commission for Integrated Transport and the Shadow Strategic Rail Authority. He became a Working Peer in 1999. He has written extensively about rail and bus transport and has contributed frequently to broadcasts on these subjects.

Clive Charlton is a senior lecturer in the Department of Geographical Sciences at the University of Plymouth. His teaching and research interests include transport policy and practice, rural tourism and development, and environmental management issues in Spain and Latin America. He has published many articles about rail issues and is closely involved with the Devon and Cornwall Rail Partnership, which seeks to promote and develop the railway branch lines of the two counties on behalf of the rail operators and local authorities.

Julia Clarke is the Director of Freight at the Shadow Strategic Rail Authority. She was formerly an official at the Department of Transport, before establishing her own consultancy dealing with rail freight issues. She published the first Rail Freight Handbook in 1990. Julia has been a member of the National Transport Forum for Scotland and the Chartered Institute of Transport's Rail Working Group and was recently elected a fellow of the Institute of Logistics and Transport. She was a non-executive director of English, Welsh and Scottish Railway until 1997 and Director of the Rail Freight Group, a lobbying organisation, until July 1999.

John Edmonds, a career railwayman, joined the then British Transport Commission in 1960 and subsequently held senior positions in all the railway businesses. He was Director of Provincial Services from 1984–88 during the period when the rolling-stock was renewed and the services revamped. After setting up the new Anglia Region as General Manager, he became a full-time member of the British Railways Board in 1989. He was appointed Chief Executive of Railtrack in 1993 and retired in 1997.

Roger Ford trained as an engineer with English Electric and on qualification joined the company's railway division. In 1976 he became a full-time writer specialising in railways and, since then, has been contributing editor of the monthly trade and technical magazine *Modern Railways*. In March 1995 he became the founder editor of the subscription newsletter *Rail Privatisation News*, originally created to provide the rail industry with inside information about the BR sell-off but now renamed *Rail Business Intelligence* to reflect its post-privatisation coverage. His experience in the commercial and technical aspects of the railways has been tapped by a number of organisations, and consultancy clients during privatisation included OPRAF, international leasing groups and City finance houses.

Sir Christopher Foster was a partner in Coopers & Lybrand from 1978 to 1986 and again from 1988 to 1994, becoming a member of its Board. He first became interested in railway economics as an Oxford academic. He discussed railway pricing and investment problems and how rail might be co-ordinated with other modes of transport in his book, *The Transport Problem* (1963). As Barbara Castle's chief economist and special adviser he was deeply involved in the new deal for railways provided for in the 1968 Transport Act. During the 1980s he was engaged successively in the privatisation of BAA, BT (on whose management board he was a Commercial Adviser from 1986 to 1988) and electricity supply. He wrote *Privatisation, Public Ownership and the Regulation of Natural Monopoly* (1992), during which he explained his disillusionment with nationalisation as a way of running the railway which would serve rail-users well and discharge its social responsibilities efficiently. He became John MacGregor's non-political special adviser on rail privitisation in the same year. He was a non-executive member of the board of Railtrack from 1994–2000.

Roger Freeman was a partner and managing director of Lehman Brothers investment bank until 1986, and was the Member of Parliament for Kettering from 1983 to 1997. During his time as an MP, he held a number of ministerial positions within the Conservative governments of Margaret Thatcher and John Major, including Cabinet Minister for Public Service and Chancellor of the Duchy of Lancaster. As Minister of State for Public Transport between 1990 and 1994, he was heavily involved in formulating and implementing the policy of rail privatisation. Granted a life peerage in 1997, Lord Freeman is now a consultant for PricewaterhouseCoopers and Chairman of Thomson (UK) Holdings Ltd.

Arthur Leathley has been transport correspondent for *The Times* since 1997, covering in detail the developments in the privatised railway industry. Before that, he worked for 5 years as political correspondent for the same newspaper, during which time he reported on the passage of the Railways Bill through parliament. He has worked for national newspapers for 12 years, previously specialising as a freelance medical journalist.

John Prideaux joined BR as an operational research specialist in 1965. He was Director of InterCity between 1986 and 1991, during which time patronage increased and profitability was achieved. He subsequently became managing director of New Ventures for BR and oversaw its role in setting up the Heathrow Express and Channel Tunnel rail-link projects. Dr Prideaux has also served on research committees associated with transport in the UK and, after leaving BR, has advised the government on numerous transport projects. He was the first chairman of Angel Train Contracts, one of the three rolling-stock companies in Britain's privatised railway industry. He remains a director of Angel and has recently become chairman of the Manchester Metrolink light-rail system.

Jon Shaw is a Lecturer in Human Geography at the University of Aberdeen and secretary of the Transport Geography Research Group of the Royal Geographical Society (with the Institute of British Geographers). His recent work has examined the evolution and initial outcomes of the policy used by the Major administration to privatise and liberalise the British railway industry. Dr Shaw has published numerous articles about rail privatisation and often contributes to broadcasts dealing with railway issues. He is currently undertaking further transport-related research, placing particular emphasis on the effects of 'on-rail' competition and the impact of rail privatisation on socially disadvantaged groups in rural areas.

John Swift was appointed Rail Regulator in December 1993, following an 11-year period as a QC specialising in competition law and utility regulation. As the first Rail Regulator, he played an important role in establishing the ORR and devising the legal and administrative frameworks used to police the privatised railway industry. He also took many important decisions affecting future development of the rail network, including changing Railtrack's licence to increase its public accountability and approving the upgrade of the West Coast Main Line. On the expiry of his 5-year term in 1998, he returned to full-time practice at the Bar as Head of Monckton Chambers of Grays Inn.

Christian Wolmar has been a journalist for 25 years and has written extensively about transport issues since 1992, when he became transport correspondent for *The Independent*. His previous books include *The Great British Railway Disaster*, a humorous critique of rail privatisation and *Stagecoach: A Classic Rags to Riches Tale from the Frontiers of Capitalism*. He is currently a freelance writer for a wide variety of publications including the London *Evening Standard*, the *Daily Express*, *The Independent* and the *New Statesman*. Since 1995, he has also written a fortnightly column on railway policy for *Rail* magazine.

List of Abbreviations

ASI	Adam Smith Institute
ATOC	Association of Train Operating Companies
BNFL	British Nuclear Fuels Limited
BNOC	British National Oil Corporation
BP	British Petroleum
BR	British Rail
BRB	British Railways Board
BRIS	British Rail Infrastructure Services
BRIL	British Rail Investments Limited
BRML	British Rail Maintenance Limited
BT	British Telecom
CEGB	Central Electricity Generating Board
CI	Compulsory Interavailability
CPS	Centre for Policy Studies
CRD	Conservative Research Department
CRUCC	Central Rail Users' Consultative Committee
DETR	Department of the Environment, Transport and the Regions
DoT	Department of Transport
DRS	Direct Rail Services
DTI	Department of Trade and Industry
EWS	English, Welsh and Scottish Railway
GNER	Great North Eastern Railways
GWH	Great Western Holding
HMRI	Her Majesty's Rail Inspectorate
HSE	Health and Safety Executive
ICCR	Inter Capital and Regional Railways
ITT	Invitation to Tender
LCR	London and Continental Railways
LT	London Transport
LTS	London, Tilbury and Southend Rail
MBO	Management Buy-Out
MMC	Monopolies and Mergers Commission
MP	Member of Parliament

NAO	National Audit Office
NBC	National Bus Company
NEG	National Express Group
NFC	National Freight Corporation
NMS	Network Management Statement
No. 10	10 Downing Street
NRES	National Rail Enquiry Service
O for Q	Organising for Quality
OIG	Objectives, Instructions and Guidance
OPRAF	Office of Passenger Rail Franchising
ORCATS	Operational Research Allocation of Tickets to Services
ORR	Office of the Rail Regulator
PIP	Punctuality Incentive Payment
PIXC	Passengers in Excess of Capacity
PLC	Public Limited Company
PRIO	Passenger Rail Industry Overview
PSBR	Public Sector Borrowing Requirement
PSO	Public Service Obligation
PSR	Passenger Service Requirement
PTA	Passenger Transport Authority
PTE	Passenger Transport Executive
PUG	Passenger Upgrade
QC	Queen's Counsel
Rosco	Rolling Stock Company
RPI	Retail Price Index
RSG	Revenue Support Grant
RUCC	Rail Users' Consultative Committee
SNCF	Société Nationale de Chemins de Fer Françaises
SNCB	Société Nationale de Chemins de Fer Belges
SOR	Save Our Railways
SR	Southern Region
SRA	Strategic Rail Authority
SSRA	Shadow Strategic Rail Authority
SWT	South West Trains
TERFF	Trans European Rail Freight Freeway
TLF	Train Load Freight
TOC	Train Operating Company
TOPS	Total Operations Processing System
TOU	Train Operating Unit
UK	United Kingdom

1. Designing a Method of Rail Privatisation

Jon Shaw

The privatisation of British Rail (BR) was the last in a series of high-profile industry sell-offs undertaken by the Thatcher and Major administrations between 1979 and 1997. According to the Conservatives, the principal motive for selling BR was the same as it had been for previous privatisations: to harness the "management skills, flair and entrepreneurial spirit of the private sector to provide better services for the public."[1] But privatising the railways would be much more complex than earlier sell-offs. Although BR ran one of the most efficient railways in western Europe, most of its passenger operations still made heavy losses. Many of BR's routes, although unprofitable, were seen as socially and politically neces- sary and any method of sale would need to maintain pre-privatisation service levels and therefore incorporate a means of providing private-sector rail operators with continuing subsidies from the state. Experience from other sell-offs had also taught ministers that merely converting public monopolies into private ones was not satisfactory and that the promotion of service competition would be important if all the potential benefits of privatisation were to be realised. Furthermore, those in government – particularly Margaret Thatcher – were aware of a peculiar attachment the British people felt towards their railways and that any policy designed to tamper with the structure of BR would most likely be met with stubborn consumer resistance.

In the event, however, it was decided that continuing as before could not be an option. Although BR had restructured itself during the 1980s and produced significant improvements in its performance, the government became convinced that further reorganisation would be necessary before the railways could be privatised. In July 1992 the White Paper *New Opportunities for the Railways* heralded the official beginning of the privatisation process and committed the government to radically changing the structure of the rail industry. As Chapter 2 will show, the method of privatisation eventually adopted, the "track authority" model, would resolve the subsidy question by franchising passenger rail services and would seek to promote competition by splitting BR into almost 100 com- panies to create an internal market. The public was assured that although BR was about to be dissolved, this was necessary in order to "see better use made of the railways, greater responsiveness to the customer, and a higher quality service and better value for money for the public who travel by rail."

The aim of this chapter is to trace the evolution of rail privatisation policy in Britain. It reviews the various models of rail privatisation which were considered, the attitudes of ministers towards them and the circumstances in which the track authority model was finally selected. Before the chapter turns specifically to the rail sell-off, it briefly examines the concept of privatisation in general in order to place its later discussion – and the rest of this book – into context.

The Conservatives and Privatisation

The privatisation programme undertaken by the 1979–97 Conservative governments was very extensive. During the Thatcher and Major administrations, two-thirds of Britain's state industrial sector – some 50 major businesses – were sold, raising over £65 billion; around one million jobs were transferred from the public to the private sector; and almost one in four adults, compared with one in ten in 1979, had become shareholders as a result of privatisations. As Oliver Letwin, an adviser to former Prime Minister Margaret Thatcher, points out, privatisation became a successful British export in the sense that it has been adopted by governments of both the left and the right all around the globe.[2] It is easy in retrospect to view the privatisation programme in Britain as an inevitability, the corollary of a political shift to the right after years of post-war welfare-state consensus. Yet in the sense of a sustained programme of divestitures, privatisation came to Thatcher as an afterthought and there was no statement of a coherent policy on the subject until John Moore sketched one out in 1983.[3] So how *did* the privatisation programme come about? How did it develop? Why was it seen as being necessary in the first place? And what exactly *is* it?

Privatisation is the transfer of at least part of the operations of a state-owned enterprise to private control. It can be accomplished in numerous different ways, although the three most practised in Britain have been: *denationalisation*, which involves the direct sale of public assets; *contracting out*, where the production of state-financed goods and services is franchised to private firms, usually for a finite period; and *liberalisation*, which requires the abolition of statutory monopoly to promote competition in markets previously characterised by restricted entry. Each of these policy strands can be pursued separately – for example, the denationalisation of British Telecom (BT) in 1984, the contracting out of municipal services throughout the 1980s and the liberalisation of long-distance coach services in 1980 – or all together, as was the case in the sale of BR.

Support within the Conservative Party for an extensive programme of privatisation began to crystallise in the late 1960s, although it was concentrated initially around a small group of free-marketeers on the right of the Party. Keith Joseph in particular became obsessed with the "ratchet effect" of British politics – that is, he believed the influence and power of the state was continuously increasing because new Conservative governments were unwilling to reverse nationalisations undertaken by previous Labour ones. In 1968, a confidential report by the Conservative Research Department's (CRD's) Policy Group on Nationalised

Industries, chaired by Nicholas Ridley, explicitly objected to public-sector corporations and went on to suggest a policy of sustained privatisation:

> *we have listed a number of small concerns which should be denationalised – £60 million worth – and these should be tackled at once. Steel, the airlines and road haulage represent £900 million worth of assets. We believe it is possible to sell them back ... [but denationalisation] should be a continuing process of which our proposals are only the first stage.*

The official Conservative Party position on privatisation in the late 1960s and early 1970s was not swayed by the free marketeers. Although occasional sales of state assets – such as the Thomas Cook Travel Agency – took place, the Heath administration remained opposed to large-scale divestiture.

A noticeable shift in the Party's stance did not occur until after the election of Margaret Thatcher as leader in 1975. Thatcher had a wish to roll back the borders of the public sector, and she allowed fellow right-wingers to portray publicly the nationalised industries as "lame duck" concerns, "part of the soft morass of subsidised incompetence".[4] The Party leader and her "New Right" colleagues argued that because the nationalised industries were not subject to market forces, they were necessarily complacent, inefficient and offered poor standards of service. Moreover, it was claimed that they were run for the benefit of politicians and bureaucrats rather than consumers, with many of the state's profitable corporations being required to forego important capital-investment programmes because their cash surpluses were siphoned off to help fulfil the government's macroeconomic objectives. Conservative Party literature began to emphasise the need for more privatisation in order to foster a competitive free market and to remove as far as possible government involvement in industry. Norman Fowler's statement of transport policy, *The Right Track*, is a case in point:

> *Conservatives reject the idea that transport ought to be regarded primarily as a social service to which the taxpayer must be forced to contribute huge and continuing subsidies in order to secure social and political objectives selected by government ... The best way to ensure the public interest is to promote free competition between the providers and free choice between the users.*[5]

Despite the rhetoric in opposition, the Conservative Party's 1979 election manifesto was circumspect regarding privatisation. Indeed, the word did not even appear, and pledges were made only to sell shares in the National Freight Corporation (NFC), to relax bus-licensing controls and to reconsider the ownership of British Aerospace, British Shipbuilders and the British National Oil Corporation (BNOC). The Queen's speech of 1979 was equally vague, outlining only "proposals [to] reduce the extent of nationalised and state ownership and increase competition."[6] Two key reasons seem to explain why the manifesto did not reflect the Conservative Right's enthusiasm for privatisation. First, the concept was opposed by many, including public-sector industry, Conservative backbenchers and especially some quarters of the civil service, who regarded large-scale privatisation as dangerously radical. Thatcher, despite her often belligerent outward appearance, was politically cautious and was concerned that the concept – at this stage unfamiliar to the electorate – could lose her the election before it even took place. Geoffrey Howe, Chancellor of the Exchequer in Thatcher's first government, has recalled that Thatcher "had been fearful that a more extensive catalogue might frighten the floating voter."[7] Secondly, the Conservatives had not actually formulated privatisation policy in any great detail during their time in opposition. Although the Party's right wing had embraced the concept of privatisation because of their ideological beliefs, a blueprint regarding how it could actually be executed in practice had not been produced. Letwin admitted in 1988 that although:

> we had a fundamental distrust in the state running things ... we had no coherent policy. It was not the case that we knew that privatisation would bring in millions of new shareholders. It was not the case that we knew all these shareholders would benefit from premiums. It was not the case that we knew companies would do better in the private sector. Almost nothing that has happened since was known in advance.[8]

Thus the privatisation programme developed slowly during Thatcher's first term in office. Even after her election victory, the Prime Minister would not risk embarking upon a major programme of sales because "she didn't want to stir up the lobbies in the public sector. She felt we could come to that in a few years' time."[9] As a result, the first industries to be privatised were the most convenient and least controversial to dispose of – such as those which had only recently been nationalised – rather than the most strategically important. Five per cent of British Petroleum was sold, which reduced the government's share to 46 per cent and thereby officially returned the company to the private sector, and before the 1983 general election a further nine firms were privatised by asset transfer to the private sector (see Table 1.1). These sales were complemented by the "Right to Buy" scheme, which entitled sitting tenants to purchase their council houses at a discounted rate, and the contracting out of local authority services such as street cleaning and refuse collection.

The cautious flow of divestitures during the first term of the Thatcher administration was generally successful in terms of policy outcome. Upon leaving the public sector, most of the privatised companies became more competitive and achieved efficiency gains – the NFC, for example, increased its profitability sevenfold. The Conservative Right was provided with some empirical justification for its previously theoretical assertions and a considerable number of former sceptics were converted to the privatisation cause. Yet although this precedent was necessary in preparing for the ambitious programme of asset disposal which was shortly to begin, it was certainly not sufficient. Prominent authors now argue that the Conservatives were driven into large-scale privatisation not just by ideology, but also by fiscal necessity.[10]

During her first term in office, Thatcher had learnt that privatisation could help restore some order to public finances. The Conservatives had committed

Table 1.1 Companies privatised by asset transfer during the first Thatcher administration. Source: Bishop, M. and Kay, J. *Does Privatisation Work?* London Business School, 1988.

Date	Company sold	Proceeds (£m)
November 1979	BP	290
June 1980	Fairey Engineering	22
June 1980	Ferranti	54
February 1981	British Aerospace	149
November 1981	Cable & Wireless	224
February 1982	Amersham International	63
February 1982	National Freight Consortium	7
February 1983	Associated British Ports	22
March 1983	International Aeradio	60
March 1983	British Rail Hotels	45

themselves to reducing the Public Sector Borrowing Requirement (PSBR) in their 1979 election manifesto but, partly because of pledges to increase spending on defence and health, and partly because of rising unemployment, they found themselves unable to curtail public expenditure. It was quickly realised that sales proceeds from privatisations could offset reductions in public expenditure as a means of cutting public borrowing. As Geoffrey Howe has since admitted, "the sensible disposal of public-sector assets had grown in urgency [by the early 1980s], not least as a short-term way of helping reduce the PSBR."[11] Added to this were the investment requirements of some of the nationalised industries. BT, for example, needed vast sums to modernise its network in the face of increasing demand, but the government could not fund this without it severely affecting the PSBR.[12] Ministers and officials increasingly accepted that the most pragmatic way around this problem was to sell off BT and let the private sector find the investment capital. Although commentators such as Samuel Brittan argued that it was ludicrous to suggest major industrial decisions such as whether to dena-tionalise BT were being taken to massage public finances – and of course ministers echoed this sentiment in public at the time – in reality it was politically easier to sell public assets than to raise taxes or make real-terms cuts in public expenditure.

BT was sold in 1984 and was quickly followed by a host of other companies in a variety of industrial sectors. The gas and water utility companies were privatised in 1986 and 1989 respectively and in the transport sector the government disposed of the National Bus Company, British Airways, the British Airports Authority and the Scottish Bus Company. In addition to being financially ben-eficial (see Figure 1.1), the large-scale privatisation programme was also found, at least initially, to be politically useful as it promoted "popular capitalism", widen-ing share ownership and increasing the chances of new investors voting Conservative.[13] Such public enthusiasm for privatisation was relatively short-lived, however, as people's perception of the policy began to change in the late

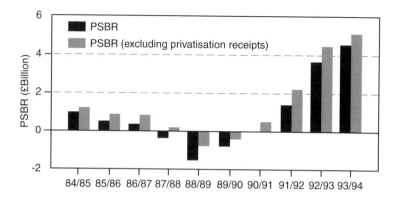

Figure 1.1   PSBR 1984/85–1993/94, showing the effect of privatisation revenue.
Source: Central Statistical Office. *Financial Statistics, 368, 395,*
HMSO, 1992, 1995.

1980s. As the scope of privatisation policy had broadened, so attention naturally began to focus more critically on its outcomes. While *generally* favourable in terms of productivity, some ministers and officials became increasingly concerned about the variable standards of efficiency and service quality of the privatised companies, especially where they continued to trade as monopolies (indeed, some public-sector monopolies, particularly the Post Office, were achieving greater efficiency gains than private ones).[14]

Anecdotal and, later, survey evidence suggested that the performance of the utilities in particular had disappointed the public. To some, this was no surprise: academics and a few within government had warned Thatcher before BT was sold that there was not necessarily a direct cause-and-effect relationship between ownership and performance. They argued that what mattered was competition – and a key reason for the success of early privatisations (such as that of the NFC) was that they had sold companies into an already-competitive market place.[15] Thatcher had defended her decision to sell BT as a monopoly on the grounds that splitting it up to produce an internal market would have taken too long and alienated the company's management. She argued that the support of high-level managers for privatisation was important if the policy were to proceed successfully – their co-operation was needed in order to prepare the business for sale – and BT's directors were known to be hostile towards a break-up. It is easy to forget how radical the privatisation of BT was at the time and, in this sense, Thatcher's wish to simplify as far as possible its transfer into the private sector is understandable. On the other hand, however, a cynic might suggest, as did *The Economist*, that BT and the gas and water companies were sold as monopolies primarily because they would fetch a higher sale price – and thus impact more positively upon the PSBR – than a host of competing companies.[16]

A notable reorientation of government policy became apparent when the Conservatives came to sell the electricity industry. The then Energy Secretary, Cecil Parkinson, was by now convinced that a lack of competition was primarily

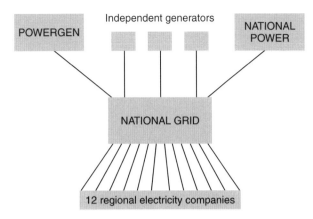

Figure 1.2   The structure of the electricity industry following privatisation.

responsible for the utilities' poor standards of performance. Seeking to align the outcomes of utility privatisation policy with the rhetoric of his Party's right wing during the 1970s, he declared that the government should "never again do a BT", and transfer a state monopoly into private hands. Perhaps to his surprise, Parkinson found he enjoyed Thatcher's support. In contrast to her stance on BT, she now insisted that whatever structure was adopted for electricity privatisation should promote genuine competition – although it is possible that her change of heart came about because any financial imperative behind previous monopoly sales had disappeared by the late 1980s. The economic "boom" at that time had improved the government's finances such that the Treasury now believed "the objective of reducing public expenditure ... [can] be achieved without bringing privatisation receipts into the reckoning."[17] As long as the economy was strong, Thatcher knew that the government could afford to experiment with restructuring state-owned monopolies before it privatised them.

The economy had in fact fallen back into recession by the time the Conservatives finally privatised the electricity industry, but by this time it had already been restructured and was sold accordingly. The industry was separated vertically into three component parts – generation, the national grid and supply (see Figure 1.2). The Central Electricity Generating Board (CEGB) was further split to allow competition among generating companies and entry into this market was liberalised following privatisation. By 1993, 14 licences had been issued to electricity producers and efficiency in the generating sector had improved significantly. Competition among suppliers was delayed as it was technically difficult at the time and the National Grid was recognised as being a natural monopoly and was therefore not broken up any further.[18] Following the sale of the electricity industry, the Conservatives began to liberalise the markets of the other utilities where possible and entry restrictions on the telecommunications, gas and electricity supply markets were lifted during the 1990s. A considerable drop in prices to the consumer occurred in all three as a result of efficiency gains which ensued. Principally as a result of these benefits, the Conservatives would no longer be content to transfer monopolies into the private sector: despite the recession, the promotion of competition was finally to become established as an explicit dimension of utility privatisation policy. The government's plans for the BR sell-off essentially represented further experimentation with those adopted for the sale of the electricity industry and it is against this background that the remainder of this chapter explains how the decision to adopt the track-authority model of rail privatisation came about.

Privatising British Rail

Debate within the Conservative Party regarding the privatisation of BR can be traced back to the late 1960s. The CRD's Committee on Nationalised Industries, which had identified the need to begin a sustained programme of privatisation, considered divesting BR's core activities but concluded that denationalisation would be inappropriate because "there would be no takers at the price which would be acceptable to us." Following the election of Thatcher as Party leader, support for the liberalisation of BR's market began to materialise among the Conservative Right. The Young Conservatives' *Key Policy Statement* in 1976 called for the rail industry to be liberalised by allowing private operators onto the network to compete with BR. As we have already seen, the shadow transport spokesman emphasised his support for market, rather than state, determination of transport provision.

Considering Thatcher's cautious outlook towards privatisation in the early 1980s, plans to attract private-sector capital into the railway industry materialised remarkably quickly. A likely reason for this is that both the new Minister of State for Transport, Norman Fowler, and the British Railways Board (BRB) favoured private investment in BR's subsidiary concerns. Proposals to achieve this were developed during 1980 and the result was the creation of a new holding company, British Rail Investments Ltd (BRIL), as a wholly owned subsidiary of the BRB. The assets of Sealink UK, British Transport Hotels, British Rail Hovercraft (Seaspeed) and British Rail Property Holdings were transferred to BRIL in order that private sector involvement could be administered separately from BR's core activities (Figure 1.3). The BRB saw its new subsidiary as a means of expanding the total level of investment in the existing businesses on top of government grants. *Modern Railways* magazine noted at the time that:

> for BR, the benefit of privatisation is seen as being twofold: in addition to receiving the proceeds of sales, BR will also face reduced calls on the finance available within its investment ceiling as the investment requirements of the subsidiaries in the holding company will be met in part from the private sector.[19]

The government's primary motivation for establishing BRIL was soon revealed to be different to that of BR. When ministers realised that revenue from asset sales could be used in order to reduce the PSBR, they gave priority to the divestiture of

Figure 1.3 Sealink ferry leaving Calais for Dover. Source: Milepost 92½.

BR's subsidiaries in order to cut the overall level of its subsidy and raise money for the Exchequer. A former BRB member recalls:

> the [government] got to work on all public assets and simply stripped them. A 1970s merchant banker couldn't have done better. "Get rid of your hotels, get rid of your hovercraft, get rid of your ships, we don't want all these engineering works, we don't want any of this catering, get rid of it. But most of all get rid of your property. And give us the money."

Table 1.2 BR's subsidiary business sales, 1981–1989 (excluding various property disposals). Source: *Hansard*, **256**, Col. 53w, 1995.

Business sold	Date of sale
BR Hovercraft	October 1981
BR Hotels	1982–1984
Superbreak Mini Holidays	February 1983
Slateford Laundry	September 1983
Sealink UK	July 1984
British Transport Advertising	August 1987
Doncaster Wagon Works	October 1987
Horwich Foundry	August 1988
Traveller's Fare	December 1988
British Rail Engineering Ltd	April 1989
Golden Rail	May 1989

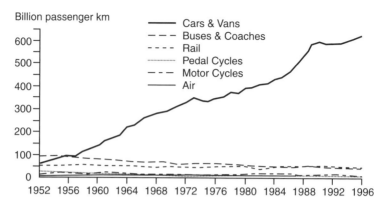

Figure 1.4   Passenger travel by mode, 1952–1996. Source: Department of the
Environment, Transport and the Regions. *Developing an Integrated
Transport Policy: An Invitation to Contribute*, DETR, 1997.
Crown copyright. Reproduced with the permission of
the Controller of Her Majesty's Stationery Office.

The 1981 Transport Act provided for BR to dispose of its subsidiary businesses
and these were sold throughout the 1980s (see Table 1.2).

Having established the concept of privatisation in the rail industry, the
Department of Transport (DoT) was keen to press ahead with selling at least
some of BR's rail operations. A Monopolies and Mergers Commission (MMC)
report on BR's Southern Region (SR) in 1980 had recommended that more
investment was needed in order to improve rail services in the area. Increased
government expenditure was ruled out because this would clash with the policy of
reducing BR's overall subsidy (and the PSBR) and instead Fowler asked his
officials to study as an experiment the potential for privatising the SR. In addition,
the DoT examined proposals for selling rail operations in Scotland and Wales, but
early privatisation plans were crude and the approach was to let the private sector
formulate proposals of its own and present them to the Department, rather than
the other way around.[20]

These early moves towards privatisation were ultimately overridden by the
Cabinet because many ministers viewed a BR sale as being complex and potentially unworkable. The most influential objector to rail privatisation was Thatcher.
She felt sure that "Middle-England" held an inexplicable affection for its railways
and that to tinker with BR would precipitate a political disaster. Moreover, BR
was different to other privatised industries, including its former subsidiaries,
because its market share was small (see Figure 1.4) and it was heavily subsidised
by the state. Any arrangements for rail privatisation would have to involve either
significant network rationalisation or devising a means to ensure the continued
payment of subsidy. Route closures were always unlikely, especially following the
publication of the Serpell Report in 1983. Serpell had reviewed the prospects for
improving BR's short-term finances and concluded that in order to make BR
profitable, 84 per cent of the rail network would need to be closed. This would

have reduced BR's route miles from around 11,000 to just 1,630. Less dramatic options were also proposed, but Serpell's suggestions encountered public hostility and it was announced in Parliament that although they constituted a "basis for decisions and for action ... the extreme options were not acceptable."[21] Thatcher also maintained that ensuring continuing subsidy payments following privatisation would be problematic. If BR were sold, either outright or in parts, how would future levels of subsidy be determined? This dilemma, as we shall see, was ultimately resolved through franchising, but at the time Thatcher was unwilling to experiment. Although she was shortly to sanction the sale of the loss-making National Bus Company (NBC), an insider recalled her being adamant – rather presciently, given the controversy which was ultimately to surround rail privatisation – that selling BR should not proceed as it would "be the Waterloo of this government."

On and off and on again

The issue of rail privatisation was not seriously considered by a government minister again until 1988, when Paul Channon, as the Secretary of State for Transport, "flew a kite" at the Conservative Party conference of that year. Channon was publicly circumspect in that he committed himself only to investigating whether privatisation might be a viable option in the future, but he was personally committed to the idea. Driven primarily by positive developments elsewhere in the privatisation programme – not least the sales of the NBC and British Airways – but also his own experience on the Southend to London "Misery Line", Channon disagreed with Thatcher's view that the railways should not be sold:

> *I became convinced that the government ought to grasp the nettle and do something about British Rail privatisation ... It was something a Tory minister was bound to want to do, bound to want to look at, but I found it astonishing that it hadn't been looked at earlier in a big way ... I was the first person to take a big step on it.*

With Thatcher so opposed to rail privatisation, how had Channon convinced her that his conference speech should make such an overt reference to it? The answer to this question unfortunately remains a mystery, even to Channon himself:

> *I casually let it be known that I wanted to announce at the [1988] Party conference the fact that the government was going to privatise BR ... I went to some meetings in September 1988 and asked permission to make this announcement at the Party conference. There were all sorts of wise people saying "oh, you can't do that, it's much too dangerous, the ground hasn't been prepared" and all that, and Mrs Thatcher was fairly lukewarm. She said I could say something if I would submit the exact form of words to her before the Party conference. So about a week before the Party conference, I wrote to her with the paragraphs that I wanted to use in my speech about rail privatisation. To my astonishment, within 48 hours I had them back with no comment.*

Table 1.3 Advantages and disadvantages of possible rail privatisation models identified by the DoT in 1988. The limited number and nature of points raised suggests that the proposals were still being considered at a ground level. Source: Redwood, J. *Signals from a Railway Conference*, Centre for Policy Studies, 1988.

Model	Advantages	Disadvantages
Regional	Some competition but largely indirect; improved morale through local loyalty; improved flexibility and efficiency	Problems with through trains between regions; possible loss of economies of scale; business "mix" within each region requires division of management attention
Track authority	Promotes competition	On-rail competition limited by railway practicalities, e.g. economics, capacity; track authority still a monopoly and difficult to regulate; track authority remote from rail users; investment decisions difficult; potentially high transaction costs
BR plc	Continuity of style and structure; minimal cost of privatisation	Not even limited competition; size of BR has engendered "diseconomies of complexity"; lack of operational transparency
Sectorisation	Avoids problems of operational transparency	Difficulties with track ownership
Hybrid	Better features of other models can be incorporated while their drawbacks can be avoided	

Whatever Thatcher's reasoning, rail privatisation had been returned to the political agenda and, shortly after the 1988 Party conference, Channon announced that the DoT was considering five models by which BR might be sold. In a speech at a Centre for Policy Studies (CPS) conference he listed them and outlined in general the pros and cons of each (see Table 1.3). It is worth noting that all the sale options were designed primarily to address the needs of the passenger, rather than the freight, railway. Largely for political reasons – passengers are more numerous and therefore have more electoral muscle than freight hauliers – the needs of the passenger railway were always given priority during both the formulation and implementation of rail privatisation policy. In this context, Chapter 8 discusses some of the issues which have arisen in the post-privatisation freight sector.

Two of the sale options, the regional and track authority models, had been proposed by right-wing think-tanks, the CPS and the Adam Smith Institute (ASI) respectively.[22] Both sets of proposals argued that BR should be broken up before privatisation, although for different reasons. The regional option proposed splitting BR's services into around 12 groups and also that ring-fenced subsidies would be provided to support loss-making services on a route-by-route basis within each group. It was argued that regional rail companies would be able to respond to customers' needs through concentrated management initiatives and staff would feel a sense of corporate "pride" because of local loyalty. The track-authority option, on the other hand, was much more radical in its approach. The ASI, following the economist David Starkie, suggested that BR should be vertically separated; that is to say, its infrastructure and operations should be split from each other. The principal reason for doing this was not to engender corporate pride or to ensure ease of subsidy payments, although these were obviously important, but to promote "on rail" competition. The idea was that any number of train-operating companies would be able to compete with each other between various destinations over track provided by a neutral agent.

A similar line of thought had underpinned bus privatisation and deregulation in 1985. The Conservatives split up the loss-making NBC into numerous, smaller companies in order to promote intra-industry competition on the assumption that this would increase efficiency and improve the overall level of service to passengers. The bus industry had seen a long-term decline in patronage (see Figure 1.4) and financial viability and it was hoped privatisation would reverse these trends. Routes which were not commercially viable, where the government acknowledged there was little chance of competition developing *in* the market, were contracted out generally to the bidder who required least subsidy in an attempt to stimulate competition *for* the market.[23]

The outcome of this policy was not as successful as its chief protagonist, Nicholas Ridley, envisaged. It quickly became apparent that much of the bus market, even routes which before privatisation had been regarded as commercially viable, was not sufficiently robust to withstand internal competition. Although services along some, mainly urban, routes improved, provision along others, particularly those in semi-urban and rural areas, was cut back. Service patterns across all types of routes became more volatile and timetabling information became fragmented and sometimes unreliable. Government subsidies were reduced, although arguably this was as much to do with fare increases and cutting employee pay as it was with efficiency gains. It is not surprising that, especially given a backdrop of rising car ownership, bus patronage continued to decline. The deregulated bus industry has now achieved a measure of stability – reliable service networks have been re-established and patronage is beginning to level off in places – but this has been at the expense of competition. Many smaller companies have gone bankrupt or have been bought out by larger rivals and a limited number of local and regional monopolies, who often tacitly co-operate rather than plunder each others' largely incontestable markets, has been established.

Of course, in 1987 (when the ASI's suggestion was first published) these trends were yet to emerge, but some people nevertheless feared that given the loss-making nature of BR, and therefore the likely incontestability of many of its routes, overemphasising the importance of intra- rather than intermodal competition might prove counter-productive (or at least self-defeating). On-rail

Figure 1.5   InterCity HSTs at King's Cross Station, October 1988.
Source: National Railway Museum.

competition was seen as unnecessary by those who felt that BR – like the NBC – already faced healthy competition from other transport modes. The ASI maintained that the adoption of the track-authority model was essential because, as David Starkie had noted in 1984, BR was "still not as efficient as it might be" despite the existence of inter-modal competition.[24]

The remaining three models, "BR plc", sectorisation and a "hybrid", were advanced by the DoT itself. The "BR plc" option involved a direct transfer of BR from the public to the private sector in the same way that BT or British Gas had been sold some years before and the advantage of this model was that it would minimise the disruption and cost of privatisation. The sectorisation model was an extension of BR's existing management structure. Until 1982, BR had been largely organised on a regional basis, with each region managing its own planning, marketing and operation of services, as well as maintaining its own infrastructure. For commercial and accounting purposes BR was reorganised in 1982 into five business sectors each defined to be relatively homogenous in the type of traffic it carried. InterCity provided high-speed services between major conurbations (Figure 1.5); London and South East served the densely populated markets in that area; Provincial operated the remainder of passenger services; and Freight and Parcels handled non-passenger operations.[25] Although some further reorganisation would have been necessary before privatisation, it was these sectors which would have been sold to the private sector.[26] Finally, the form of the hybrid model had not been determined by 1988. Channon noted only that this "option would allow some of the better features of the other [proposals] to be incorporated, while avoiding some of the drawbacks."[27]

Speculation in the press indicated that Channon was most impressed by the sectorisation and "BR plc" options. Not only would these obviate the need for a complex restructuring exercise, but they were also known to be favoured by BR's management. The BRB, according to a former member, preferred the unitary solution but was prepared to accept sectorisation as an alternative (a report by Coopers & Lybrand in 1989 found in favour of the latter and the BRB endorsed its findings). In fact, Channon was not particularly swayed by the feelings of the BRB and instead favoured the regional model, chiefly because he felt it could be a potential vote-winner:

> *it would be in different regions again . . . That's the solution that I would have done – at least, when I left, that was the front runner. I was very keen to do that . . . I thought it would be nice, people would like to go back on the Great Western or whatever and that was certainly the chief runner at that stage.*

Before Channon could make significant progress on the regional model, he was replaced as Secretary of State for Transport by Cecil Parkinson. Parkinson's success at introducing competition into the electricity industry led him to sympathise with Starkie's view that a degree of market liberalisation was needed although, in the absence of a sufficiently thorough policy analysis, he did not necessarily favour Starkie's suggestion of how it should be secured. As it stood, Channon's regional model did not really encourage the development of competition – in general it could only have taken place along the territorial borders of different companies – but circumstances were to militate against Parkinson selecting an alternative. Upon arrival at the DoT, he became aware that Thatcher had again lost interest in selling BR after becoming alarmed at public reaction to Channon's plans. Parkinson sent Thatcher a draft copy of his speech for the 1989 Party conference, which built upon Channon's announcement of the previous year, but recalls: "I got a message back saying she'd be grateful if I would leave the subject alone and not say anything." Press speculation had already begun to suggest that the government was planning to shelve indefinitely its plans to sell the railways, so Parkinson felt it was necessary to emphasise this was not the case: "I actually went to see her in Blackpool and said 'look, if I don't say anything that will be seen as a retreat and . . . I don't think we should be seen to be backing off.' So we agreed a form of words like 'studies continue.'" Parkinson stated publicly after the conference that plans for selling BR "are not at the top of my list of priorities at the moment," but he continued to pressure Thatcher into giving a firm commitment to privatise. This he achieved in 1990 (again, it is uncertain why she changed her mind) and he was finally able to announce to Parliament that the government was now "determined to privatise British Rail."[28]

The working group

Although the government had now announced a firm intention to sell the railways, a final decision still had to be taken regarding which of the five options would be employed to accomplish this. A working group comprising ministers and officials from the DoT, the Treasury and the Department of Trade and Industry (DTI) was established in the autumn of 1990 to resolve this issue, but Parkinson left the DoT before he could contribute in any meaningful way to the group's deliberations. Thatcher was also replaced as Prime Minister at that time, although the group was able to proceed without significant objections from Downing Street as her successor, John Major, was a keen advocate of rail privatisation.

Parkinson's replacement, Malcolm Rifkind, shared some of his predecessor's enthusiasm for market liberalisation but concluded that Starkie's model of vertical separation would be unnecessarily complex. Rifkind was particularly concerned that separating infrastructure from operations might place too high a proportion of a train operator's costs at the whim of the track authority. He argued on this basis that vertical separation was not advisable and his initial thoughts were to modify Channon's regional solution in two ways. First, the InterCity business would be kept intact, possibly on a vertically integrated basis. Not only would this allow a degree of continuity for passengers and rail managers, but it would also provide scope for some competition between origin/destination pairs served by both InterCity and a regional company. Secondly, "open access" operators – i.e. new entrants not part of an established train company – would in certain circumstances be allowed to run services in competition with incumbents. Rifkind was keen to establish an open-access regime as soon as possible and even wrote (with no impact) to BR asking them to consider admitting new entrants onto their network before privatisation had taken place. These two modifications would allow most operations still to be undertaken by rail companies who owned and maintained at least some infrastructure.

By contrast, the Treasury and the DTI supported the track-authority model. The bulk of the Treasury's enthusiasm for the track-authority model came about because of its apparent ability to promote competition. Treasury officials in particular were convinced by Starkie's argument that BR behaved like a monopoly, especially in major commuter areas such as London, and were fully persuaded by the case for vertical separation. As we have seen, the break-up of the CEGB and the liberalisation of the electricity-generating market had stimulated significant efficiency gains and, in comparing the performance of the electricity generators with that of BT and British Gas, the Treasury came to believe that the fundamental requirement of privatisation policy was the promotion of genuine competition: greater efficiency and investment, improved levels of service, enhanced customer care and, in the case of BR, the potential for reducing government subsidy would all *automatically* follow.

Whereas technical factors had prevented competition from being extended beyond the generating sector of the electricity industry, rail privatisation was seen as an opportunity to experiment further with vertical separation. Undeterred by the consideration that competition might be difficult to introduce into a loss-making industry (this was highlighted by both the Coopers & Lybrand report and the initial outcomes of bus privatisation which were now apparent) the Treasury drew an analogy between the structure of the privatised electricity industry and the track-authority model of rail privatisation. One senior official remembers that:

> *they [the Treasury] were convinced that the model was to try and strip things down to the natural monopoly . . . accept that was a monopoly and regulate it, but everywhere else bring in competition. So when they approached BR, they said "where is the natural monopoly in BR? Let's strip it down, let's isolate that, let's try and break the rest of it up into units which can be open for competition in a variety of ways" . . . And that's the model they were convinced of, as being right.*

In the light of this disagreement between Departments, the working group's conclusions, outlined in a report in early 1991, were a compromise. A hybrid solution was recommended, which suggested that there should be a separation of infrastructure and operations throughout most of Britain, but that the London commuter area should remain vertically integrated. Although Treasury officials thought that competition would be difficult to introduce in the South East if rail companies were vertically integrated, they accepted this compromise because they estimated that the amount of rail congestion around London would preclude most theoretical competitive opportunities there anyway. At this stage the Treasury did not know that its wish to create a network-wide track authority would subsequently be granted.

The conclusions of the working group were adopted in principle by the Cabinet and the DoT and the Treasury were cleared to finalise policy detail in the run-up to the 1992 general election (the DTI had stepped back from proceedings by this stage). Although the hybrid model had been agreed upon, the practicalities and implications peculiar to it had still to be analysed and legislation drafted. Key officials had hoped to undertake these tasks before the next general election, due no later than spring 1992, in order that the policy could be implemented quickly in the new Parliament. As things were to turn out, however, a definitive policy decision was not taken as soon as many both within and outside government would have liked.

Adopting a Model for Rail Privatisation

Although the conclusions of the working group were clear, Rifkind soon had second thoughts. The Secretary of State, as already noted, disliked the idea of a track authority and began to distance himself from the hybrid model (for which, of course, his Department was partly responsible). Rifkind attached a new importance to sectorisation, mainly because he now viewed it as the most straightforward way of retaining a vertically integrated InterCity business. As such, he devoted manpower to re-examining sectorisation and temporarily halted the development of the rail privatisation Bill. The ensuing delay intensely frustrated the Treasury because it had wanted to forge ahead with drafting legislation, but officials were able to use the extra time to subject their conception of a track authority to some further analysis and this was to prove beneficial because academics and transport economists had identified several operational shortcomings with the idea by this stage.

The advent of franchising

Although there is an apparent analogy between the separation of generation and distribution activities in the electricity industry and the creation of a track authority for the railways, it is in fact far from perfect.[29] It has already been noted that BR, unlike the electricity industry, lost money. In terms of operations, however, the most obvious difference is that, while electricity generated by competing companies can be supplied simultaneously to different customers using the same cables, it is clearly impossible to run two or more trains along a given piece of track at the same time. Services between origin/destination pairs have to be run according to a series of dedicated train paths monitored by the track authority. According to one official, the Treasury had intended simply to auction available paths to whoever offered the highest bid or required the lowest subsidy:

> They had a view ... that, if they had the time, they would have devised a rather more sophisticated structure of allocating railway slots, which was effectively a system of auctioning ... [but] with some minimum requirements to prevent grossly anti-competitive behaviour like running a train fractionally in front of another train and all that kind of stuff.

In this way, not only would there be competition in the market, between train services, but also competition for the market, through the auctioning of paths.

It quickly became evident that such a scheme would be inoperable, at least in the short term. The heterogeneous nature of rail services – trains serve different markets by running at different speeds and frequencies – means that they are vastly interdependent. For example, any company bidding for rights to run a half-hourly stopping service between London Euston and Birmingham New Street would generate certain train-path requirements over a route shared with other operators. Running this service would thus affect the availability of paths for other operators wishing to offer a different type of service on the same, or different, routes. (Two stopping trains per hour could seriously constrain the opportunities to run fast services, and so on.) Conflicts arising in this way were resolved by BR through co-ordination in the timetabling process, but in practical terms it would be extremely difficult to reproduce this through market mechanisms. Bids from different companies for potential services over the whole network would inevitably clash and a first auction would become impossible – unsuccessful tenderers would therefore need to reconsider their need for paths in the knowledge that some were already allocated to a competitor. Not only would assembling a timetable in this manner be tortuous, but it would also introduce considerable financial uncertainty for bidders.

Even if paths could be efficiently allocated, day-to-day operational problems were identified in the form of *externalities* and the loss of *network benefits*. Externalities can be divided into two categories, "train to train" and "track to train". The former occur as delays to one service, perhaps owing to locomotive breakdown, affect the running of others, whereas the latter arise as trains are delayed by a failure of the infrastructure. Both have a "snowballing" effect because of the interdependency of rail services and their resolution presents a host of complex problems. Each late train requires a consequential decision: shall following trains be delayed? Whose train? Who should then compensate whom for lost traffic?[30] Even with a logical (yet elaborate) accounting scheme, such problems would probably not be resolved without considerable goodwill from the multitude of operators. The existence of such goodwill in a "new" industry could not be guaranteed.

Network benefits are advantages which accrue to passengers from the existence of a unified railway network. Tickets can be purchased from any one station on the network to any other and are "inter-available" – that is to say, passengers can purchase one ticket and use it on any train between an origin/destination pair. The fragmentation of rail operations can result in problems with co-ordinating the sale of "through" tickets, which involve numerous changes of operator, and/or the cessation of ticket inter-availability if it is deemed anti-competitive.[31] In cases of the latter, rail would lose its "turn up and go" facility because passengers would have to buy operator-specific (or "dedicated") tickets. A passenger wishing to travel from, say, Plymouth to Exeter St David's might purchase a cheap ticket to use an infrequent Regional Railways train but, in so doing, would forfeit his right to travel by more numerous – and therefore convenient – InterCity services.

Arguments unconnected with train-path auctioning had also been advanced in opposition to the track authority model. In addition to Rifkind's concerns about track-access costs, the DoT had noted at the time of the 1988 CPS conference that effecting a track–train split could result in the track authority abusing its monopoly; that the track authority would be remote from rail users and responsibility for service shortcomings would be difficult to pin down; and that investment would be difficult to attract and co-ordinate. The combination of all the above factors led some to debate over whether vertical separation was an appropriate means of reorganising the railway industry. Bill Bradshaw, a former BR manager and now transport academic (and author of Chapter 10 of this volume), went further suggesting that the track authority offended "every professional principle of railway operation" and was "likely to result in an outcome which will be expensive, unsuitable and unsafe."[32]

The Treasury was forced to concede that its plans for a system of train-path auctioning would be unworkable given the limited time available to address the above issues. It suggested passenger-rail franchising as an alternative. Franchising was a tried-and-tested method of privatisation, the Conservatives having contracted out numerous municipal services since they took office in 1979. In the context of the railways, it would mean combining groups of train paths – perhaps geographically discrete, perhaps not – and offering them to the private sector as one package. In this way, some competition for the market would be retained by inviting tenders for the whole package of routes and competition in the market would still occur in border areas where operating territories overlapped. The Treasury argued in addition that open-access operations should be permitted where a market for them existed, subject to as yet undefined operating constraints arising from franchise commitments. All open-access services would have to be run on a strictly commercial basis and would be ineligible for subsidy.

A senior official remembers that the Treasury saw passenger-rail franchising as a much cruder model than slot auctioning, but recognised that it was a means of at least partially addressing the problems which would have arisen under the more sophisticated regime. By combining the path requirements of numerous services, the potential for reducing the number of operators on the network – and thus the complexity of inter-operator dealings – would be considerable: trains could be co-ordinated in a central timetable before franchises were let (with a degree of flexibility retained for private operators to rearrange service patterns in the future); the majority of train to train externalities could be "internalised" because delays to any given service would principally affect other services run by the same operator; the resolution of track-to-train externalities would be simplified for the same reason; and attempts to secure network benefits would be somewhat more straightforward with a smaller number of operators working to a co-ordinated timetable. Furthermore, once a framework to resolve these issues in the context of franchise operation had been established, it was suggested that open-access services could be slotted in around existing services with relative ease.

Franchising did not provide a complete solution to the train-path auctioning problems – it only moderated them – and there was still no guarantee that they would be straightforward to resolve. Nevertheless, Treasury officials had at least been working within the framework of the hybrid model advanced by the working group. In contrast, the DoT's position on rail privatisation, following Rifkind's decision to re-evaluate sectorisation, had fallen into disarray. An insider recalls Rifkind "agonising over whether InterCity should be vertically integrated or not," and that, as a consequence, the remainder of 1991 was a "saga of . . . grief within the DoT." So long as the DoT failed to commit itself to a formal policy option, the government was unable to draft legislation. With hindsight, it is obvious that decisive action from Downing Street was required at some point during this period in order to restore a sense of direction to rail privatisation policy. What actually happened was precisely the opposite. Rather than instructing the DoT to accept the hybrid model, on the basis that it had been formally adopted by the Cabinet, John Major's Policy Unit began advancing solutions of its own based around the regional concept. Downing Street's action served only to confuse matters further and there was, according to a DoT source, "tremendous faffing around . . . between the Department [of Transport], the Treasury and the cabinet secretariat who were trying to pull it all together – and not succeeding." At least three models were now being considered – hybrid, sectorisation and regional – with none, other than the track-authority element of the hybrid model, having received much more than a cursory analysis.

Framing the policy

The government was obliged to call a general election by spring 1992, but at the beginning of that year there was still no consensus between Departments about rail privatisation. A White Paper had been promised for late 1991 but was being delayed as ministers and officials continued to argue over the most appropriate industry structure. As polling day neared, policy necessarily became considered in the context of an election campaign. One civil servant pointed out that, "by the end of [1991] we'd lost a whole bloody year faffing around ... and Number 10 suddenly said 'we've got to write an election manifesto'." Thus:

> *the deal was brokered not in the context of considered papers or great meetings; [it] was brokered by a guy, Jonathan Hill, in the policy unit at Number 10 essentially – almost literally – walking around Whitehall with the bit for the manifesto. That was the way the final deal was done.*

It is perhaps an overstatement even to refer to the manifesto commitment as a "deal". The only firm policy decision which seems to have been taken in terms of industry structure by April 1992 was that of ruling out Rifkind's sectorisation model. The manifesto promised a track authority ("one part of BR will continue to be responsible for all track and infrastructure") and at the same time kept alive the possibility of regions ("our aim will be ... to reflect regional and local identity ... we want to ... recapture the spirit of the old regional companies"). The wording could have referred to the hybrid solution, where BR would maintain control of operations in the Network SouthEast territory (which or how many franchises would be created was not mentioned in the manifesto); the universal track authority solution; or a variant of the regional solution, where the infrastructure would be split among several divisions of the same track-authority to coincide with the territories of train operators.

John MacGregor, appointed as Secretary of State for Transport following the Conservatives' surprise election victory in 1992 (almost all polls had predicted a Labour majority), now admits that there was "not quite a blank sheet of paper as our election commitment, but very close to it. Just a few outlines about how [rail privatisation] might work." An official added that because of 1991 being "blown out of the water and things being resolved in the context of drafting the manifesto, when [the Conservatives] won the election we had nothing drafted at all. There was no base." MacGregor's job was to resolve once and for all the debate over industry structure and present a Bill before Parliament as soon as possible. Although ministers were quoted as saying privatisation would be gradual and might take up to 10 years, the real intention was always to complete the sale before the next general election (due by May 1997 at the latest). As the then Minister of State for Public Transport, Roger Freeman, has since declared, "you either did it or you didn't – and if you did it, you had to complete it in one term."

Along with officials and ministerial colleagues, MacGregor undertook a "huge amount of work" in May and June 1992 to frame final proposals outlining how BR would be privatised:

> *I spent the first 2 months [after the election] making up my own mind as to whether the framework – almost the blank sheet of paper in the manifesto – was*

the right framework or whether we should go differently. Horizontal and vertical integration was one crucial aspect of that.

MacGregor was also assisted by Sir Christopher Foster, then a partner at Coopers & Lybrand, who had been appointed as a special adviser on rail privatisation. Foster was, like the Treasury, a proponent of the track authority model although his enthusiasm for vertical separation was based on different reasons than the Treasury's. For reasons that will become apparent in Chapter 6, he warned that on-rail competition would be difficult to achieve straightaway and played down its significance accordingly; instead, he saw opportunities for efficiency gains through the franchising process and the need to formalise by economically based contracts the relationships between the various components of the industry. Foster outlined his views in his subsequent publication, *The Economics of Rail Privatisation.*

Foster's arrival at the DoT was nevertheless to suit Treasury ministers and officials because it increased the likelihood of them realising their original aim of a network-wide track authority as opposed to the partial one included in the hybrid model. Following Rifkind's example of abandoning the hybrid in favour of his own preferences, the Treasury had by now decided to do likewise and seek a complete vertical separation. Just 6 weeks after the Conservatives' election victory, this is exactly what they got: although Foster recalls initial misgivings regarding this option on the part of some within the DoT, a policy outline advocating the creation of a network-wide track authority was "hammered out" and accepted by MacGregor.

A key point to note here is that the decision to adopt the track authority model should not be regarded as the result of a detailed policy analysis. Despite the protracted evolution of rail privatisation policy and the existence of numerous models advanced by academics, think-tanks and civil servants, there is a strong possibility that MacGregor did not have the time to choose the track authority model on the strength of a lengthy and thorough evaluation of which would be the most effective or successful means of rail privatisation. Given the time constraints in which he was operating, it is likely that he was forced into accepting vertical separation as it was effectively his only choice. With Rifkind's sectorisation plans rejected and the DoT's half of the hybrid model still incomplete, the track authority had at least been subjected to an evaluation of sorts. If the railways were to be sold within the 1992–1997 Parliament, there would not have been time to analyse further the remaining alternatives. Moreover, both the Treasury and Foster were able to contend – somewhat disingenuously – that a new European Directive, introduced in 1991 to require a split in accounting in member states' railway industries, now further supported their case for a network-wide track authority.[33] Freeman implies that he, along with many DoT officials, had resigned himself to the inevitability of vertical separation:

Put it this way. MacGregor stood back and reviewed the options to familiarise himself with his brief at Transport. He just wanted to make sure that vertical separation would work. He may have said in public, "we're doing another

consultation", but in reality we all knew what the outcome [of his decision]
would be.

Former BR chairman Sir Bob Reid identifies Foster's view as being the primary
influence behind MacGregor's decision to adopt the track authority model. In
1995, Reid opined that the debate over how to privatise BR "was a dogmatic
argument of 3 or 4 years ago. We lost [BR had, of course, supported a vertically
integrated solution]. It means we now have a structure that is more complicated
than necessary."[34] Foster's support for vertical separation was no doubt high in
MacGregor's mind when he took the decision to adopt it, but Reid's view
overlooks the influence of the Treasury, whose desire to maximise competition
had seen it campaigning for a track authority of one form or another since 1990.
More significant, however, is the fact that although Foster did not support the
enthusiastic and immediate pursuit of on-rail competition, *New Opportunities for
the Railways* was to emphasise heavily its importance (see below) and this would
suggest that in drafting the White Paper MacGregor deferred to the preferences
of the Treasury rather than those of his special adviser. MacGregor argues that
he knew on-rail competition would not work but delayed announcing this for
tactical reasons. Given the circumstances in which rail privatisation policy had
developed, this is understandable – in the sense that his primary aim was to
secure the earliest possible publication of the White Paper and he could not risk
any further delay which might have arisen if the Treasury had protested – but
there was still a compelling reason for him to avoid publicly endorsing the
Treasury's proposals at that time. As will be seen below and in subsequent
chapters, the idea of on-rail competition – which by the time of the White
Paper's publication was already being met with considerable hostility – would
trouble MacGregor politically throughout much of his time as Secretary of State
for Transport.

The Treasury, of course, favoured vertical separation as it was perceived to be
the most effective means of liberalising BR's market. Officials believed that
competition would improve the efficiency and quality of rail services while decreasing their cost in the same way that it had in the electricity industry. Their
assumption was that the model used to sell the CEGB could, with only a few
minor changes, simply be transferred to the privatisation of BR. Yet relatively little
consideration had been given to whether or not this approach was entirely
suitable for privatising and liberalising the railway industry. Although both
Starkie and the ASI had advocated competition through vertical separation
before it was embraced by the Treasury, their analyses, in the context of exploring
potential implementation strategies or even a broad range of likely outcomes, had
been rather elementary (an editorial in *Modern Railways* described the thinking
behind the ASI's arguments as being of less than A-level standard).[35]

The Treasury's own evaluation was hardly rigorous; although it had acknowledged some of the more obvious shortcomings in the analogy between a track
authority for BR and the National Grid for the electricity industry, it could only
provide MacGregor with a framework, beyond which there was very minimal
detail. Little had been worked out regarding: the calculation and allocation of

track-access charges; the formation and vesting of successor rail companies; the specifications and administration of franchises; the precise functions and responsibilities of the regulators; the likelihood of privatising the structure within one Parliament or the probable cost of the exercise. Perhaps most surprisingly, given that a fundamental objective of the Treasury's plans was to promote competition between train operators, MacGregor had not been provided with a proper examination of the opportunities for, and appropriateness of, liberalising the rail-service market. The government did not know whether such competition – and all the associated benefits the Treasury believed would follow as a result – would be sustainable or even attainable in the proposed industry structure.

The outcome of bus privatisation and deregulation, which had differed considerably from that which was intended, should have given ministers cause for thought at this point. Although the markets of BR and the NBC were by no means identical, they shared key characteristics such as their relative insignificance in terms of the transport market as a whole, their dependence on public subsidy to support loss-making yet socially necessary services and their general incontestability. Attempting to introduce competition into the bus industry had been a largely superfluous exercise, often creating instability and uncertainty – not to mention the resurgence of monopoly – rather than service improvements and market growth.

Foster argues that there had been "substantial analysis of many points" within the government before MacGregor made his decision and he identifies that ministers had taken time to satisfy themselves regarding basic concerns such as safety (see Chapter 3). The Secretary of State may or may not have been secure in his conviction that the railways could operate in a vertically integrated environment but, having made the decision to adopt the track authority model, he could only hope that it would now deliver, as the White Paper *New Opportunities for the Railways* was to claim, "a higher quality of service and better value for money for the public who travel by rail."

The White Paper and the Railways Bill

Having finally decided upon vertical separation, MacGregor was now faced with the task of producing a workable industry structure. This was essentially undertaken over a 3-year period between 1992 and 1995, beginning with the publication of the White Paper in July 1992. The document noted that "the introduction of competition . . . and the ending of BR's monopoly in the operation of services will be instrumental" in improving rail services and the government's wish to liberate private-sector management from state control in order to harness its "skills, flair and entrepreneurial spirit" was also emphasised. The White Paper set out the government's commitment to establishing a track authority, Railtrack, and to splitting BR's passenger services up into franchises which would be awarded by competitive tendering. In addition, the document noted the intention to provide for open access operations:

> *companies wishing to provide new railway services . . . will have a right of access to the railway network . . . [At present], there is no choice of operator for the rail passenger . . . liberalising access to the network will [provide] the opportunity for new operators to run services. This will give . . . rail operators the stimulus of competition to provide better service quality and value for money.*

Responsibility for negotiating, awarding and monitoring franchises would be transferred to a new Franchising Authority, whilst the rights of access for both franchised and non-franchised operators would be overseen by a new Rail Regulator. Some debate had gone on within government about the regulation of the industry, particularly over whether there should be one or two regulators. Two were eventually chosen because of the potential for a single regulator to be faced with conflicts of interest as he provided government subsidies to train operators on the one hand, but attempted to maintain independence from ministers on the other (see Chapters 6 and 9).

New Opportunities for the Railways immediately attracted numerous hostile commentaries, not least because the plans appeared ill-considered and lacking in detail. Of course, a White Paper is not necessarily the place in which a thorough exposition of a new government policy is found, but *New Opportunities for the Railways* was seen by many as being exceptionally vague. The then Chairman of the Transport Select Committee, the late Robert Adley MP, argued that a green paper should have preceded the White in order to allow a fuller debate of the policy and its likely implications before legislation was published. He further suggested to MacGregor that:

> *the Secretary of State, the Minister of State and Department [of Transport] officials have appeared before [the Transport Select] Committee and . . . it seems to me that none of them, quite frankly, have a clue about how all this is going to be worked out.*[36]

MacGregor, in Parliament, had admitted that "in working through some of the proposals, it is clear that much work remains to be done,"[37] and Freeman now acknowledges that "in an ideal world" the whole process would have been slower, allowing a green paper to be produced. But, considering the difficulties and associated delays the government had already experienced in deciding to adopt the track-authority model, he pointed out that:

> *in all honesty there would not have been time within the lifetime of that parliament to go through the process of drafting a green paper, putting the green paper out to consultation, re-running the argument which had gone on within government about the structure, then drafting a White Paper, then drafting a Bill, then implementing it . . . That process, in my judgement, would easily have lasted two parliaments . . . There was just not time.*

Crucial policy details were not completed when the Railways Bill was presented to the House of Commons in early 1993. As later chapters will show, certain issues had proved complicated to resolve and, because of the need to proceed with rail privatisation as soon as possible, it was decided not to wait until the plans were fully formulated before drafting legislation. The solution was to produce a Bill which contained numerous enabling powers and to continue policymaking during – and after – its passage through Parliament. One official remarked that "the Bill was a mess and it had lots of enabling powers rather than specific proposals . . . [because] the thing wasn't properly prepared."

During the Bill's second reading, Liberal Democrat MP Nick Harvey mocked its vague content when he pointed out that:

> *the Bill comprises 132 clauses and 11 schedules and gives massive powers to the Secretary of State . . . It might have been preferable to have had a Bill of one clause which simply said "the Secretary of State can do what he likes, how he likes when he likes and where he likes." It would have had more or less the same effect.*[38]

MacGregor, in contrast, argued that "the principles and the main structure of the Bill are entirely consistent with [those in] the White Paper."[39] It is true that the offices of the Rail Regulator and Franchising Director were included, along with the concept of franchising and several technical details such as closure procedures. Beyond this, however, MacGregor's assertion is somewhat spurious. Although a deviation from the White Paper was *unlikely* because of the circumstances in which the policy had been adopted, the Bill was not necessarily consistent with *New Opportunities for the Railways* in several crucial areas precisely because it was vague. To illustrate, no details were provided for: the structure of the industry (the Bill did not even mention Railtrack and noted merely that the Secretary of State could instruct the BRB to form a number of companies); the framework within which on-rail competition could develop (it was stated only that a facility owner might be instructed to allow more than one company access to its assets); or how rail companies would be regulated (although some duties were assigned to the Regulator and the Franchising Director, the majority of their functions were to be prescribed by the Secretary of State at a future, unspecified date).

The Railways Bill finally received Royal Assent on 5 November 1993, after a difficult passage through both Houses of Parliament. The new railway structure (which was still not outlined in the Railways Act),[40] was due to take effect from 1 April 1994 and this is described in Chapter 2. Although the government had succeeded in getting the Bill passed, much of the hard work was only just beginning as key areas of policy detail still had to be worked out. Moreover, this task would have to be undertaken in the face of mounting and vociferous criticism of rail privatisation. The high level of opposition to the Railways Bill in Parliament had simply reflected public and media sentiment: by late 1993 the BR sell-off had become the most disliked privatisation ever undertaken in Britain. It is probably true to say that perceptions of the rail privatisation project were to a degree being affected by the now-dwindling popularity of the Conservative government, but ministers' inability to produce concrete and detailed plans for the new industry structure as the Bill passed through Parliament had also exacerbated critics' concerns. The strength and depth of opposition facing ministers and officials as they sought to sell BR is discussed elsewhere in the book and it is sufficient here to record that many commentators, some rather gleefully, began speculating that rail privatisation could not possibly be completed before the 1997 election given the high level of uncertainty which surrounded almost every aspect of the policy. The fact that it was, while due in part to good fortune (the economy recovered from recession, patronage levels began to rise accordingly and some in the private sector were willing to take risks), is testament to the efforts and achievements of those involved in formulating and implementing the policy between 1992 and 1997. It is against the background outlined in this chapter that the remainder of the book describes and evaluates the privatisation of British Rail.

Acknowledgements

This chapter is based upon research funded by the Department of Geographical Sciences, University of Plymouth. Thanks are due to Ian Bailey, Steve Bennett, Clive Charlton, Dr Mark Cleary, Dr Richard Gibb, Professor Phil Goodwin and Chris Price whose incisive comments on, and criticisms of, early drafts have greatly improved the text. Errors and/or omissions are, of course, my own.

Notes

1. Cmnd 2012. *New Opportunities for the Railways*, 1992.
2. Letwin, O. *Privatising the World*, Cassell Publications, 1988.
3. Jenkins, S. *Accountable to None: The Tory Nationalization of Britain*, Penguin, 1995. Moore, J. "Why privatise?" in J. Kay, C. Meyer and D. Thompson (eds), *Privatisation and Deregulation: The UK Experience*, Clarendon Press, 1986.
4. Blackaby, F. *British Economic Policy, 1960–74*, Cambridge University Press, 1978.
5. Fowler, N. *The Right Track: A Paper on Conservative Transport Policy*, Conservative Political Centre, 1978.
6. Quoted in McLachlan, S. *The National Freight Buyout*, MacMillan, 1983.
7. Howe, G. *Conflict of Loyalty*, MacMillan, 1994.
8. Quoted in Walker, M. *Privatisation: Tactics and Techniques*, Fraser Institute, 1988.
9. Ridley, N. *My Style of Government*, Hutchinson, 1991.
10. Foster, C. *Privatization, Public Ownership and the Regulation of Natural Monopoly*, Blackwell, 1992.
11. Howe, op. cit.
12. This was because of the so-called Ryrie rules (named after Sir William Ryrie, the civil servant then in charge of public expenditure). The rules stated that any borrowing by nationalised industries remained public-sector borrowing because the ultimate risk still lay with the government.
13. Foster, op. cit.

14. *The Economist*, 11 March 1995.
15. The telecommunications firm Mercury was licensed to compete with BT following the latter's privatisation, but its impact was minimal at first. See Moore, J. "The success of privatisation", in Kay, Meyer and Thompson, op. cit.
16. Thatcher, M. *The Downing Street Years*, HarperCollins, 1993. *The Economist*, 11 March 1995.
17. Mitchell, J. "Britain: privatisation as myth?" in Richardson, J. *Privatisation and Deregulation in Canada and Britain*, Dartmouth, 1990.
18. Natural monopoly occurs where a single firm can produce total industry outputs more efficiently than two or more firms.
19. *Modern Railways*, No. 384, 1980.
20. *Modern Railways*, No. 429, 1984.
21. *Hansard*, **35**, Cols 489–499, 20 January 1983.
22. Gritten, A. *Reviving the Railways: A Victorian Future?* Centre for Policy Studies, 1988. Irvine, K. *The Right Lines*, Adam Smith Institute, 1987.
23. See Knowles, R. and Hall, D. "Transport deregulation and privatization" in B. Hoyle and R. Knowles (eds), *Modern Transport Geography*, John Wiley, 1998. Buses in London were privatised in the 1990s but were not deregulated. Routes were franchised to private-sector companies, but open-access competition was not allowed. This model of privatisation is generally regarded as having been more successful than that employed for the sale of the NBC.
24. Starkie, D. "BR – privatisation without tears" in *Economic Affairs*, October–December 1994.
25. London and South East was later renamed Network SouthEast and Provincial became Regional Railways.
26. There were some idiosyncracies in the sectorisation structure of the mid-1980s, in particular the continuing existence of some regional management. See Nash, C. and Preston, J. "Franchising Rail Services" in A. Harrison (ed.), *From Hierarchy to Contract*, Transaction Books, 1993.
27. Channon, P. "Speech to conference" in J. Redwood (ed.), *Signals from a Railway Conference*, CPS, 1988.
28. Stephens, P. and Brown, K. "BR sell-off 'not a high priority' " in *Financial Times*, 13 October 1989. *Hansard*, **181**, Col. 606, 26 November 1990.
29. Adamson, M., Jones, W. and Pratt, R. "Competition issues in privatisation: lessons for the railways" in D. Banister and K. Button (eds), *Transport in a Free Market Economy*, MacMillan, 1991. Jones, I., Marks, P. and Willis, C. *Franchising Passenger Rail Services*, National Economic Research Associates, 1993. Nash, C. *The Role of Rail in Future Transport Policy*, Rees Jeffreys Road Fund, 1990.
30. Foster, op. cit.
31. Under a system of inter-availability, customers can use one ticket to travel between an origin/destination pair on trains operated by more than one company.
32. Bradshaw, W. *A Review of Policies for the Future of Britain's Railways*, Paper presented to the Railway Studies Association, 13 November 1991.
33. EC directive 91/440 requires that member states' railways account for their infrastructure and operations business independently of one another. It does *not* require the formation of separate infrastructure and operations companies, however. The idea is that trans-European freight and passenger movements will increase as one member state's rail operator can gain access to another's tracks following the simple calculation of a track-access fee. Because the whole process is transparent, discriminating in favour of the incumbent becomes more difficult.

34. *The Guardian*, 25 February 1995.
35. *Modern Railways*, No. 481, 1988.
36. *House of Commons Papers*, Session 1992–1993, 246iii.
37. *Hansard*, **211**, Cols 971–986, 14 July 1992.
38. *Hansard*, **218**, Cols 156–255, 2 February 1993.
39. Ibid.
40. House of Commons. *Railways Act 1993*, HMSO, 1993.

2. The Structure of the New Railway

Clive Charlton

This chapter provides a basic underpinning to the in-depth accounts of rail privatisation that follow. The aim is to familiarise the reader with the structure and organisation of the privatised rail system, with particular emphasis on the main "actors" and their responsibilities. An understanding of the shape of today's railway depends in part on an appreciation of its background under British Rail (BR), so the salient features of this era are also reviewed briefly. There is no pretence that the coverage of the privatised system is exhaustive – not least because Britain's railway industry is now a remarkably complex enterprise – and a fuller description is found in the *Passenger Rail Industry Overview*.[1] Neither is there an attempt to evaluate the outcomes of rail privatisation, as this is undertaken in the following chapters.

The Railway Under British Rail

BR underwent a major organisational transformation in the decade preceding its privatisation. Although the Thatcher administration had rejected the Draconian pruning of the rail network proposed in the Serpell Report of 1983 (see Chapter 1), its determination to reduce the level of subsidy flowing to the public-sector railway stimulated a drive within BR for substantial efficiency improvements. Central to these reforms was the partial replacement of the existing structure based on regions by one formed around distinct rail business sectors, each with managers responsible for meeting objectives in terms of marketing, cost allocation and investment decisions. The regions continued to physically run the trains, however. The intention was that this shift to "sectorisation" would foster more responsible, innovative, customer-oriented management in comparison with the previous approach, which had responded more to the operational demands of the rail system rather than to the needs of the market.

A further major reform in BR's management strategy came in 1991, with the launch of "Organising for Quality" (O for Q). Completed by April 1992, this initiative finally abolished the old regions and defined separate profit centres within each of the business sectors. While the British Railways Board (BRB) maintained responsibility for overall policies, finances and standards, O for Q further devolved responsibility for rail operations, with each profit centre having its own managing director and dedicated management team. Each profit centre assumed direct responsibility for the costs of track on which they were the "prime user", as well as maintenance of rolling stock. Importantly, the higher degree of autonomy encountered under O for Q gave BR managers experience of the market and cost-oriented principles that would become still more central in the privatised railway.

The impacts of the substantial reorganisation and the accompanying efficiency improvements undertaken by BR in its final decade should not be underestimated. In some respects they generated the conditions that made privatisation a more viable policy. The new business sectors formed at least in part the basis for the structure of the privatised railway (the O for Q profit centres provided the template for the subsequent reorganisation of BR's passenger operations – see below and Chapter 6) and showed that the railway system could be operated as a series of relatively independent components, rather than only as a monolithic structure. The reforms, streamlining and perhaps even cultural change involved in the restructuring of BR also made the industry more attractive to the private sector.

The marked reduction in the Public Service Obligation (PSO) payments paid directly to BR by the government in support of loss-making services lends support to this interpretation. The PSO system of sector-based subsidy had been established under the 1974 Railways Act, at a point when the government had turned away from any further significant passenger service withdrawals. In 1988–89, PSO grant-support income was 42.9 per cent of BR's other receipts, but had fallen to 31.95 per cent by 1992–93. From 1988, InterCity services were excluded from subsidy entirely, whereas the sector had made a loss of £100 million in 1984. Revenue support for the Network SouthEast and freight sectors fell substantially (although rail's share of the freight market also declined). The Regional sector also enjoyed a range of improvements that helped boost passenger traffic, including the introduction of new "Sprinter" trains, new longer distance cross-country services and station openings and re-openings (Figure 2.1).

Privatisation

The 1993 Railways Act provided the legislative authority for the reorganisation and privatisation of the rail system. Although the structure of the new railway was not fully outlined in the legislation (see Chapter 1), it at least enabled the government to proceed with the track-authority method of privatisation. BR's operations business was divided into almost 100 individual – and, where possible, competing – businesses for sale to the private sector and a new regulatory regime was created in an attempt to ensure the White Paper's basic objective of "improving the quality of rail services."[2]

In outline, the main rail businesses that emerged to provide the organisational framework for privatisation fell into the following groups:

Figure 2.1   Regional Railways Class 142 at York Station, June 1987.
Source: National Railway Museum.

- Railtrack – ownership of all rail infrastructure;
- Passenger Train Operating Companies (TOCs) – operators of designated passenger train services on a franchised basis;
- Rolling Stock Companies (Roscos) – three businesses set up to own and lease out passenger trains to the TOCs;
- rail-freight companies – operators of rail-freight services and owners of freight rolling stock;
- companies concerned with the maintenance of track and signalling – initially within British Rail Infrastructure Services (BRIS);
- companies concerned with the heavy maintenance of locomotives and rolling stock – initially within British Rail Maintenance Ltd (BRML);
- ancillary businesses – a miscellany of units providing services in support of the rail industry such as communications and research.

The key regulatory bodies established under the Railways Act were:

- Office of Passenger Rail Franchising (OPRAF), headed by the Franchising Director – to franchise passenger rail services and allocate financial support;
- Office of the Rail Regulator (ORR), headed by the Regulator – to oversee the fair and effective operation of the rail system and to license railway operators;
- Rail Users' Consultative Committees (RUCCs) – to work in conjunction with the ORR to protect the interests of the users of rail services and facilities.

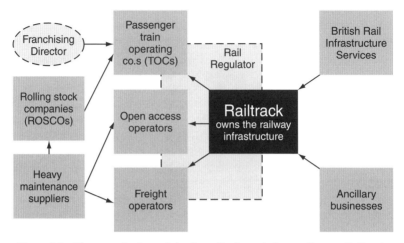

Figure 2.2   The organisation of the "new" railway industry. Source: Railtrack.

The business groups interact with each other on a contractual, commercial basis with some falling under the supervision of one or more of the regulatory bodies (see Figure 2.2). The nature and activities of these main components of the rail system are now considered in rather more detail throughout the remainder of the chapter.

Railtrack

On 1 April, 1994 – the date from which the Railways Act took effect – all of British Rail's "fixed assets" were transferred to the monopoly ownership of a single independent company, Railtrack (see Chapter 3). This infrastructure included around 11,000 route miles of track, structures such as 750 tunnels and 40,000 bridges, 2,500 stations, signalling and other property. At this stage there was no clear policy regarding when Railtrack would be privatised and it was at first retained in government ownership. When the government subsequently determined to privatise the whole rail system, Railtrack was floated on the London Stock Exchange in May 1996.

A contract-based charging regime was established enabling Railtrack to sell track, station and depot access to train operators on a commercial basis. It is responsible for allocating and co-ordinating all train paths and movements, managing the national passenger timetable, operating the signalling and control system and maintaining, renewing and enhancing rail infrastructure. This latter function is contracted out on a competitive basis to specialist engineering companies.

The main source of Railtrack's revenue is the charges levied on passenger-train operators for access to track, stations and depots, with a lesser input from operators of freight and other rail services. Overall, access charges contribute over 90 per cent of Railtrack's income and also account for a large element of the costs falling on the TOCs. The precise nature of the costs arising from the operation of passenger and freight services is complex, as is the extent to which the charges applied by Railtrack accurately reflect the costs concerned. Given the prime importance of Railtrack's charges on the financial condition of the TOCs, and the performance of the rail system in general, the Regulator launched a detailed Periodic Review of Railtrack's access charges in 1997, with a view to implementation of any revised charging regime from April 2001. A central aim is a better understanding of the costs involved in operating the rail network.

Further Railtrack income comes from station leasing and the rental and disposal of other property. The company's extensive property portfolio represents a very valuable asset base. Although most of the stations on the network are leased to, and operated by, nominated TOCs, Railtrack maintains direct responsibility for managing 14 major stations with especially strong commercial potential.[3] Railtrack is organised into seven (initially ten) geographical zones of broadly comparable scale, namely Anglia, Great Western, London North Eastern, Midland, North West, Scotland and Southern (see Figure 2.3). The zones are important as they are the main point of contact between Railtrack and its clients and suppliers, as well as other stakeholders such as local authorities and user groups.

In recognition of its fundamental position as a privatised monopoly on which the rest of the rail industry depends, Railtrack's performance is closely scrutinised by the Regulator — a relationship that has proved one of the more contentious encounters in the privatised railway. An important instrument in this regard is the requirement that Railtrack should produce an annual Network Management Statement (NMS). This document outlines the company's expenditure proposals for the maintenance, renewal and enhancement of the network. The NMS also includes information on Railtrack's expectations for the growth of passenger and freight traffic capacity and demand. The statement includes the identification of current and potential traffic bottlenecks, as well as the company's performance in terms of a range of output and quality indicators and targets.

Railtrack is also bound into a contractual performance regime with its main customers, the TOCs. If substandard service performance arises from deficiencies in the standard of Railtrack infrastructure and management, the company is liable to make compensatory payments. Conversely, if Railtrack exceeds predetermined reliability targets, it receives a bonus payment from TOCs. If passenger service delays are attributed to train failure, the TOC concerned is required to pay compensation to other TOCs affected, which Railtrack administers.

Passenger Train Operating Companies

The 1993 Railways Act specified that passenger rail services should be provided by private-sector TOCs on the basis of franchises, to be awarded for a specified period following a competitive bidding process organised by OPRAF. Services can also be provided by non-franchised, "open access" operators although the Regulator currently restricts this type of train operation. Initially, a target was set for the first six franchises to be let by the end of 1995, with at least half of BR's

Scotland

London
North Eastern

North West

Midlands

Midlands

East
Anglia

Great Western

Southern

Figure 2.3 Railtrack's operating zones. Source: Railtrack.

services operating under franchises by 1 April 1996. Although this particular deadline proved over-optimistic, one of the more striking features of the privatisation process is that all franchises were transferred to the private sector by April 1997 (see Chapters 6 and 7).

In order to prepare the organisational model for the passenger franchises, 25 new Train Operating Units (TOUs) were established from 1 April 1994, when the business sectors InterCity, Network SouthEast and Regional Railways ceased to exist. The TOUs were subsequently vested as separate subsidiary Train Operating Companies of BR, which operated as "shadow franchises" to provide a clearer indication of the likely financial and operational conditions facing potential franchise bidders. As already noted, the new units were essentially based on the BR O for Q sub-sectors that they replaced, although there were some modifications (see Table 2.1). The operating "territories" of the TOCs are shown in Figures 2.4–2.6.

Each TOC was allocated responsibility for operating specified train services, rolling stock, stations and maintenance depots. However, because ownership of these resources lay elsewhere – with either the Roscos or Railtrack – a complex range of contracts between the TOCs and their suppliers had to be drawn up. In addition to the access agreements with Railtrack, rolling-stock leases had to be devised. The terms that TOCs took on with the Roscos include not only rental payments, but also establish responsibility for light and heavy maintenance, insurance, who should pay for mandatory modifications to rolling stock and the position at the end of the lease. In theory, there is a competitive market for the supply of rolling stock although, in practice, many trains were leased on contracts of similar length to the TOCs' franchises. This will probably change after the first generation of franchises has expired. TOCs procure various other services, such as telecommunications and research, from the range of ancillary businesses created at the time of BR's reorganisation.

Franchising of the TOCs was phased, both in terms of the stages in the process itself and the timing of the "release" of tranches of franchise tenders. As the process got under way, there was uncertainty and controversy over its viability and validity; it was not clear at this stage just how much competition there would be to enter the market for passenger-train operation. However, after a cautious start, the bidding for franchises made available later in the programme was considerably more enthusiastic, to the undoubted relief of ministers who were committed to transferring the entire rail system to the private sector before the end of the Parliament. The escalating vigour and evident optimism of the contest took many of the more sceptical observers by surprise and the final franchise, ScotRail, was awarded in February 1997 and started operating on 1 April of that year.

As Table 2.2 shows, the franchise period agreed varied somewhat between individual franchises. Whereas the norm is around 7 years, some operators were able to negotiate extended periods in return for extra commitments to invest in upgraded services; examples include the two Virgin Trains franchises (15 years), Connex South Eastern (15 years), Midland Mainline (10 years) and First Great Western (10 years). Franchises differ markedly in terms of their scale, complexity,

All Change: British Railway Privatisation

Table 2.1 The "evolution" of O for Q profit centres into TOCs. Throughout the book, pre-privatisation references to passenger-train operators will be by their TOC name (the nationalised London, Tilbury and Southend (LTS) Rail is the privatised c2c and so on).

BR Business Sector	BR Train Operating Unit	Privatised Train Operating Company
InterCity		
Anglia and Gatwick[1]	Anglia[2]	Anglia Railways
	Gatwick Express	Gatwick Express
East Coast	InterCity East Coast	Great North Eastern Railway
Great Western	Great Western	First Great Western
Midland and Cross Country[3]	Midland Main Line	Midland Mainline
	CrossCountry	Virgin Trains
West Coast	West Coast Trains	Virgin Trains
Network SouthEast		
Great Eastern	Great Eastern	First Great Eastern
London Tilbury and Southend	London Tilbury Southend Rail	c2c
North	North London Railways	Silverlink Train Services
South Central	Network South Central	Connex South Central
South East	South Eastern	Connex South Eastern
South West[4]	South West Trains	South West Trains
	Isle of Wight	Island Line
Thames and Chiltern[5]	Chiltern Lines	Chiltern Railways
	Thames Trains	Thames Trains
Thameslink	Thameslink	Thameslink
West Anglia and Great Northern	West Anglia and Great Northern	West Anglia and Great Northern (WAGN Railways)
Regional Railways		
RR Central	Central	Central Trains
RR North East	North East	Northern Spirit
RR North West[6]	North West	First North Western
	Merseyrail Electrics	Merseyrail Electrics
RR South Wales and West[7]	South Wales and West	Wales and West
	Cardiff Valleys	Cardiff Railway Company
ScotRail	ScotRail[8]	ScotRail

[1] InterCity Anglia and Gatwick was split into separate TOUs.
[2] The Anglia TOU and franchise combined British Rail's InterCity Anglia operation with the rural services operated in East Anglia by Regional Railways Central.
[3] InterCity Midland and Cross Country was split into separate TOUs.
[4] Isle of Wight was split from the former Network SouthEast South West sub-sector.
[5] Network SouthEast Thames and Chiltern was split into separate TOUs.
[6] Merseyrail Electrics was split from RR North West.
[7] Cardiff Valleys was split from RR South Wales and West.
[8] Anglo-Scottish sleeper services were transferred to ScotRail.

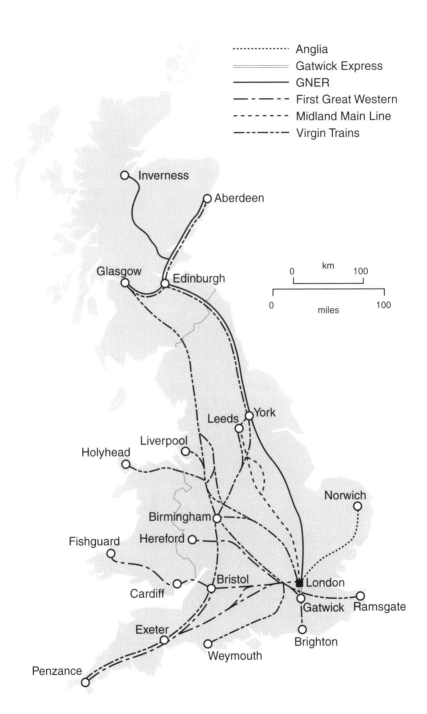

Figure 2.4 Route plans of the former InterCity TOCs. Reprinted from *Transport Policy*, vol. 5, Shaw, J. 'The competitive spirit re-awakens the ghost of railway monopoly', pp. 37–49, 1998. With permission from Elsevier Science.

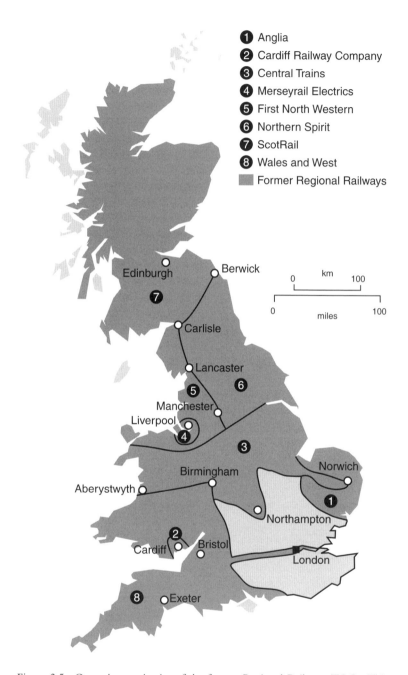

1 Anglia
2 Cardiff Railway Company
3 Central Trains
4 Merseyrail Electrics
5 First North Western
6 Northern Spirit
7 ScotRail
8 Wales and West
▮ Former Regional Railways

Figure 2.5 Operating territories of the former Regional Railways TOCs. This
representation is in part schematic to aid clarity. There are numerous territorial
"incursions"; for example, Northern Spirit runs its "Transpennine Express"
trains to Liverpool. Reprinted from *Transport Policy*, vol. 5, Shaw, J.
'The competitive spirit re-awakens the ghost of railway monopoly',
pp. 37–49, 1998. With permission from Elsevier Science.

2. The Structure of the New Railway

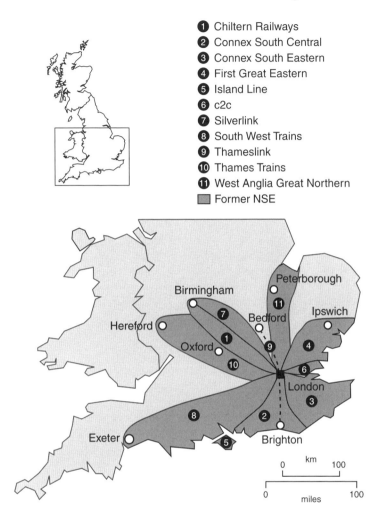

1 Chiltern Railways
2 Connex South Central
3 Connex South Eastern
4 First Great Eastern
5 Island Line
6 c2c
7 Silverlink
8 South West Trains
9 Thameslink
10 Thames Trains
11 West Anglia Great Northern
☐ Former NSE

Figure 2.6   Operating territories of the former Network SouthEast TOCs. Again, this representation is partly schematic. Reprinted from *Transport Policy*, vol. 5, Shaw, J. 'The competitive spirit re-awakens the ghost of railway monopoly', pp. 37–49, 1998. With permission from Elsevier Science.

traffic densities, commercial viability and geographical characteristics. As evident from Figures 2.4–2.6, there are also many points of overlap between franchises; for instance, the Penzance–Bristol corridor is served by First Great Western, CrossCountry and Wales and West.

Franchise awards were made to the company offering to take on the operation of each TOC's services for the lowest subsidy, while committing themselves to a programme of service enhancements, improved reliability and punctuality performance and investments in trains and stations (see Table 2.3). Thus, while undoubtedly the most significant factor, it would be wrong to say that money

Table 2.2 Franchise award/commencement dates, holder and length (TOCs listed in order of letting). Sources: Knowles, R. 'Passenger rail privatisation in Great Britain and its implications, especially for urban areas' in *Journal of Transport Geography*, 6, no. 2, 1998, pp. 117, 133. With permission from Elsevier Science.

Train Operating Company	Franchise awarded/ commenced	Franchise holder	Franchise length (yr/month)
South West Trains	19 December 1995/ 4 February 1996	Stagecoach Holdings	7
First Great Western	20 December 1995/ 4 February 1996	Great Western Holdings	10
c2c	9 May 1996*/ 26 May 1996*	Prism Rail	15
GNER	29 March 1996/ 28 April 1996	Sea Containers	7
Gatwick Express	3 April 1996/ 28 April 1996	National Express Group	15
Midland Mainline	22 April 1996/ 28 April 1996	National Express Group	10
Connex South Central	12 April 1996/ 28 May 1996	CGEA	7
Chiltern Railways	26 June 1996/ 21 July 1996	M40 Trains	7
Connex South Eastern	21 August 1996/ 13 October 1996	CGEA	15
Wales & West	17 September 1996/ 13 October 1996	Prism Rail	7/6
Cardiff Railway Company	17 September 1996/ 13 October 1996	Prism Rail	7/6
Thames Trains	19 September 1996/ 13 October 1996	Victory Railways	7/6
Island Line	20 September 1996/ 13 October 1996	Stagecoach Holdings	5
Virgin CrossCountry	29 November 1996/ 5 January 1997	Virgin Rail Group	15
First Great Eastern	4 December 1996/ 5 January 1997	First Group	7/3
Anglia Railways	6 December 1996/ 5 January 1997	GB Rail	7/3
West Anglia Great Northern	6 December 1996/ 5 January 1997	Prism Rail	7/3
Merseyrail Electrics	20 December 1996/ 19 January 1997	MTL Trust Holdings	7/2
First North Western	5 February 1997/ 2 March 1997	Great Western Holdings	7/1
Silverlink	7 February 1997/ 2 March 1997	National Express Group	7/6

Northern Spirit	10 February 1997/ 2 March 1997	MTL Trust Holdings	7/1
Thameslink	11 February 1997/ 2 March 1997	Go-Ahead/VIA	7/1
Central Trains	17 February 1997/ 2 March 1997	National Express Group	7/1
Virgin West Coast	19 February 1997/ 9 March 1997	Virgin Rail Group	15
ScotRail	25 February 1997/ 1 April 1997	National Express Group	7

* The TOC was originally awarded in December 1995 but this deal was called off and the franchise was re-let (see Chapters 6 and 7).

was the only criterion considered in the franchising process. Franchisees committed themselves to accept a declining level of year-on-year support from OPRAF. Acceptance of this "subsidy taper" reflects a general trust in the ability of private-sector firms to achieve cuts in operating costs as well as to stimulate growth in business – often by unprecedented levels. In some cases, TOCs undertook to move to a reversal of the flow of payment, whereby they will pay OPRAF a steadily increasing premium, rather than draw a subsidy (see Table 2.4). The overall effect of these agreements implies a reduction in the total annual payment (in real terms) by OPRAF and Passenger Transport Executives for passenger rail services from £1.704 billion in 1997–98 to £806 million by 2002–03, after which date subsidies should continue to fall. The reduction varies considerably between franchises. Whereas the subsidy drawn by South West Trains will fall by £26.3 million from 1997–98 (£63.2 million) to 2002–03 (£36.9 million), Virgin West Coast agreed to switch from a £76.6 million subsidy to a premium payment of £4 million over this period (an £80.6 million difference). Under the terms of its 15-year franchise agreement, the company is set to return a massive £227.8 million premium payment in 2011–2.

It is important to acknowledge, however, that the earlier years of privatisation brought a significant rise in passenger rail subsidy; the government grant to BR in 1993–94 had been £1,092 million whereas in 1994–95 it almost doubled to £2.16 billion. This increase in overall subsidy was necessary to fund the substantial rise in the TOCs' expenditure on Railtrack access charges, leasing payments to Roscos and fees for other services all now purchased externally at true market prices rather than supplied "in house". In the period immediately before the sale of the various rail businesses to the private sector, the "surplus" generated as profits by Railtrack and the Roscos flowed back to the Department of Transport and on again to BR as subsidies and grants – the so-called "money-go-round". Once privatisation was established, however, much of this flow was necessarily siphoned off as profits for the companies concerned, although substantial sales receipts were received for Railtrack and the Roscos and some funds still return to the Treasury as taxes (see Figure 2.7). The "costs" of rail privatisation are discussed in more detail in Chapter 7.

Table 2.3 Quality-of-service enhancements secured during the franchising process (TOCs listed in order of letting). Reprinted from Knowles, R. "Passenger rail privatization in Great Britain and its implications, especially for urban areas", *Journal of Transport Geography*, 6, no. 2, 1998, pp. 117, 133. With permission from Elsevier Science.

Train Operating Company	Rolling-stock investment	Stations upgrade	New services	Improved passenger's charter
South West Trains	No	Yes	Bus links	Yes
First Great Western	Refurbished	No	Bus links	Yes
c2c	Fleet replacement (new and refurb)	Yes	Bus links, off peak	Yes
GNER	Refurbished	Yes	Bus links	Yes
Gatwick Express	New	No	Off peak	Yes
Midland Mainline	New and refurbished	Yes	Extra and faster	Yes
Connex South Central	No	Yes	Off peak and faster	Yes
Chiltern Railways	New	Yes	Extra and faster	Yes
Connex South Eastern	Fleet replacement	Yes	Extra and bus link	Yes
Wales & West	Refurbished	Yes	New routes	Yes
Cardiff Railway Company	No	Yes	New routes and bus links	Yes
Thames Trains	No	Yes	Extra and faster	Yes
Island Line	No	Yes	No	Yes
Virgin CrossCountry	Fleet replacement	Yes	Extra, faster and bus link	Yes
First Great Eastern	Refurbished	Yes	Extra and bus link	Yes
Anglia Railways	New and refurbished	Yes	Extra, faster and bus/air link	Yes
West Anglia Great Northern	Refurbished	Yes	Extra, faster and bus links	Yes
Merseyrail Electrics	No	Yes	No	No
First North Western	New and/or refurbished	Yes	Extra and new	Yes
Silverlink	Yes	Yes	Extra, new and bus link	Yes
Northern Spirit	Yes	Yes	Extra and faster	Yes
Thameslink	Refurbished	Yes	Extra	Yes
Central Trains	No	Yes	New, extra, bus link, park and ride	Yes
Virgin West Coast	Fleet replacement	Yes	Extra, faster and electrification	No
ScotRail	Yes	Yes	Extra	Yes

Table 2.4 TOCs' subsidy profiles, 1995/96–2011/12 in 1998 money terms. Source: Office of passenger Rail Franchising. Annual Report 1997–98, OPRAF, 1998, Appendix 5. With permission from OPRAF.

Train Operating Company	1995/ 1996	1996/ 1997	1997/ 1998	1998/ 1999	1999/ 2000	2000/ 2001	2001/ 2002	2002/ 2003	2003/ 2004	2004/ 2005	2005/ 2006	2006/ 2007	2007/ 2008	2008/ 2009	2009/ 2010	2010/ 2011	2011/ 2012
Anglia Railways		8.8	36.2	26.9	22.8	16.5	13.4	8.8	6.5								
c2c		25.4	27.6	25.8	24.1	22.6	21.2	19.9	18.7	17.6	16.5	15.5	14.5	13.6	12.8	12.0	1.8
Cardiff Railway Company		10.2	20.6	18.7	17.6	16.3	15.5	14.7	14								
Central Trains		11.5	187.5	173.4	153.7	145.8	140.9	136.6	132.6								
Chiltern Railways		11.6	14.3	12.9	10.2	6.9	4.8	3.4	0.4								
Connex South Central	75.8	76.0	56.2	48.5	44.8	39.6	37.1	34.6									
Connex South Eastern	57.7	114.6	87.4	63.2	50.7	41.7	33.7	28.5	24.5	19.8	16.8	11.8	8.1	3.3	-1.3	-1.6	
First Great Eastern		5.6	28.6	14.4	8.4	2.8	-0.3	-5.2	-9.8								
First Great Western	9.4	61.8	58.9	55.5	49.4	42.8	35.1	28.2	18.2	8.7	-2.7						
First North Western		12.5	100.3	92.4	84.3	77.4	74.1	71.3	69.0								
Gatwick Express		-4.1	-6.2	-8.1	-10.1	-11.0	-11.8	-12.4	-13.7	-15.1	-16.7	-17.3	-18.8	-20.5	-22.1	-23.9	-1.9
GNER		61.4	55.0	37.4	17.0	6.4	2.0	0.1	0.0								
Island Line		0.9	1.9	1.9	1.9	1.8	0.9										
Merseyrail Electrics		7.5	7.4	6.7	6.1	5.8	5.5	5.7	5.4								
Midland Mainline		16.1	8.2	2.5	0.9	-0.5	-2.6	-4.5	-6.4	-8.4	-10.5	-0.9					
Northern Spirit		12.3	224.5	197.1	175.8	164.3	156.3	150.5	145.6								
ScotRail		280.1	264.8	250.5	234.9	220.4	209.3	202.5									
Silverlink		4.2	49.3	36.5	30.6	27.3	23.8	20.6	17.4	16.3							
South West Trains	9.3	63.2	62.6	62.7	57.5	52.2	46.7	36.9									
Thameslink		1.3	2.5	-6.9	-16.7	-23.2	-24.0	-27.9	-29.4								
Thames Trains		18.7	33.5	25.6	17.5	14.0	7.8	3.9	0.0								
Wales & West		38.3	73.5	64.2	59.3	53.1	49.1	45.5	40.5								
West Anglia Great Northern	14.0	54.5	35.9	26.2	13.5	4.4	-15.0	-26.3									
Virgin CrossCountry		30.6	115.9	95.5	80.0	72.0	66.0	49.2	38.4	21.5	13.4	6.9	3.0	0.8	0.0	-5.0	-10.0
Virgin West Coast		5.8	76.6	70.4	58.0	55.5	54.0	-4.0	-54.5	-57.7	-74.4	-130.9	-156.7	-173.3	-201.8	-209.1	-227.8
Total		1,703.9	1,449.8	1,236.7	1,092.7	984.5	806.4										

Notes: Positive figures represent subsidies payable by OPRAF, negative figures represent premiums payable to OPRAF.
Figures in extreme left and right columns may indicate part-year payment/premiums, depending upon the commencement date of franchises.

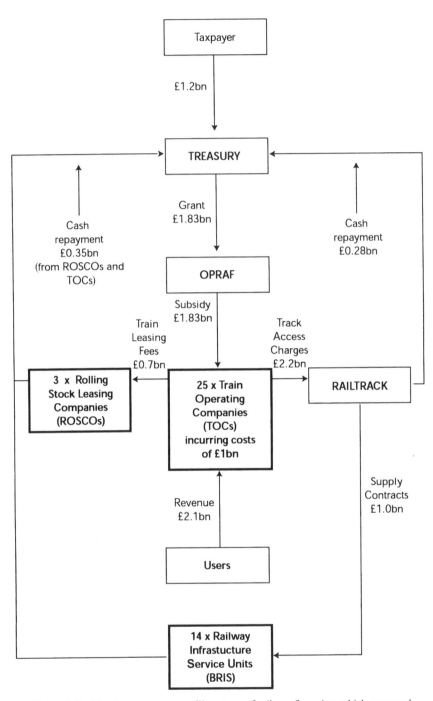

Figure 2.7 The "money-go-round" system of railway financing which operated whilst the restructured BR was still in public ownership.
Source: Steer Davies Gleave.

Figure 2.8   Eurostar test train at Ashford International station, December 1995.
Source: Railtrack.

To safeguard the level and quality of passenger services, OPRAF negotiated Passenger Service Requirements (PSRs) for the passenger operations of each franchise. PSRs laid down for each route a minimum service frequency, maximum journey times, the time of the earliest and latest trains and, in certain cases, minimum capacity levels. Although they were broadly in line with existing service patterns, the minimum frequencies embedded in PSRs were often set at levels somewhat below those the TOCs inherited. This adjustment was designed to enable TOCs to adjust their timetables according to demand and has offered limited potential for TOCs to cut costs through marginal service reductions, thereby helping them adjust to the tapering subsidy payments they have taken on in their franchise agreements. Although PSRs essentially set the "bottom line" for passenger service provision for the duration of the franchises, OPRAF has permitted a limited number of changes. For example, Anglia was allowed to discontinue its daily service between Peterborough and Harwich that featured in its original PSR.

Several significant rail passenger transport operations were excluded from the franchising process. The former European Passenger Services, set up as an independent business under the BRB to operate Eurostar high-speed services from London through the Channel Tunnel to Paris and Brussels in partnership with SNCF of France and SNCB of Belgium, passed to the ownership of London and Continental Railways (LCR) (Figure 2.8). This company had a

Figure 2.9   Heathrow Express Class 332 at Paddington Station, March 1999.
Source: National Railway Museum.

number of key firms among its major shareholders, including Ove Arup, Bechtel, Sir William Halcrow and partners, National Express, SBC Warburg, Virgin Group and SNCF/Systra. LCR ran into difficulties when its patronage failed to reach predicted levels and the Eurostar business has passed to Inter-Capital and Regional Railways (ICCR), a consortium including National Express and British Airways.

The Heathrow Express electrified train service from Paddington to London Heathrow Airport is an entirely commercial operation owned by BAA plc (formerly the British Airports Authority) (Figure 2.9). In addition, certain urban rail operations are also outside the general privatised rail framework. The most significant is the London Underground, although there are others on Tyneside and in Glasgow, as well as a slowly expanding number of light rail systems such as those in Manchester, Sheffield, Croydon and the West Midlands.

The Association of Train Operating Companies (ATOC) was established in 1994 to foster co-operation between the 25 TOCs by running a range of compulsory joint schemes and by acting as a focus for industry representation. Among the interoperator activities administered by ATOC are through ticketing, ticket interavailability and railcards (see Chapter 6), as well as the management and contracting out of the National Rail Enquiry Service (see Chapter 7) and staff travel arrangements. Each of these ventures is governed by its own "scheme council" formed of representatives of each participant, with funding varying according to the nature of participation.

Rolling Stock Leasing Companies

The structure of the new railway has established the principle that TOCs should lease their passenger trains from separate companies, rather than take on the burden of direct ownership. This division of control recognised that the lifespan of rolling stock is far longer than that of the franchises and therefore that it would have been unrealistic to require TOCs to purchase trains and amortise their investment within the confines of a short contract period. Consequently, Roscos were created and these were: Angel Train Contracts, Eversholt Leasing (now HSBC Rail) and Porterbrook Leasing (their curious names were derived from the names of the streets on which their offices were located) (see Chapter 5). Nearly all passenger rolling stock was allocated to one of these three Roscos.[4] Each Rosco was provided with a varied "portfolio" of equipment that would serve a varied customer base and mix of passenger rail markets and also offer the potential for competition between companies servicing the demand for rolling stock. In 1995, the Roscos were transferred to the government in preparation for sale to the private sector.

At the outset, the sale failed to attract serious sustained interest from investors outside the rail industry and two of the three Roscos passed to companies formed by ex-British Rail managers. The exception, Angel Train Contracts, was sold to the GRSH consortium led by the Japanese Nomura group (although Angel's first Chairman, John Prideaux, was a former Director of InterCity). The value of railway rolling-stock leases was to become markedly more impressive, however, for all three Roscos later became targets for takeover at substantially higher prices than the original buyout costs. Porterbrook was taken over by Stagecoach, Eversholt was sold to Forward Trust, part of HSBC Holdings, and Angel Train Contracts was purchased by the Royal Bank of Scotland.

Normally, everyday servicing and repairs are the responsibility of the TOC and several have constructed new facilities for this purpose, such as Central Trains' depots at Nottingham and Birmingham. Some operators subcontract their maintenance to other TOCs or to train builders. For example, the new fleet of electric trains ordered for c2c will be maintained by their manufacturer, ADTranz. Generally, periodic heavy maintenance remains the duty of the Rosco.

Rail Freight

Rail freight operations in Britain saw massive rationalisation through the 1960s and 1970s as rail steadily lost its share of the market to road transport (see Figure 2.10). Across the country there was severe retrenchment which resulted in the closure of terminals and a reduction in services and rolling stock. In several ways, however, private investment had played an important role in the operation of the rail freight system well before the emergence of rail privatisation *per se*. Most freight was carried to and from private terminals, often in privately owned wagons (for example, those owned by stone aggregate companies or by specialist leasing firms). Indeed, BR was somewhat reluctant to invest directly in new freight

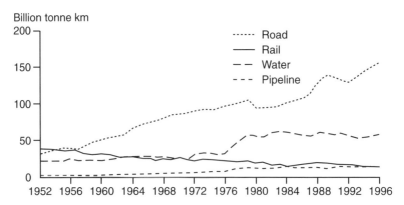

Figure 2.10 Goods moved by mode, 1952–1996. Source: Department of the Environment, Transport and the Regions. *Developing an Integrated Transport Policy: An Invitation to Contribute*, DETR, 1997. Crown Copyright. Reproduced with permission of the Controller of Her Majesty's Stationery Office.

rolling stock, preferring to allow private-sector clients to take on the investment risk. Three companies, Foster Yeoman, ARC (both carrying stone from their quarries in the Mendips) and National Power (coal traffic) had also purchased their own locomotives.

As privatisation policy gathered pace in the early 1990s, the decision was taken to restructure BR's existing freight businesses and six new companies were formed. The trainload freight market was carved up between Loadhaul, Mainline and Transrail; Railfreight Distribution would essentially be concerned with European freight services via the newly opened Channel Tunnel; container operations were allocated to Freightliner; and BR's Royal Mail contract became the responsibility of Rail Express Systems. The trainload freight companies were organised along geographical lines (see Figure 2.11), but the intention was that a significant degree of competition should develop between them. In the event, this ideal proved to be stillborn in practice. When Loadhaul, Mainline and Transrail were offered for sale to the private sector, the government found that a market for three individual companies did not exist and they were all eventually sold to a single bidder, a consortium led by the US-based company, Wisconsin Central. The consortium unified its newly acquired freight operations into a single company, English, Welsh and Scottish Railway (EWS) and also purchased Rail Express Systems and Railfreight Distribution. More recently, EWS has taken on the already privately owned rail operations of National Power (see Chapter 8).

EWS does not have a total monopoly over freight operations, however, as Freightliner was privatised through, and remains, a management buyout. Moreover, Direct Rail Services (DRS), a subsidiary of British Nuclear Fuels, transports spent nuclear fuel and low-level waste for the nuclear industry. While the company is essentially a niche rail freight operator, it has extended

Figure 2.11 The geographical division of the trainload freight companies. Reprinted from *Applied Geography*, vol. 16.

its operations to include haulage of track maintenance and freight distribution trains and even some passenger charter services. Elsewhere, Mendip Rail is responsible for the operation of heavy stone trains from quarries in Somerset belonging to Foster Yeoman and Hanson.

Track Renewal, Heavy Maintenance and Ancillary Companies

At the start of privatisation, responsibility for the maintenance of railway infrastructure was allocated to BRIS, which had been created as part of the reorganisation of BR in the early 1990s. BRIS was divided into 13 separate businesses, divided between infrastructure maintenance companies and track-renewal companies (which are closely interdependent). These units were organised on a broadly geographical basis and were contracted to work on behalf of Railtrack in return for a collective payment in excess of £1 billion. The BRIS companies were sold in 1996; some went to management-buyout teams, although most of the maintenance companies have now passed into the hands of major UK construction companies such as Jarvis, Balfour Beatty, Amey and Tarmac.

The heavy maintenance of BR's locomotives and rolling stock was carried out at the various engineering works operated by BRML. In preparation for privatisation, the seven major repair units were established as stand-alone businesses, which were all sold in 1995. The works at Chart Leacon, Doncaster and Ilford, together with the Swindon Electronics Centre were sold to ABB (which became part of ADTranz), those at Glasgow and Wolverton passed to Railcare (a joint venture between Babcock International and Siemens), while the Eastleigh unit was sold to a management-buyout business, Wessex Traincare.

Privatisation saw numerous other ancillary service units detached from BR and sold to the private sector. Examples include BR Telecoms (sold to Racal) and Transmark, BR's consultancy business (sold to Sir William Halcrow and partners). Generally, much of the specialised expertise required by the rail industry that was available "in house" is now supplied by a considerable battery of consultancy firms. These compete to offer a wide range of services to the rail industry such as engineering consultancy, financial advice, planning, quality management, IT, engineering, design, marketing, publicity and training.

The Regulatory Framework

Although privatisation of the rail network was based on the belief that commercial freedom and enterprise would generate a more effective system, it was recognised that market forces alone could not safeguard wider social objectives. As with the privatised utilities, it was therefore essential to regulate the railways in order to sustain the integrity of the national rail network and to protect the interests of passengers.

In contrast to the other privatised utilities, however, a "dual" system of regulation was established for the railways which included OPRAF and the ORR. These two bodies have powers and responsibilities that are in theory complementary, although in reality there is a degree of overlap (see Chapters 6 and 9). Further regulatory oversight is provided through the contributions of the RUCCs and Her Majesty's Railway Inspectorate (HMRI), with its overall responsibilities for safety matters as part of the Health and Safety Executive (HSE).

Office of Passenger Rail Franchising

OPRAF has several key functions and duties. First, it was responsible for managing the sale of the passenger rail franchises, by inviting tenders for each of the TOCs and awarding the franchise to the most competitive bidder. OPRAF also considered the financial and corporate reliability of the franchisees. Secondly, OPRAF administers the operation of the franchises. A central part of the franchising process was the contract drawn up between each successful TOC and OPRAF – the Franchise Agreement. The Agreement included, among other things, the level and pattern of services (the PSR), the subsidy payable and duration of the franchise. All successful franchisees also made additional commitments to improve their product, detailed in a Franchise Plan. This included promises on such developments as new trains, improvements in reliability and punctuality, new bus connections, provision for cyclists and station improvements. OPRAF must police both the Franchise Agreement and the Franchise Plan.

Thirdly, OPRAF disburses subsidy payments to TOCs for those passenger-train operations needing financial support and, in the case of the more commercially viable franchises, receives the agreed premium payment from the TOC. In certain cases OPRAF works with the Passenger Transport Executives (PTEs) when providing subsidy in the major conurbations outside London. PTEs were set up by the 1968 Transport Act and were given powers to secure and subsidise suburban rail services provided by BR in their areas. Additional payments to support rail services which otherwise would not have been run by BR were drawn from an extra element in local authorities' Revenue Support Grants (RSGs). With the reorganisation of the railway in 1994, however, there was a significant increase in the charges PTEs had to pay the fledgling Railtrack (for track and station access) and the Roscos (for train leases) as a result of their being established as profitable entities. This required an enhanced "bolt on" element in the RSG to meet the higher costs. PTEs are parties to the Franchise Agreements with TOCs and OPRAF that apply to those train services which they support above the level of the Passenger Service Requirement. The Central Trains, Merseyrail Electrics, First North Western, Northern Spirit and ScotRail franchises all derive part of their funding from their local PTEs.

Fourthly, OPRAF operates a system of financial performance incentives and penalties to secure the quality of passenger services. Bonus incentive payments are paid to those TOCs operating suburban commuter and regional services at levels of punctuality and reliability above those set in their Passenger's Charters (see

Chapter 6). Conversely, the TOCs are liable to pay OPRAF penalty payments if they fall short in terms of service quality criteria such as train capacity and cancellations. OPRAF's incentive regimes operate in addition to that agreed between the TOCs and Railtrack.

Finally, OPRAF protects consumers by regulating ticket prices. The Franchising Director is tasked with ensuring that fares are "reasonable". A fundamental feature of this aspect of regulation is that fare increases for many tickets were broadly pegged to the Retail Price Index (RPI) in the first 3 years of the franchise, but are now reduced to RPI minus 1 per cent. However, only unrestricted standard class fares, "saver" fares, certain single fares for shorter journeys and some standard-class season tickets, including weekly tickets, are regulated.

Under the 1993 Railways Act, OPRAF's activities were put under the control of the Secretary of State for Transport through a set of Objectives, Instructions and Guidance (OIG). These require the Franchising Director to protect the interests of both taxpayers and rail passengers, to follow relevant government policy and also to maintain close relationships with a range of relevant organisations. Thus although OPRAF was given some degree of flexibility and discretion in its activities, it remains subject to fairly close governmental control. In 1997, the OIG were adjusted to make the protection of passenger interests the top priority (as opposed to the initial concern to transfer the passenger franchises to the private sector as rapidly as possible). This new emphasis has been activated for instance by negotiating an additional "passenger dividend" package (including station improvements) from TOCs when sanctioning changes in ownership, as in the case of FirstGroup's recent takeover of Great Western Holdings.

Office of the Rail Regulator

The Regulator was set up as the second element in the "dual" system of regulation established under the Railways Act, with duties that include: protecting the interests of rail passengers, promoting the use and development of rail freight, promoting the use and development of the rail network, promoting competition and efficiency, overseeing the financial, safety and environmental health of the railway system and enforcing through-ticketing agreements and the maintenance of network benefits.

The Regulator has four main functions. First, he issues, modifies and enforces licences and these fall into four categories: the Network Licence issued to Railtrack, Operating Licences for Train Operating Companies (including freight operators), Station Licences and Light Maintenance Depot Licences. The Regulator can use his powers with respect to licences to ensure that the quality of service for rail passengers is maintained and improved. Secondly, he approves access agreements between train operators and owners of track, stations and light maintenance depots. Given its overwhelmingly dominant control of the national rail infrastructure, Railtrack is clearly the principal target for regulation under this heading, which includes the control and monitoring of track-access charges. The Regulator acts as arbitrator in any disputes between Railtrack and train operators, which gives him an important role in the economic regulation of the railway. Generally, the Regulator has become a strong defender of the rail system in the interests of rail users in his often critical and confrontational dealings with Railtrack (see Chapter 4).

Thirdly, the ORR applies legislation and regulation with regard to competition. The Regulator was given the statutory duty to promote competition between train operators, although in practice his role has emphasised moderation and restriction of competition to protect franchise holders, rather than any concerted attempt to foster open-access operations (see Chapters 6 and 9). Indeed, the Regulator promotes co-operation between TOCs if this is considered to be beneficial to rail passengers. The Regulator's fourth main function is to ensure that, in all his tasks, he protects consumers of rail services.

The Regulator has no statutory obligation to follow government objectives for the railways; he has more independence than OPRAF, having been subject simply to "guidance" from the Secretary of State until the end of 1996 rather than the more prescriptive and enduring OIG. The requirement for statutory guidance was replaced by a voluntary concordat between the Regulator and the government as a mechanism for communication in the public interest.

Certain core contracts within the rail system are not subject to direct regulation, notably the leases undertaken by TOCs with Roscos for their rolling stock and contracts between Railtrack and maintenance firms. It should also be noted that the regulatory framework established under the Railways Act has less potential to influence the development of rail freight traffic than for the passenger market; there is, for instance, no "Freight Franchising Director". A further "gap" in the regulatory system established under the 1993 Act is the absence of an overarching focus for strategic planning of the national railway system (see Chapter 10).

Rail Users' Consultative Committees

Eight regionally based RUCCs were recognised by the 1993 Railways Act (the Committees had actually existed for over 40 years at the time of privatisation) and charged to protect the interests of rail users, essentially by representing the views of rail passengers on such matters as punctuality and reliability, timetable changes, service quality and fares, as well as the consequences of any rail closure proposals. The Regulator funds and supports the RUCCs and also appoints their members, who represent a spectrum of rail users. The activities of the RUCCs are co-ordinated and given a national focus by the Central Rail Users' Consultative Committee (CRUCC). The CRUCC also incorporates the London Regional Passengers' Committee.

Her Majesty's Railway Inspectorate

HMRI is now part of the HSE, and has responsibility for overseeing safety on the rail system. A long-established, independent safety regulator, HMRI's duties include the provision of guidance on safety matters to train operators, monitoring of safety procedures, inspection of new infrastructure and rolling stock and accident investigation. HMRI validates Railtrack's own "Safety Case", which sets out the systems and standards used to ensure safe rail operations, but Railtrack itself is responsible for validating the Safety Cases of train and station operators (see Chapter 3).

Post-Privatisation Developments

The structure of the rail industry has not remained static since privatisation was completed in 1997. There have been continual adjustments, especially in the control of rail businesses. A prominent tendency has been the resale of units initially sold to management-buyout teams to commercial firms, with a degree of organisational concentration, although ownership and control of the railway system is still relatively fragmented. This transfer of control was the case for the Roscos (see Chapter 5), several TOCs (see Chapter 7) and various infrastructure and train maintenance-businesses.

With respect to regulatory control, the major change has been the emergence of the Strategic Rail Authority (SRA), initially in "shadow" form, on 1 April 1999, with Sir Alistair Morton as its Chairman. The SRA will take over the functions of OPRAF in terms of awarding and overseeing passenger franchises and consumer protection, but its brief will be extended to include much wider ranging degrees of strategic planning and co-ordination of rail policy and investment. It is intended that the SRA will work closely with local and national organisations in the public and private sectors to ensure the railway plays an appropriate role within an integrated transport system.

Notes

1. Office of Passenger Rail Franchising. *Passenger Rail Industry Overview*, OPRAF, 1996.
2. Cmnd 2012. *New Opportunities for the Railways*, 1992.
3. These are: Charing Cross, Euston, King's Cross, Liverpool Street, London Bridge, Paddington, Victoria and Waterloo, Birmingham New Street, Edinburgh Waverley, Gatwick Airport, Glasgow Central, Leeds and Manchester Piccadilly.
4. A limited amount of rolling stock was allocated to the Special Trains Unit, responsible for charter-train hire, which was initially sold to Waterman Railways.

3. Creating Railtrack

John Edmonds

However intensive the debate may have been amongst policy makers on the merits of a vertically separated railway with franchising and an independent track authority, the adoption of the concept came as a surprise and culture shock to the industry itself. Railway company directors had never needed advice from staff colleges or consultants to persuade them to operate on a vertically integrated basis. For many years – in some cases up to the beginning of the Second World War – railways worked at the leading edge in their marketing, operating and engineering disciplines and the companies' instinctive approach remained to design, build, operate and maintain most of their own resources. It took the influx of new blood under Richard Beeching in 1963 to provide the first serious challenge to what by then had become a long outdated approach and, by the late 1980s, under Sir Robert Reid's leadership, there remained only the core railway activities within vertically integrated businesses. With privatisation by then on the agenda, it was generally assumed within the industry that these businesses would form the basis for the privately-owned companies although the resurrection of the old regionally based companies was advocated by a few romantics.

Opponents of the track-authority model briefed their press and parliamentary colleagues accordingly, pointing out that such an arrangement did not exist anywhere else in the world, apart from a limited experiment in Sweden working to quite different ground rules.[1] Despite the European Directive 91/440, other railway companies within the EU had resisted change and looked on in disbelief at the UK debate. By the time a firm political decision was taken to proceed, opinion had hardened into outright opposition from all sides and catchphrases such as "fragmentation", "unworkable", "unsafe" and "poll tax on wheels" became common currency. Furthermore, there was at this stage no public-relations machine to counter the briefings readily provided by "industry spokesmen". Those who did understand the proposals were totally preoccupied in developing a working model from the bare bones of the political decision. The attitudes and actions of key industry players during the period in which Railtrack was created has to be understood in the context of these factors, in some cases overlaid of course with the usual consequences of change: loss of empire and different career prospects. Whether with a more reasonable period

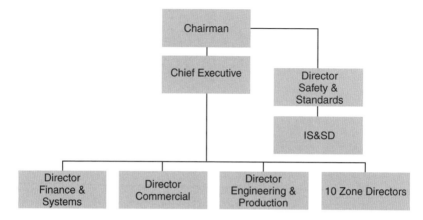

Figure 3.1   Railtrack's organisational structure. Source: Railtrack.

of preparation and a "hearts and minds" exercise to help understanding and change attitudes it would have been possible to organise a smoother transition is a moot point.

The recruitment of directors and managers to set up Railtrack took place against this unpromising background. Railtrack was initially formed as a division of British Rail (BR) in April 1993 with Robert Horton as Chairman designate and myself as Chief Executive designate. In the months that followed, the broad structure of the company was drawn up and some early recruitment was possible against a target vesting date of 1 April 1994. The main Board structure, given the political decision that Railtrack should assume overall responsibility for safety within the railway industry (see below), provided for the Chief Executive assuming responsibility for the line management of Railtrack with the Safety Director reporting directly to the Chairman and Board. The main Board and its supporting committee structure evolved as senior appointments were made and is shown in a simplified form in Figure 3.1. Initially, ten Zonal Directors were appointed to take on the geographical management task, the boundaries of the zones closely mirroring the preceding BR profit centres and the embryo Train Operating Companies (TOCs) so that management system changes were kept to a minimum (as Chapter 3 points out, there are now seven operating zones).

This chapter outlines the process of vesting Railtrack out of BR and its subsequent sale and then examines in detail the key issues policy makers were forced to consider (and those which received most interest in the media) as the company was created: safety, contracts with rail service operators and the associated performance regime, contracts with suppliers and investment. Railtrack's performance in these areas until the end of the 1996–97 financial year is also reviewed. Commentary on the company's recent record, in the period following my retirement as its Chief Executive in 1997, follows in the next chapter.

Creating Railtrack

The first step in the process of transferring the assets from BR to Railtrack was a draft of the main Railtrack transfer scheme in January 1994, produced by BR using the services of City lawyers Clifford Chance. Terence Jenner from BR played a significant co-ordinating role in designing the "structure" of the main scheme and the other transfer schemes which had to be made by BR for other vestings to take effect. The law firm Simmons & Simmons acted for Railtrack with Simon Osborne in the lead and further draft schemes were produced, each of which was considerably longer than its predecessor, as the various policy strands were agreed and formalised.

Gareth Davies, a partner at Simmons & Simmons, looked back on the 1994 meetings in which legal teams quickly "absorbed a cultural change" in learning about the railways. He remembers a fraught atmosphere: "As lawyers, we were used to going into adversarial situations to negotiate a deal, argue a dispute or to present a case in court. It was essential in the limited time that we didn't get distracted."[2] The incredible workload involved for the legal and property professionals and their advisers is summed up in Table 3.1

One of the most time-consuming and difficult areas was the division of the asset base, that is the process of agreeing which assets stayed with BR (for the time being) and which were vested to Railtrack. An instinctive desire to acquire assets and memories of the National Freight Corporation's acquisition and subsequent lucrative development of railway land after the 1968 vesting ensured that all the players fought their corner – particularly those players who, rightly or wrongly, felt able to anticipate their future employer. The basic ground rules, set by the government, provided that the freehold of stations, yards, depots and all the infrastructure itself should pass from BR to Railtrack, who in turn would lease

Table 3.1 Legal documents on transfer schemes in the vesting process. There were a further seven volumes (that is, large ring-binders) of documents relating to the transfer schemes for Railway Claims Limited, Hallmark, BRT, Eversholt Train Leasing Company Limited, Porterbrook Leasing Company, Angel Train Contracts Limited and Gatwick Express. Each volume contained between twenty-one and thirty-one individual documents. Source: Railtrack.

Railtrack Transfer Scheme	(2 volumes)	41 documents
Licence documents and approvals for 1 April 1994	(1 volume)	29 documents
Waterloo and City Putney Bridge to Wimbledon Transfer Scheme	(1 volume)	27 documents
Railtrack Transfer Scheme supplemental agreements	(5 volumes)	54 documents
Railtrack Transfer Scheme ancillary agreements	(1 volume)	22 documents
Railtrack Transfer Scheme track access agreements	(3 volumes)	28 documents
Railtrack Transfer Scheme station access agreements	(2 volumes)	43 documents
Railtrack Transfer Scheme freight access agreements	(4 volumes)	224 documents
Derby Railway Technical Centre, Railfreight Distribution and Rail Express Systems	(1 volume)	26 documents

certain assets back to the new operating companies on terms which reflected the needs of those companies. It was particularly important that these terms took account of the companies' imminent sale. In view of the criticisms of earlier privatisations in which property had been seriously undervalued leading to wind-fall profits, the government made it clear that all non-operational land must stay with BR and only clearly defined operational land should pass to Railtrack; in addition the government decided that certain key assets had to be reserved for the Channel Tunnel Rail Link.

In addition to these tangible assets, there were also the intangible assets such as brands, logos, engineering drawings and plans and, in particular, the issue of where BR's extensive intellectual property rights would rest. BR suggested that intellectual property relating to "what is" should vest in Railtrack, while property relating to "how to" should remain with BR, so that the latter could be transferred, as necessary, to the new generation of infrastructure maintenance and track–renewal companies when they were formed; by and large this approach has worked.

The vesting of Railtrack also involved the setting up a series of template contracts with Railtrack's customers and suppliers which, at the time of vesting, were still part of BR. These contracts, as the chapter will later explain, were superseded by a second suite of "commercially negotiated" contracts which were introduced in the run-up to Railtrack's flotation. Work proceeded between Clifford Chance for BR and Simmons & Simmons for Railtrack in drawing up literally hundreds of agreements which had to be entered into when Railtrack vested. Although global passenger track-access agreements and station-access agreements sufficed at that stage, freight access required separate freight track-access agreements in respect of some 220 traffic flows.

The result of this preparatory work was that on 1 April 1994 almost all of BR's infrastructure was transferred to Railtrack, encompassing some 11,000 miles of track with associated signalling and electrical control equipment, around 40,000 bridges, viaducts and tunnels, some 2,500 stations, 90 light maintenance depots and over 9,000 level crossings. A key objective of "vesting" had been that customers would not be aware of the change; this was duly achieved with the operational control systems passing uneventfully to Railtrack while designated signatories from BR and Railtrack spent the night signing the transfer documents listed in Table 3.1.

Railtrack's flotation

The White Paper *New Opportunities for the Railways* had not specified when Railtrack would be moved into the private sector but the rail privatisation process began to fall behind schedule for a whole variety of reasons: the original timescale was overambitious and underestimated the scale and complexity of the task. It became increasingly clear that if Railtrack was to be privatised at all, it would have to be undertaken while the Conservatives, facing a dwindling majority, were still in power and before the general election, due no later than May 1997, was called.

After much discussion, the decision to float the government-owned company in 1996 was formally announced in July 1995. Roger Freeman remembers that:

> *When the Railways Bill entered Parliament in 1992 it had not been planned to privatise Railtrack, but the position changed during 1993. Robert Horton was constantly lobbying ministers to put Railtrack in the private sector. He just never gave up. In the end, ministers wanted investment in the railways and there was no way of doing that unless it was in the private sector. There was absolutely no chance of an increase in rail spending from the government.*

It is true that the funding difficulties BR had faced within the External Financing Limit were unchanged as long as Railtrack remained a government-owned company – if anything, they would have become more difficult because of the need to determine with government the split of available funds between Railtrack and BR.[3] Railtrack's support for early privatisation was unequivocal although it wanted to make sure the terms would be right for the company. In particular it sought a 100 per cent sale, a strong share register to protect against subsequent political interference, a realistic balance sheet (enabling in due course an AA credit rating) and a regulatory and contractual framework which left the company to perform against defined financial and operational targets. The Directors also wanted recognition by the government and the new Rail Regulator that although Railtrack was a monopoly in the sense that it owned all the track, rail transport's position with its customers was weak, with low market share except for a handful of InterCity and suburban routes into London and what was left of bulk freight traffic.[4] Railtrack wanted ministers to acknowledge that its taking on inherited financial burdens and commitments would in the long term depress still further rail's market share.

The government in fact shared these objectives, although the detailed negotiations inevitably took time as civil servants were naturally anxious to avoid the mistakes of earlier privatisations. For example, whilst attractive contract terms were necessary to ensure the successful trade sale of the engineering companies, they looked constraining and very unappealing to Railtrack, which was anxious to establish competition in supply at the earliest possible stage.

Ministers took the decision to privatise Railtrack through a public sale because of the size of the business and a view that it had many characteristics of a regulated monopoly utility with which the UK retail investor was familiar. It also met the government's objectives of wider share ownership and avoided the potential criticism of concentrating too much power in too few hands that may have been levelled at a trade sale.

Railtrack's management and its advisers were particularly keen that one of the prerequisites for the sale should be that a substantial proportion of the former BR be in the private sector. They felt it was important to be able to demonstrate to the market that the new industry could work in the private sector and, as such, a good proportion of Railtrack's customers and suppliers would need to have been sold. The original timescales for the railway privatisation had sought to achieve this objective but, as already noted, in practice the sales programme fell gradually

Table 3.2 Key milestones in Railtrack's flotation. Source: Railtrack	
July 1992	Proposals for new institutional regime for rail detailed by government White Paper: *New Opportunities for the Railway*.
November 1993	The Railways Act passed providing the legislative framework for the break-up of the rail industry and to appoint the regulatory bodies.
December 1993	John Swift appointed as Rail Regulator.
April 1994	Railtrack vested out of BR.
November 1994	Regulator determines structure of access charges for franchised passenger services.
January 1995	Regulator sets passenger-access charges for period through to 31 March 2001.
July 1995	Government announced its intention to float Railtrack before end of current parliament (i.e. before the election which subsequently took place in May 1997).
December 1995	Performance regimes became operational.
January 1996	Government announced Railtrack to be floated in May 1996.
March 1996	Railtrack's balance sheet formalised: government wrote off £1,459 million of Railtrack debt leaving £585 million of borrowings in the company.
26 March 1996	Retail marketing campaign launched with mail shots to 5 million households and media advertising.
15 April 1996	Pathfinder prospectus published and government announced its intention to sell 100% of Railtrack.
17 April 1996	Marketing roadshows begin to institutions.
1 May 1996	Railtrack prospectus published and launch of UK public offer.
15 May 1996	Close of the UK public offer.
20 May 1996	Railtrack shares start trading on London Stock Exchange.

behind the original schedules. By the time of flotation, around 40 per cent by turnover of the former BR (excluding Railtrack) had been privatised. Five of the 25 TOCs had been transferred to the private sector and the franchising of two more was nearly complete. Four of the six freight companies had been sold as had ten of the thirteen maintenance and renewal companies. Table 3.2 outlines the early milestones of the rail privatisation process and situates Railtrack's sale among them.

As a newly formed company there were a great number of fundamental functions and processes to put in place. Some of these were what any large undertaking would require – such as the development of the business plan, policies for health and safety, employment contracts, new systems and so on – and there were other commitments specifically required for the flotation process itself such as synthesising a 3-year financial track record. Naturally, given the demanding timescales established by the proposed flotation date, the latter tasks, for the most part, had to take priority during this period.

A key task for Railtrack and the Department of Transport (DoT) was establishing the capital structure that would be put in place for flotation and the detailed negotiations were led for Railtrack by its Finance Director, Norman Broadhurst. Important points in the debate included the characteristics of the initial track-access pricing regime, the development of Railtrack's accounting policies until the publication of its first set of accounts in the autumn of 1995 and the creation of a performance regime with an attempt to make its outcome financially neutral but with incentives for Railtrack to outperform. Funding issues surrounding the company's substantial investment programme were crucial to resolve and the level of debt appropriate to the company at flotation had to be decided upon. The government had to balance the debt and equity to maximise value, as Robert Jennings, of its bankers SG Warburg, noted:

> *To secure maximum enterprise value for the government, it was essential for us to leave debt in Railtrack even though the company's capital-expenditure programme meant that it would be cash-flow-negative for several years. Understandably, the company felt differently about this.*[5]

In the event, the government wrote off £1,459 million of the £2,044 million debt which Railtrack had acquired from BR.

One of the Stock Exchange's requirements for a company coming to the market is a robust 3-year financial record of a company's trading. This posed significant problems since Railtrack was required to create its financial track record in part from its own trading data and in part from BR's accounts which had been compiled on an entirely different basis. The financial information for the 2 years ended 31 March 1994 which related to those activities which were transferred from BR to Railtrack had to be recreated for the purposes of the financial track record in the prospectus. Broadhurst commented:

> *This was a challenging task. Not only were the assets split between BR and Railtrack making the accounting separation complicated but BR had a different approach to accounting policies. We all worked very hard in an attempt to create some meaningful data.*

The sale process was relatively simple in that it followed the well-trodden path that had been established by the Conservative government's privatisation programme. There were, however, aspects of the Railtrack sale that were different; notably, this was the first open-priced book-built privatisation in the UK.[6] Bookbuilding was chosen because it was considered to be more likely to maximise the proceeds than an underwritten structure – the process adopted for previous privatisations. The offer to the UK public was largely made through the Share Shop network, an approach which had proved successful in the past.

Railtrack was sold in May 1996 for a total of £1.9 billion. The sale was clearly a success in terms of meeting the timetable set by ministers and attracting investor interest. The total offer was seven times oversubscribed, some 665,000 retail investors applied and eventually accounted for over 50 per cent of the total offer and over 90 per cent of Railtrack's employees became shareholders. The company was sold at the top of the price range set out in the prospectus although, as has been pointed out many times, this range was strongly influenced by the political climate at the time and the proceeds to the taxpayer suffered accordingly. In a subsequent analysis of the flotation, Robert Lilja commented that:

> *The main factors contributing to the success of the sale were: the institutional investors believed in the robust nature of the new industry structure and Railtrack's future revenue base, the regulatory framework seemed relatively secure, the offer structure was flexible allowing momentum to be built and the syndicate was small, the management did a good job on the roadshow, there was a comprehensive and successful marketing campaign and retail investors had done well on previous privatisations.*

The National Audit Office (NAO), in a subsequent enquiry, suggested that a higher price could have been achieved if the sale had been delayed to allow Railtrack to show greater experience or if there had only been a partial sale of the shares.[7]

Safety Management in the New Industry

Of the many critical determinants which had to be met for the ambitious time-scales set for rail privatisation to be achieved, the most important had to be sustaining safety. Whilst the financial elements could be manipulated to meet the demands and expectations of the market, a single serious accident involving loss of life would have scuppered the entire process and all those closely involved were well aware of this.

Railways provide the safest form of land transport and railwaymen in this country have every reason to be proud of past achievements. However, the serious accident at Clapham in December 1988, followed by accidents in March 1989 at Purley, Surrey and Belgrove, Glasgow had given them a severe jolt and the very thorough subsequent enquiry led by Sir Anthony Hidden in November 1989 revealed many shortcomings in the rail safety-management systems and procedures. Public concern was further highlighted by the P&O ferry accident at Zeebrugge and the London Underground fire at King's Cross in so far as both enquiries also revealed weaknesses in safety-management processes.

In the years following the Clapham accident, BR worked hard to implement the Hidden recommendations and Sir Bob Reid, with his extensive experience of disciplines in the oil industry, successfully led a personal crusade to improve safety awareness and to accelerate the process of defining standards and monitoring compliance. By the time the government had announced its determination to press ahead with rail privatisation and that vertical separation was the chosen framework, it was clear that several years' work would be necessary simply to complete the documentation of standards and the analysis of proper systems and processes. Particular attention would be needed in difficult areas like the commissioning of new rolling stock, new signalling systems and the development of cost-effective train protection. Conceptually, many railway safety professionals were concerned that vertical separation would mean the loss of a single command structure thereby making it more difficult to define technical standards and operational procedures and also monitor compliance.

In July 1992 John MacGregor, then Secretary of State for Transport, asked the Health and Safety Commission, and through it the Health and Safety Executive (HSE), to advise on the way ahead. In January 1993 their report, *Ensuring Safety on Britain's Railways*, was published in which proposals for assuring safety "following the liberalisation of access to and privatisation of British Railways" were set out. The most important was that, under the revised arrangements, the railways should come fully within the scope of the 1974 Health and Safety at Work Act. This meant that all parties would be held accountable for the safety of those aspects over which they had control. The report also proposed the concept of the "infrastructure controller", recognising that because the infrastructure company would have central control functions and a relationship with all the other players, it would need to impose conditions of access and monitor compliance with them. The infrastructure controller was therefore given the duty to validate the safety arrangements of users – i.e. train operators – and to audit compliance with the promises made at the validation of their "safety case". The infrastructure controller's own arrangements would be vetted by the HSE.

Following the Clapham accident, the British Railways Board (BRB) had set up a Group Standards Organisation and there were very strong representations that it should remain intact, either as an independent unit or linked with the Railway Inspectorate of HSE. However, a political decision was made immediately prior to vesting on the advice of the HSE to transfer the Group Standards Organisation in its entirety to Railtrack to become its Safety and Standards Directorate. This would give Railtrack key safety responsibilities across the whole industry, as well as introducing another level in the safety chain.

Misgivings were expressed in some quarters that Railtrack would be influenced by commercial factors in exercising these responsibilities, but the government nevertheless accepted *Ensuring Safety on Britain's Railways* as defining the way ahead. A DoT official explained:

> *Here was an industry that had demonstrated itself to be very safe, whether set against other modes of transport or against railways overseas. The advice of HSE was clear – that the Group Standards unit should transfer to Railtrack. We took the expert advice and, frankly, there was no mood to tamper with a safety system that had been working very effectively.*

As a consequence of the government's decision, the Regulator introduced Condition 3 to Railtrack's Licence which required the Safety Directorate to be adequately funded and independent of Railtrack's commercial business and established the Regulator as the appeals body in the event of any dispute. Three new sets of Regulations were made under the Health and Safety at Work Act to give legal substance to the proposals. The most important was the Railway (Safety Case) Regulations 1994, which brought the concept of safety cases, as developed

Table 3.3 Summary of fatalities and other incidents, 1992/93–1995/96. Source: Railtrack Safety and Standard Directorate.

Date	1992–93	1993–94	1994–95	1995–96
Passenger fatalities*	14	9	17	16
Workforce fatalities*	9	5	7	2
Level-crossing fatalities*	13	13	10	9
Passenger-train collisions and derailments	35	52	40	38
Signals passed at danger on or affecting the running line	749	790	735	702
All accidental/equiv. fatalities per million train miles†	0.67	0.66	0.65	0.61

* Accidental fatalities.
† Measures annual change in harm on the railway network.

by the nuclear and offshore oil industries, to rail. Railtrack was required to document its arrangements for managing safety and formally commit to them and to compliance with railway group standards. This would have to be accepted by the HSE. The operators of both trains and stations would produce similarly structured safety cases to be accepted by Railtrack's Safety and Standards Directorate. The principle of the safety case "cascade" was thus established and has proved very powerful. Further regulations require operators to make a written commitment to comply with the infrastructure controller's "reasonable requests" with regards to safety, create a general duty for operators to co-operate on safety matters and give Railtrack the effective authority to lead the management of safety for the industry.

It had become the practice of BR to produce an annual Safety Plan, incorporating a set of safety objectives and monitoring their achievement. Railtrack maintained this practice, with the lead role taken by the Safety and Standards Directorate and the results presented to the Railtrack Group Board via the Safety, Environment and Health Committee. Almost all the key safety-performance indicators showed sustained improvement throughout this period of radical structural change. Table 3.3 sets out a summary of fatalities and other incidents for the 5 years from 1992 to 1997. Taking a broader view, the public fatality rate and significant train accidents per million train miles showed a continuing downward trend during this period (see Figures 3.2 and 3.3).

Whilst the formal process of producing a safety case can seem tedious and over-bureaucratic, in the newly vertically separated structure the results proved very encouraging. With greater experience and understanding, it should be possible to reduce the time and paperwork involved. Four main areas of difficulty proved to be the technical acceptance of new rolling stock, the continuing need to define and revise standards, the management of Railtrack's contractors and train protection. Difficulties under the first two headings would have arisen irrespective of privatisation or indeed the form of privatisation. The interaction

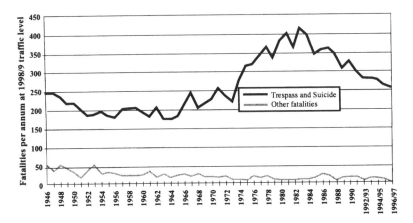

Figure 3.2   Fatalities per annum, 1946–1996/97. Source: HMRI Annual Report.

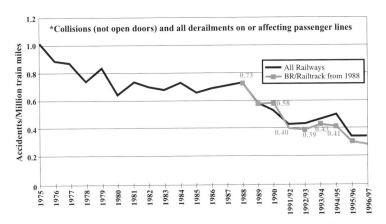

Figure 3.3   Accidents per million train miles, 1975–1996/97.
Source: HMRI Annual Report.

between new electric locomotives/units and existing/potential new signalling systems created a number of uncertainties and the straight-forward question – "Is it safe to use these vehicles on this infrastructure?" – proved difficult to answer. Better proficiency in risk-assessment techniques and better collaboration between train designers and infrastructure engineers have improved understanding but the potential for delays remains as delivery of the new rolling stock builds up. The full extent of the programme of defining and rationalising standards could not be finalised until after the spring of 1997, but safety was maintained through a process of risk management and registering non-compliance and this had no adverse effect on safety in the short term.

The third problem – the management of Railtrack's contractors – arose directly from the privatisation process, which had assumed the principle of the "competent contractor". In fact, many skilled staff had moved on during the various regroupings which had taken place during the sale process and Railtrack, following a series of incidents, had to step up the arrangements for the supervision and monitoring of its contractors and the registration of personnel competent to work safely on the network.

Train protection, the fourth issue, refers to systems guarding against the risks of driver error in passing red signals and overspeeding. In the aftermath of Clapham and the Hidden Report, BR had committed itself to installing Automatic Train Protection (ATP) – which automatically stops trains passing red signals and slows speeding trains down – system-wide. This proved inordinately costly relative to its benefits and BR's risk-based report recommending withdrawal from this commitment was accepted by BR, Railtrack and HSE in 1994 and endorsed by the government in 1995. Railtrack developed an alternative train protection strategy, based on a range of short, medium and long-term measures which offer fewer safety benefits than ATP but at a much lower cost and this has since been endorsed by all parties as the Train Protection Warning System (TPWS). Recent developments in safety issues, particularly with regard to this last point, are discussed in the next chapter.

Contracts with Rail-Service Operators

The negotiation of the passenger track-access contracts, initially for vesting and then for flotation/franchising, was a testing experience for all the parties involved and although they had to form the basis of the commercial relationship between Railtrack and its customers, the TOCs, there was all too often nothing particularly "commercial" about their style and content. At the outset, there were doubts about how they would be constructed or what they would contain. As Gareth Davies remembers:

> No one really understood [what] the principles of a track-access agreement should be at that [early] stage ... Frankly, if you look at the first contracts, each one is very different and yet, ignoring the fact that the trains run to different places and provide a different quality of services, they should be substantially similar contracts, but they're not. And what we learnt from that was the need for – the advantages of – standardisation.[8]

This realisation enabled Davies' team to proceed with the task far more quickly than would otherwise have been possible.

The overall level of the track-access charges was established prior to Railtrack's vesting through a joint industry committee called the Charging Implementation Group, which was chaired by DoT officials. The overall level was based on an analysis of the breakdown of assets and expenditure budgets for the various parts of BR that were being split up. Access charges were set to cover operating costs, current cost depreciation and a return on capital. This return was based on an assessment of Railtrack's assets in terms of their Modern Equivalent Asset Value (MEAV) and a rate of return of 5.1 per cent. It was expected that the annual rate of return would increase to 8 per cent over the 3 years following vesting, without any increase in access charges in real terms, as a result of efficiency savings. It was also determined that Railtrack's revenues should be considered as a "single till", that is, the revenue required from access charges for franchised passenger services was calculated by deducting income from freight operators, open-access operators and property, including property sales.

Once the overall level of charges had been determined, their structure had to be devised and this was developed by Railtrack and Coopers & Lybrand. The track-access charges comprised three elements: an electricity for traction charge, based on a geographical tariff to cover expected costs from the supply contracts in operation; a track-usage charge – a national tariff was developed for a pence-per-vehicle mile depending on the type of vehicle; and a fixed charge – this is the remaining portion which represents some 91 per cent of the total charge and takes account of other single-till income.

The track-access charges were then disaggregated for each train operator based on the characteristics of their vehicles and the route over which they operated. An insider recalls that this was important because, until the TOCs' charges had been worked out, there was no way of knowing anything concrete about the economics of the new passenger railway: "they had to concentrate on the charges, [which were] disaggregated by reference to complicated models, so that each train operating company would know what it was expected to pay." These charges were put in place for Railtrack's vesting.

The Rail Regulator, immediately upon assuming his powers in April 1994, launched a review of the passenger track-access charges. He concluded in January 1995 that the access charges should be rebased to a level on average 8 per cent lower in real terms in 1995–96 than in 1994–95 and that they should then fall by 2 per cent a year in real terms in the 5 subsequent years. Broadly, the structure of the charges stayed the same. The reasoning behind these changes is discussed in Chapter 9.

The passenger track-access contracts were unquestionably lengthy, complicated documents, especially when the associated access conditions are also taken into account. It should be remembered, however, that similar trading relationships have to exist even within vertically integrated structures and the fact that they may not always need to be formalised can sometimes lead to ill-disciplined performance, with no financial sanctions for non-achievement of objectives. The lack of transparency and specificity in the contracts (response to different train service patterns and so on) was a disappointment as much to Railtrack as to the train companies. Under the business structure within BR, a series of conventions had been developed assuming "route ownership" by the dominant user, thus enabling the businesses to take informed decisions within the defined framework. The timescales and the fact that the data had not been assembled in this way for the track-authority model meant that the access charges had to be structured in broad rather than specific terms. They were, for example, largely insensitive to changing traffic volumes.

There are, however, several points to bear in mind when seeking to understand why and how the access contracts took the form they did. First, the parties which would be affected by the outcome of the negotiations were owned or controlled by the government and were being prepared for sale simultaneously. Contractual issues were thus frequently determined by ministers with an eye to the wider objectives of selling the whole of the railway industry in the extremely tight timescale they had imposed upon themselves. Thus, although Railtrack and the Office of Passenger Rail Franchising (OPRAF) were both prepared to develop innovations such as trial revenue-sharing contracts, it was decided that the risks to the timetable were too great.

Secondly, the standardised contracts referred to by Davies were usually handed down to individual TOCs and Railtrack Zones in the form of templates and this was particularly frustrating for those in the field who might have worked long hours together to secure local agreement. As Brian Burdsall, now Managing Director of Midland Mainline who led an unsuccessful bid for GNER, commented:

> *The process of converting central templates into workable access agreements was at times tedious. The civil servants seemed at times to be unable or unwilling to make decisions and on more than one occasion on contentious issues we had escalated to the centre I wanted a decision – any decision – rather than being left in limbo. Thus it was hardly a normal commercial process.*

Thirdly, Passenger Transport Authorities/Executives – key customers of the rail industry and significant players in funding and planning passenger services prior to the 1993 Act (see Chapter 2) – made clear their displeasure both with the whole process and their exclusion from it. Strathclyde unsuccessfully challenged the access contracts in the courts and Greater Manchester withdrew PTE support from local services. Eventually, the government adjusted their Section 20 grants to allow for the full recovery of costs in the new access charges, involved them positively in the franchise specifications and in due course effective co-operation was resumed. Finally, Railtrack and the TOCs were at varying stages in their development and both, at times, showed some insensitivity in the early stages of their divorce proceedings.

Whatever their weaknesses, the contracts were completed to form the basis of the successful franchising process which heralded the private ownership of the TOCs and with it the opportunity for a new chapter in Railtrack/TOC relation-ships. At the outset, Railtrack's new private-sector customers had to determine their own plans and priorities and they found the tightly drawn access contracts constraining. The West Coast Main Line contract was a significant exception in that coming at the end of the process, provision had been made in the franchise for a subsequent high-speed enhancement, with the option of further enhance-ments left for agreement between Railtrack and the chosen franchisee (Virgin). The contract, which established revenue sharing in various forms as a potential way forward for the future, is discussed in more detail in Chapter 4.

Turning to the freight business, it is important to note that there are significant differences between the freight and passenger businesses and how they were treated when contracts were being drawn up. First, access for freight operators represents a relatively small part of Railtrack's business (8 per cent by revenue in

1994–95) compared with access for passenger operators (86 per cent). Secondly, whereas the passenger-access charges were ultimately set by the Regulator during his review in 1994–95, the freight-access charges were negotiated between Railtrack and BR in the first instance and then approved by the Regulator. Thirdly, there were significant business customers of BR's freight operations whose turnover depended upon the continuing provision of freight services. The government was keen to ensure that these freight shippers (the end-users of BR's freight operations) received a continuous service from the railway and that their contracts were honoured. These contracts were parcelled up and passed to the freight companies that were formed out of BR.

BR used Mercer Management Consulting to advise on the restructuring of the freight operations who, following their review, advised that the freight business should be kept together for sale. The government, however, was keen to promote competition and was inclined to restructure BR's freight operations (see Chapter 8). This resulted in the creation of six new businesses, the Trainload Freight companies, Freightliner, Railfreight Distribution and Rail Express Systems. Railtrack employed the LEK Partnership to advise on the best structure within Railtrack to manage the relationship with these new businesses.

Railtrack was keen to establish a standard freight-access contract which each company would sign up to with schedules to reflect the differences in the traffic flows. However, the contractual structure was driven by the new freight companies. In particular, the three heavy haul businesses were keen that there was a high degree of transparency and sought individual access contracts for each of their traffic flows. This resulted in about 150 different contracts for the three companies. Freightliner, on the other hand, operated on one national contract. The freight-access charges were negotiated between Railtrack and BR and followed a principle set by the government that the charges should reflect the market value of the freight traffic. For example, higher charges resulted for the movement of coal because there is a strong market for rail and lower charges for containers where the market for rail is weaker. Both Railtrack and BR had knowledgeable freight teams which facilitated an open and transparent joint programme of work following the government's principle of market value.

As noted in Chapter 2, the government was eventually forced to sell five of the six freight businesses to a single buyer, a consortium led by Wisconsin Central Transportation, after it found that a market for six individual companies did not exist. As a result, there was no need to continue with the 150 different freight contracts reflecting the traffic flows and the consortium's consolidated freight company, English, Welsh and Scottish Railway (EWS) and Railtrack sought to renegotiate these contracts into one national contract. This renegotiation was completed in early 1997 and led to a simplified contract structure (see Chapter 4).

The Performance Regime

One of the criticisms of the new structure was that with the fragmentation of the industry, and the loss of a single-management focus, there would be a

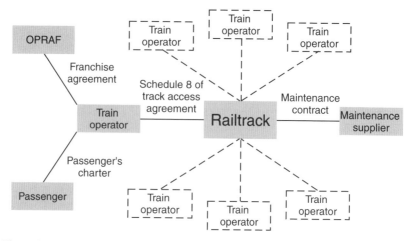

Figure 3.4   The "star model" of contractual relationships in the performance regime.
Source: Railtrack.

deterioration in train performance. It was obvious from the outset that some framework – a performance regime – would be necessary to ensure that the new companies worked constructively together, with financial benefits and penalties to reward success and failure. The DoT chaired the negotiations involving Railtrack, BR (for the embryonic TOCs and engineering companies), OPRAF and the Regulator, and each party was supported by its respective professional advisers. One official recalls that everyone involved worked "frantically hard" to get the broad principles "hammered out" and these were agreed by December 1994, although necessary development and calibration work took several months longer and the regime was not introduced into live running until 10 December 1995.

In simple terms, the scheme established by service-group average-delay benchmarks achieved for the 3 years prior to privatisation.[9] Performance was reviewed each 28 days (the industry's accounting period) and where Railtrack achieved an average delay below the benchmark then the TOC would pay Railtrack, at a rate agreed for the service group, and when Railtrack failed to achieve its benchmark then it would be penalised with payment to the TOC.

The contractual relationships of the regime involved are shown in a simplified form in Figure 3.4. This "web" of contracts is often referred to as the "star model" at the centre of which lies Railtrack. Starting with the performance contracts with the passenger on the left-hand side, the passenger has an agreement with the train operator through the "Passenger's Charter" (see Chapter 6) whereby if trains do not meet certain punctuality standards then the passengers will receive some form of refund. The train operator also has an agreement with the Franchising Director through the franchise agreement and with Railtrack through Schedule 8 of the track-access agreement. Railtrack stands between all the TOCs so if one TOC delays another, the various penalties are dealt with through Railtrack. It is the Schedule 8 agreement which is discussed here – the others are reviewed in Chapter 6.

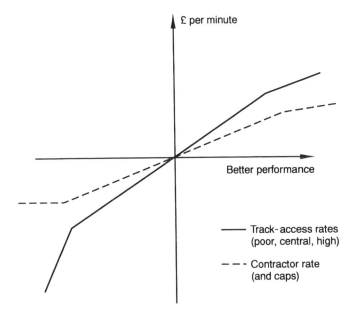

Figure 3.5   Financial incentives in the performance regime. Source: Railtrack.

A summary of the financial incentives is shown in Figure 3.5. The centre point of the graph is the benchmark – the "permitted" delay for a group of train services over a 28-day period. If Railtrack just meets this target, it receives no bonuses and incurs no penalties. In the top-right sector of the diagram, the TOC pays Railtrack for better performance (as shown by the thick line). The rate of reward reduces beyond a certain point, as shown by the less steep part of the thick line – Railtrack is paid less per minute improvement as the service improves. If Railtrack does not meet the benchmark, it pays money to the TOC, and beyond a certain point, it pays a higher rate. The intention is to penalise significantly bad performance and to limit the cost implications of performance improving beyond a certain level. From the relationships laid out in Figure 3.5, for every £1 Railtrack has to pay a TOC, it will only be able to offcharge 80p to its contractors even when the fault was theirs. Thus Railtrack was given an incentive to encourage contractors to improve, since it always pays a 20-per-cent cost for their mistakes.

The responsibility for delays are defined in principle in Schedule 8 of the passenger track-access agreements. A TOC is responsible for incidents within its control or resulting from a delay due to rolling stock faults, but Railtrack is responsible for all other incidents. These may be: (a) within Railtrack's control, (b) arising in connection with the Network (whether or not Railtrack is at fault) or (c) caused by other operators. Railtrack is also responsible for delays caused by its contractors. If a TOC delays trains of other TOCs, then Railtrack administers the payment to the disadvantaged TOC(s) and there is joint responsibility for incidents which both close a station and prevent scheduled train movements through it. All parties are obliged to avoid and mitigate delays. Average payments per minute of lateness across a range of service groups include regional services at £17 per minute, and some South-East categories of up to between £130 or £170 a minute.

The starting point for recording performance is a reference working timetable for every train movement on the network. The actual progress of trains is reported through a complex recording system and if there is a delay of more than 3 minutes somebody has to explain why and who is responsible. There are: 2,900 reporting points, 1,300 Train Running Systems (TRUST) delay-attribution points – 500 contract monitoring points and 366 passenger charter monitoring points. About 86 per cent of the data is recorded automatically as trains pass a given point; the balance – on less heavily used parts of the network – is captured manually at signal boxes.

There are about 3,000 delay incidents every day across the railway network and all delays are recorded using the real-time performance monitoring system, TRUST. The responsibility for every delay is identified to one of 204 causation codes, to the organisation responsible for the delay and to the specific manager within that organisation. Even at the outset a significant number of the attributions were agreed by the delay attribution staff before the end of a shift and this level of agreement increased as familiarity with the regime grew. Delays which are not explained are attributed an "unexplained" code which defaults to Railtrack.

Following the introduction of the attribution process early in the 1995–96 fiscal year, full trial running began in October 1995, with a daily sign-off and a help desk in operation. Draft procedures were formulated by mid-November of that year and, after consultation, were finalised late in November. Brian Mellitt, Railtrack's Engineering and Operations Director, successfully led the implementation team at Railtrack and, as already noted, full live running began on 10 December 1995. A series of external audits, conducted by Deloitte Touche and by Coopers & Lybrand, carried out from December 1995 to January 1996 confirmed that the regime was robust.

In the intitial period after privatisation, the performance regime was a major factor in improving the timely operation of trains in the privatised railway during the period under the review. Figure 3.6 gives details of passenger-service improvements for the first 2 years of its operation. For the first time in the UK, there was in place a means of measuring train performance accurately (and not just at destination) with causation properly identified and results rewarded/penalised in financial terms. The regime had a number of shortcomings associated with the quality of some of the early data and the compromises necessary to reach agreement, but Railtrack's managers accepted the challenges and with a strong centrally-directed management focus achieved significant reductions in delay, particularly in the first year of privatised operation.

Contracts with Suppliers

It was generally accepted that innovation in work practices, multi-skilling and challenging long-established, engineering-dominated procedures, was long overdue and a key feature of the vertically separated structure was that railway

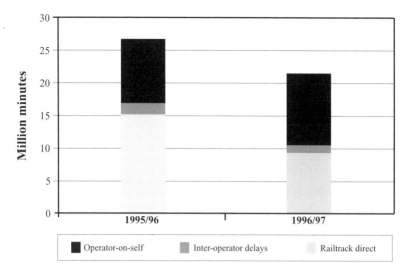

Figure 3.6   Performance-regime improvements 1995/96–1996/97. Source: Railtrack.

maintenance should be undertaken by contract, to meet defined group standards by a number of private companies. A competitive framework would provide the best way of achieving reform in due course.

The form of contract adopted by the government was output based for a fixed lump sum, with the presumption that the contracting companies had core competencies and expert knowledge; since these companies were to be formed by trade sales of the BR engineering departments, this was a reasonable assumption. Railtrack's role as client was to manage the contracts through management-system audits and quality checks, as well as being responsible for approving work programmes and providing access to the railway.

The infrastructure-maintenance companies (IMCs) (see Chapter 2) were sold by trade sale. At the outset 36 contracts at fixed lump sums, to be reduced by 3 per cent per year in real terms, were "gifted" to the incumbent contractors for periods of between 5 and 7 years. The government also decided to split routine maintenance activities from the heavy maintenance associated with track-renewal work, with track-renewal companies (TRCs) set up via trade sales. There was a widely held view that this separation was inappropriate and in the event, market-forces have operated so that the TRCs and IMCs have been consolidated.

Given the constraints imposed by the sales process, the overall results have been good with a 4 per cent per year real reduction in costs. Inevitably there have been variations in individual contract performances and while necessary standards are generally being maintained, there have been some issues which have required significant management attention by both Railtrack and the contractors' managements.

Work planning within BR was based on a work bank with significant local discretion but, given the need to plan detailed access in advance around a commercial service and the obligation to book possessions against penalty payments, it has been necessary to improve the original processes. End-product checks have also been introduced by Railtrack to provide information to confirm the maintenance work has been undertaken across all asset classes at a rate and distribution which is statistically significant. Intervention criteria have been developed to identify trends of poor performance and, in one case, Railtrack replaced the original contractor by another before the duration of the original contract. This was undertaken by mutual agreement and demonstrated that contractors could be replaced subject to careful planning and a systematic handover of responsibilities.

As explained earlier, a feature of privatisation was the specific formalisation of safety duties specified in the Railways (Safety Case) Regulations made under the Health and Safety at Work Act 1974 and Railtrack has extended the principle of safety cases to contractors working on and about the railway. The principle here is that since such contractors and their subcontractors can impose risk to the network, defined criteria for achievement of safe operation are necessary.

Investment and Network Development

Railtrack's passenger-access charges provide for the maintenance and renewal of the network to modern standards whilst investment for enhancing the railway is funded through negotiated agreements with customers. The new structure provides some significant opportunities for developing such enhancement projects. As long as Railtrack maintains its strong trading performance and the proposed investment makes commercial sense to its shareholders and lenders, then it has access to funding. It was envisaged that cost reductions, more imaginative marketing, more technical innovation and so on were more likely to be achieved and therefore improve the case for investment in those schemes where the justification had previously been marginal.

There were therefore exciting opportunities for the development of the stronger commercial elements of the rail businesses: major inter-urban passenger flows, particularly on the West Coast and East Coast main lines and bulk freight. However, it is always important to manage expectations. The scale of the benefits does not change the fundamentals of investment appraisal as they have emerged over several decades. In other words, investment in easing congestion for commuters during peak periods, in developing low-density passenger flows and inter-modal freight remains very difficult to justify commercially within the current economic framework. Partnership investment – with a variety of collaborators such as the TOCs, local authorities, the government and the European Union – is required to realise non-commercial projects and Railtrack put in place arrangements to deal with this expectation.

It is Railtrack's responsibility to produce a robust timetable; that is, to ensure that capacity is optimised and the number of trains operating over critical sections of a route is consistent with reliability and good timekeeping.[10] One of the potential weaknesses of the vertically separated structure, if this is not achieved, is that competition between train companies over a congested route and a desire to improve frequency can, in certain circumstances, increase the number of trains and actually diminish the capacity to move people and/or freight. In the previously vertically-integrated industry, this problem was dealt with by the BRB taking a view across the businesses and this critical role now passes to the Regulator who has to make judgements in a very specialised field. At the same time, he must take account of the need to source funds for network investment if more infrastructure is deemed to be necessary after full evaluation of more cost-effective alternatives. It will not be in the long-term interest of the TOCs, or of UK plc, for infrastructure investment to be undertaken which has the net effect of driving up the unit costs of rail transport still further.

Throughout the initial period following privatisation Railtrack was regularly criticised for "under investment" in the network and the frequent repetition of the accusation meant that it became an assumption in any analysis. This criticism gained particular prominence in the Autumn of 1996 when there was public correspondence between the Regulator and a sponsored pressure group. In an open letter to the pressure group in December 1996, John Swift commented:

The underspending which you cite reflects the slowness on Railtrack's part to accelerate the level of infrastructure renewal from the lower levels which applied when it was in the public sector. The current level of underspend is wholly unacceptable to me and I expect prompt action to remedy this.[11]

The Regulator's comments on Railtrack's investment record were repeated in January 1997 when he published his document, *Regulatory Objectives for Railtrack*. The Labour Party in opposition also reacted to these statements, with Andrew Smith, the shadow Transport Secretary, quoted as noting: "the fact that the company could get away with starving the railway of millions of pounds of investment showed the privatised rail set-up was a farce."[12]

After decades in which BR had had to work within Treasury-imposed funding limits, it was natural that there would be impatience for results, once private-sector funding became possible. But significant infrastructure schemes have a long lead time (3 to 5 years typically and often longer) and commercial projects have to be justified in private-sector accounts, the other side of the coin which secures the source of funds. "Under-investment" means different things to different groups: it feels very real to passengers whose journeys are unreliable and it is a useful phrase for politicians and journalists anxious to put a particular slant on events. But Railtrack was given very specific targets which it has consistently met or bettered.

The Rail Regulator's review of access charges in January 1995 for the 6 years to April 2001 was intended to enable Railtrack to spend £3.4billion (at 1994–95 prices) on renewing the network over that time in modern equivalent form. The amount was calculated on the basis that it would cover depreciation on a current cost basis. In addition, he allowed for accelerated expenditure of £500 million to cover the backlog of work which was necessary to bring Railtrack's stations and light-maintenance depots into the condition required to meet its statutory and contractual obligations. By 2001, Railtrack will have spent over £1

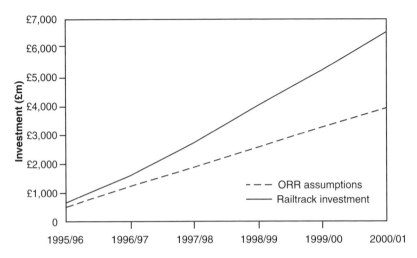

Figure 3.7   Railtrack's investment set against the Regulator's initial expectations.
Source: Railtrack.

billion more on renewals and backlog than the Regulator initially expected. As
Figure 3.7 shows, in any year Railtrack has exceeded the Regulator's assumptions.

One of the main difficulties facing Railtrack when putting over its case for its
investment record was the lack of understanding (or distrust) of its basic accounting principles, particularly during its transition from a government-owned company to the private sector. Whilst the financial community had few problems in
grasping the situation, many commentators were not convinced and found the
detailed arithmetic necessary to establish the real position both tedious and
difficult to follow.[13] For example, Labour's Brian Wilson wrote to the
Regulator in December 1995 assuming that funds intended for investment
were being set aside as a means of strengthening Railtrack's balance sheet prior
to privatisation. Mr Wilson urged the government "to delay Railtrack's privatisation until all questions relating to their accounts are resolved . . . They [Railtrack's
accounts] paint a misleading picture, to the tune of over £1 billion a year, of the
amount available for investment."[14]

Railtrack adopted a form of renewals accounting by establishing an Asset
Maintenance Plan (AMP) in which an estimate was made for the renewal costs
for track, structures and property over the next 10-year period. This estimate was
then divided by the number of years and the appropriate charge made to the
profit-and-loss account for the corresponding year. Naturally, the spend in any
one year may not exactly match the charge for that year but there is a commitment that over the long term (10 years) the expenditure will match the charge.
This is an approach adopted by many regulated businesses such as runway renewal
for BAA plc and some water networks for the water companies. The approach
was adopted in Railtrack's first accounts while the company was still in the public
sector and cash constrained because of Treasury-imposed spending limits.

Railtrack was therefore unable to spend against the full AMP charge in its accounts. The outstanding figure was carried forward as an accrual in its balance sheet to spend in the future when Railtrack had access to cash. In a similar way, the company made a £450-million provision to cover the backlog of works to bring its stations and depots into the condition required to meet its statutory and contractual obligations. By the time of Railtrack's flotation the AMP accrual was £267 million and the property backlog accrual was £442 million, giving a total accrual of over £700 million. This figure, which is given in Railtrack's accounts, was seized upon by anti-privatisation rail pressure groups as a supposedly tangible indication of Railtrack's underspend. Of course, these were amounts that were inherited from its time in the public sector as a government-owned company and Railtrack had always been on course to clear these "public sector" accruals by the end of 2000.

The general perception that Railtrack was behind on its investment programme led to increasing public concern that the Regulator should have tougher powers to be able to enforce Railtrack to invest in the network. The Regulator undertook a review of Railtrack's 1996–97 Network Management Statement which he then used as an opportunity to propose an amendment to Railtrack's Licence. Railtrack agreed to accept a modification to its licence – Condition 7 – which had the effect of: confirming Railtrack's general duties in achieving maintenance, renewal and enhancement of the rail network in a timely, economic and efficient manner; requiring Railtrack to publish criteria for prioritisation of expenditure; requiring Railtrack to define the issues which the Network Management Statement should address, including consultation and a review of progress made on the previous year's plans; and requiring Railtrack to produce an annual reconciliation of expenditure incurred, compared with the plans published in the previous year.

Some Reflections on the Creation of Railtrack

BR had organised – usually with political direction – a series of disposals over many years: docks, road operations, shipping, hotels, major rolling stock workshops. But nothing could have prepared those concerned for the upheaval and workload involved in the privatisation of BR itself and even those with wider non-railway experience found the process daunting. Railtrack's merchant banker, N. M. Rothschild, had been involved in all the public-service privatisations in the UK and it is interesting to note the perceptions of one of their directors, Simon Linnett, who played a leading role. He pointed out that rail privatisation was different from other sell-offs because it involved the sale of a subsidised industry and, as a result of the method of sale adopted, necessitated the complete break-up of the industry to a degree never before contemplated. He continued:

In addition to the sheer number of companies created, the sale of the British Rail Businesses included two characteristics never before seen: the disappearance of the Company from the industry (BRB being a shell) and the level of contracts required between the companies that were separated. No sale process has ever involved the simultaneous sale process of the components of an industry or used so many methods (trade sales of freight businesses, a flotation of Railtrack, franchising of TOCs and, effectively, the sales of leases with the rolling-stock companies which were subsequently securitised). The sales of these different components were interrelated; for example, we, as advisers to Railtrack, were very concerned that it should not be sold with a significant number of the infrastructure maintenance and track-renewal units remaining in the public sector – it was on these companies and the future competition between them that Railtrack's efficiency improvements depended.

He concluded:

[There were] challenges never before seen in any privatisation. The rail industry was (and remains) in competition with many other forms of transport in a way not experienced by many other utilities. Many perceived the business to be in irreversible decline as roads were built to meet (and fuel) demand for car travel; it had experienced years of under-investment to a level where its service performance and its privatisation had been seriously impaired; and it was experiencing a degree of separation when the units being carried on the system were not molecules or electrons but people who minded about the quality of the system and how reliably they moved through the network.

Rapid and massive change to an industry's structure whilst providing the basis for future development inevitably brings problems. With the formation of so many new companies, there are managers with new ideas who have to learn how to handle their freedom and work within the disciplines of the market place whilst recognising the consequences of trading in an industry still supported by the taxpayer. Public and private-sector managers had much to teach each other.

The imperative of improving service to the customer has to be handled and expectations managed to recognise the lead times needed for culture change on the one hand and infrastructure improvement, new systems and new rolling stock delivery on the other. Everybody recognises the contribution the greater use of railways can make to alleviate congestion and pollution, but few understand the economics of rail transport and the implications for the taxpayer. The funding of infrastructure investment to provide more capacity on routes which, on existing analysis, are inherently loss making and which after investment require more financial support, remains unresolved. If there are benefits from increasing capacity which are not presently taken into account, then it is essential that all the parties involved (including the Treasury) agree how they are to be quantified. Clear criteria for justifying investment must be established to avoid 10-year plans becoming pipe dreams, as has so often been the case in the past.

It is important that privatisation is seen as an enabling framework, providing for the funding and security of the network. It does not in itself constitute a cure for the UK's deep-seated transport problems but neither does it represent a threat to their solution.

Acknowledgements

A number of people have provided invaluable assistance to me whilst I wrote this chapter. In particular, I am grateful to Rod Muttram for his detailed information on rail safety, Professor Brian Mellitt for material on maintenance contracts and performance and Peter Durman for research, collation of material and help with drafting.

Notes

1. The post-privatisation industry structure in Sweden was relatively simple compared with that proposed in Britain.
2. Quoted in Grantham, A. *Privatisation and Reorganisation: Case Studies in Rail Policy Implementation*, Unpublished PhD thesis, University of East Anglia, 1998.
3. The External Financing Limit was the total amount of government grant and borrowing available to BR and was determined by the Treasury.
4. One of the criteria for reference of potential monopolies to the Monopolies and Mergers Commission is possession of 25 per cent or more of relevant market share.
5. Quoted in Lilja, R. *International Equity Markets – The Art of the Deal*, Euromoney Publications, 1997.
6. Bookbuilding is a pricing and underwriting method where the offer price is fixed and the offer underwritten after a book of preliminary orders from interested buyers has been built at the end of the marketing period. The approach allows the bookrunner to compile a comprehensive picture of the strength of institutional demand over a range of prices by obtaining non-binding expressions of interest from potential investors. At the end of the bookbuilding period the price is fixed, the prospectus finalised, the shares are allotted to investors and dealings in shares begin.
7. Lilja, op. cit., National Audit Office. *The Flotation of Railtrack*, The Stationery Office, 1998.
8. Grantham, op. cit.
9. Each of BR's "O for Q" profit centres consisted of one or several service groups and punctuality and reliability figures were compiled therefrom.
10. Capacity and growth need careful definition and should relate to the movement of people and freight rather than simply the number of trains.
11. Letter from John Swift QC, 17 December 1996.
12. *The Guardian*, 21 December 1996.
13. Railtrack gave clear explanations of its accounting policies for investment in each of its Report & Accounts, at press conferences and at its Annual General Meetings.
14. *Financial Times*, 6 December 1995.

4. Railtrack's Recent Performance

Arthur Leathley

This chapter examines Railtrack's recent performance, beginning at the start of the 1997–98 financial year. It picks up on the main issues raised in the previous chapter and reviews the extent to which Railtrack has succeeded in meeting continuing public and political demands for safer, more punctual train services and increased investment. The relationships between Railtrack and the TOCs, the Rail Regulator and the government have become increasingly turbulent since early 1997 and railway performance has been analysed as never before. The text will therefore focus on significant changes to the regulation of the industry and on key events that have forced a rethinking of the way Railtrack's actions are monitored.

Safety

As noted in the previous chapter, the issue of who would be in charge of ensuring safety in the "new" railway industry was easily disposed of by ministers and officials. The prevailing view within government was that an already improving trend in rail safety would continue with Railtrack at the helm, but recent events have suggested that current safety arrangements might have to be reviewed.

Despite the efforts of Railtrack in its first year of privatisation to improve safety standards, evidence of disagreements between rail managers and Her Majesty's Rail Inspectorate (HMRI) began to emerge in 1997. Safety inspectors spoke of "immaturity" among senior staff – not only Railtrack's but also TOCs' – when it came to commissioning safety improvements from contractors. In particular, there was concern that some managers began challenging inspectors' assessments. One example occurred in 1997 near Folkestone, Kent, where HMRI ordered Railtrack to erect fencing to prevent objects being thrown out of trains. Railtrack appealed against the improvement notice, but withdrew the appeal before the Industrial Tribunal hearing ended and agreed to erect the fencing. A further point of conflict emerged in April 1999, after HMRI prevented trains from running at more than 20 mph through the Severn Tunnel because of concerns about the track condition. Although Railtrack planned remedial work to be completed by October, Vic Coleman, the Chief Inspector of Railways, insisted that "more urgent action is required to enable trains to run safely at normal speed."

With a new government pressing hard for improvements to rail services, there was now a political dimension to the increasingly public disagreements between HMRI and industry personnel. Perhaps for the first time, railway inspectors were recognising that the public scolding of rail managers suited the political mood, but there were deep concerns – from both ministers and rail commentators alike – that such open criticism could undermine seriously the fledgling privatised industry's success in attracting new passengers to the railways. Such concerns appear to be unfounded, however, as passenger numbers have continued to grow despite recent rail accidents (see Chapter 7).

The most significant safety issue since early 1997 has been that of train protection. The proposed deployment of the Automatic Train Protection (ATP) system had, of course, been cancelled after a report in 1995 concluded that Railtrack's Train Protection and Warning System (TPWS) would be more cost effective. Within months of the Labour government coming to power in May 1997, however, John Prescott, the Deputy Prime Minister and Secretary of State for Transport, ordered HMRI to re-examine the benefits of the main train-protection systems available. In September 1997, the need for a decision became even more urgent, when seven people were killed at Southall, west London, after an InterCity train passed a red signal and ploughed into a freight train.

Cost remained a key issue in the HMRI's deliberations, but so too was the speed of delivery of a system seen as crucial in preventing tragedies such as that at Southall. ATP, dubbed by the media the "Rolls Royce" version, could be fitted across the network to some 35,700 signals. The system could be laid as new track and signalling were installed or, at considerably less expense, be "bolted" on to existing equipment. The system was forecast to prevent two-thirds of accidents caused as a result of "Signals Passed at Danger" (SPADs) but the estimated £1 billion price tag remained a serious concern for ministers and many in the industry.[1] In fact, as well as being costly, the British version of ATP was unproven and was already showing signs of being outdated. On routes where trials had taken place, such as the Great Western Main Line, serious deficiencies had been identified in the computer system, which led to 80 per cent of trains fitted with ATP running without it being in operation. Railway safety officials and ministers remained unconvinced that a system that had been devised 15 years earlier, and found to be unreliable, should be the basis of huge future investment.

Yet Railtrack's plans for the TPWS were also denounced, mainly by railway pressure groups, as safety "on the cheap". Railtrack had announced that the system would not have the theoretical capabilities of ATP as it could not stop trains running at speeds of over 70 mph. It would also be fitted to only half the country's signals, largely those at important junctions or that had been the scene of SPAD incidents in the past. In its favour, however, TPWS could be fitted across all affected signals within 5 years, less than half the time required for ATP to be installed. In December 1998, Prescott took the decision to fit TPWS by 2004, at a cost of between £160 and £250 million, most of which would fall to Railtrack.

As the debate over train protection had been going on, other incidents had ensured that safety had been propelled to the fore in the privatised railways.

Railtrack was accused by rail unions of failing to spend sufficiently on the maintenance and repair of the network – a charge which the company strenuously denied – but its cause was not helped when its failure to repair damaged track on a viaduct at Bexley, Kent, resulted in a train plunging down an embankment, injuring five workmen. Moreover, vandalism was emerging as a threat to railway safety and Stan Robertson, then Chief Inspector of Railways, called the rise in incidents "a massive and very disturbing increase."

Throughout this period, Railtrack pointed to a string of statistics published by HMRI indicating safety improvements across the network and Gerald Corbett, who took over as Railtrack's Chief Executive in 1997, becomes almost apoplectic when his company is accused of putting the need to protect shareholders' dividends ahead of safety considerations: "I've been amazed since joining Railtrack at the strength of the safety ethic and how ingrained it is into the culture. It is inconceivable that these people would put profit ahead of safety." Corbett has a point: despite the Bexley incident, the number of significant train accidents fell to an all-time low of 89 in 1997–98 and the number of derailments dropped sharply, from 119 to 93, two measures from which Railtrack could take comfort. A continuing trend of reducing the number of SPADs was also maintained in 1997–98 although, 1 year later, the rail industry saw an 8 per cent rise, to 643, prompting a fresh wave of concern.

In October 1999 the railway industry was consumed by the safety issue once again, after two commuter trains collided at Ladbroke Grove, in west London, with the eventual loss of 31 lives (Figure 4.1). An interim report by HMRI quickly established that one of the trains had passed a red signal. It also emerged that the signal had been the subject of past complaints by drivers and train companies, and had been passed at red eight times in the previous six years. Railtrack suffered badly in the immediate aftermath, although the signalling equipment was found to be in working order. Heavy criticism of the company's maintenance programme came from all sides, and Lord MacDonald of Tradeston, Prescott's second-in-command, announced that the government was "minded" to remove Railtrack's responsibility for the Safety and Standards Directorate which sets industry guidelines (see Chapter 3).

The key problem facing Railtrack now seems to be that, although the railway remains statistically very safe, recent events mean people no longer *perceive* it to be.[2] And when, no matter how many times Corbett trots out the statistics, perception becomes reality in the minds of the travelling public, the will for change may be too great for the politicians to ignore.

Contracts with Rail Service Operators

John Edmonds in Chapter 3 made the important point that the structure of the track-access agreements imposed upon Railtrack and the TOCs at the time of privatisation was largely insensitive to changing traffic volumes. Provided the number of trains running on the network remains static, then the current charging regime works well, but problems begin to emerge if the amount of services

Figure 4.1   Train wreckage at Ladbroke Grove, West London, October 1999.
Source: *The Times.*

operated changes substantially. In a declining industry, TOCs seeking to reduce their train miles would be unable to make significant cost savings and could face bankruptcy. In an expanding industry, Railtrack would receive hardly any additional money from TOCs increasing the amount of trains they run. The marginal cost of introducing new services under the current track-access contracts is virtually nil.

Passenger-train operators are in fact able to increase the amount of trains they run by around 8 per cent without paying additional track-access charges and, faced with high levels of patronage growth around much of the network (see Chapter 7), most TOCs have sought to do just that. There has, however, been a snag: as the number of services operating across the network has increased – from 17,096 per day in winter 1995 to 18,470 in winter 1999 – so the track has become more congested and Railtrack, which has received hardly any additional income from the new trains, is finding it difficult to ensure the smooth running of the railway.[3]

The company estimates that, under current conditions, a 1 per cent increase in the amount of trains on the network leads to a 2.5 per cent increase in congestion-related delays. Whilst it is easy for TOCs (and commentators) to demand simply that Railtrack spends more money to address this problem, it must be remembered that the company has practically no financial incentive to do so. Some operators who have looked to expand their services have thus found Railtrack an unwilling partner. As Connex Rail's Chief Operating Officer, Geoff Harrison-Mee, has said: "I'd be the first to throw tomatoes at Railtrack. Railtrack is working more like a building society than an entrepreneur. There are no big risks. All I do is put my money in and I have to give 7 years' notice if I want to change."[4]

Corbett has been quick to bemoan the "adversarial" relationship the track-access contracts seem recently to have encouraged, but much of that conflict might have been avoided had the original contracts been underpinned by more positive assumptions about growth. Given the uncertainty surrounding the rail-privatisation exercise, it is perhaps understandable that the contracts were structured in the way they were. Railtrack, after all, was guaranteed a predictable income until 2001 (to aid its sale) and the TOCs were effectively encouraged to maintain service levels (a factor which, combined with the PSRs, would help limit the amount of service cuts and associated political fallout). Equally, however – and admittedly with the benefit of hindsight – the apparent pessimism enshrined in the access contracts seems surprising in the sense that a key factor behind the Conservatives' privatisation programme was always to seek an improvement in service quality – which, in turn, should have resulted in increased business. Either way, the railway industry, thanks in part to the form of the track-access agreements, is becoming a victim of its own success.

The track-access charges are currently being reviewed by the Regulator and change is expected in 2001, when the review's conclusions are set to be implemented. Railtrack is seeking a far higher variable element in the charges which will reflect more accurately the amount of trains which operators run on its network. This clearly has advantages in a buoyant market as Railtrack will raise extra revenue from new services which, in theory, can be invested in improving punctuality and reliability. Moreover, the TOCs will be in a much stronger position to demand improvements as they can rightly claim that they are paying for the additional access and expect high standards for their outlay. But as Brian Burdsall, of Midland Main Line, points out, Railtrack could come unstuck in a future recession: "It is all very well for Railtrack to be looking at variable charges bringing in additional income. But if I am running trains that are empty and paying a high price, it might pay me to take the train off, so no one gains." Other operators are suspicious about Railtrack's motives as they fear that the company would fail to invest any additional revenue in upgrading its product. As we will see below, Railtrack's investment record since early 1997 has disappointed many both within and outside the industry.

One of the biggest upheavals of Railtrack's early dealings with operators was the 1997 renegotiation of contracts with EWS, the dominant freight operator. The original agreements, as noted in Chapter 3, comprised individual contracts for each of EWS's 150 freight routes, but EWS argued the process was absurdly complex and that, as a result, it was unable to respond quickly to potential customers' requirements. The replacement contract, signed in early 1997, was a single 4-year agreement based on high fixed charges, with EWS paying variable rates based on tonnage. The new contract has not been without its problems, however. The then Rail Regulator, John Swift, was concerned about the potential for the deal to impact adversely upon other operators and intervened to limit the number of EWS train paths through key points and prevent the freight company making block bids for services without giving precise timings. More recently EWS, and particularly its former head Ed Burkhardt (see Chapter 8), has been critical of the contract in the sense that the access charges levied by Railtrack are too high. He argues that:

Access costs paid by EWS are three times the equivalent cost incurred by the North American and Australian railways measured per gross tonne mile. No rail operator in the US, Canada or Australia could increase its track-access costs to the Railtrack level and remain in business and these extreme costs are the largest impediment to freight competitiveness and growth in the UK.[5]

Burkhardt urges EWS to "participate vigorously" in the Rail Regulator's current review of track-access charges in order to try and effect a suitable reduction.

The Performance Regime

We have seen that the performance regime was certainly a factor in improving the timely operation of trains both during and for the year after Railtrack was privatised. The regime has admirable objectives, but its continued success depends upon the reliability of both the sophisticated monitoring system and its administration. Although the former had been declared robust by independent assessors (see Chapter 3), the latter has become problematic and, despite the efforts of Railtrack, the rail industry has experienced legal disputes over the system's attribution of fault. As Charles Belcher, Managing Director of Silverlink, put it:

From a train operator's viewpoint, the performance regime has drawbacks. Firstly, the attribution is initially made by Railtrack, itself the principal cause of delay. Operators can and do challenge attribution but the bureaucracy of the systems inevitably places them on the back foot.

Christopher Garnett, Chief Executive of GNER, highlights a typical problem:

Railtrack is incentivising its managers very heavily on delays and there is pressure on them to behave in certain ways. We've got to watch very carefully where the minutes are going and it can get very complicated. A train that gets delayed leaving King's Cross in the morning can be late back in the evening, and it's all down to a problem with Railtrack that happened in the morning and you've got to make damn sure that that train is being tracked right through the system.

Although Railtrack reduced the amount of train delays attributable to the company significantly in the 2 years after the performance regime "went live", the rate of its improvement fell dramatically in the second year after privatisation to just 2 per cent. John Swift began moves to tighten up Railtrack's future performance. His efforts came amid sustained political pressure from ministers over the performance of railway companies. John Prescott announced that the Labour government was intent on curbing car-traffic growth by encouraging wider use of public transport and his call for motorists to use their cars less was inextricably linked to the success of public-transport operators to run a punctual and reliable service that could also compete with car travel on price.

Amid this pressure, Railtrack agreed with Swift in 1998 to achieve a 7.5 per cent improvement in delays to passenger services and freight movements in 1998–99. By the end of 1998, following a heavily disrupted autumn period, it became clear that Railtrack would miss its passenger target by some way and the company again achieved only a 2 per cent improvement. Swift's replacement, Tom Winsor, has now threatened Railtrack with an enforcement order which will mean fines of up to £52 million if it fails to make improvements of 12.7 per cent (the 1998–99 shortfall plus the original 1999–2000 target) in 1999–2000. Lower fines will be imposed if Railtrack achieves some improvements but falls short of Winsor's demands. Some commentators have noted that Winsor's action was rather harsh, especially when much of the increase in delays has been caused by an increase in traffic for which Railtrack has received no money, but others maintain that the company has presided over a decline in performance improvements for too long and needs more incentive to tackle the problem.

Winsor drew some satisfaction from the fact that, despite vociferous complaints from Railtrack that the new target was unrealistic, the company was almost on course to achieve it over the first 6 months of 1998–99. Yet the Regulator's apparent success drew a sceptical reaction from some operators who had fought in vain for similar improvements by Railtrack. Brian Burdsall made clear his view that "Railtrack are more concerned about public opprobrium and the Regulator fining them than about operators who need immediate investment to improve services." Indeed, other operators are calling for a substantial overhaul of the current regime to make Railtrack more accountable to its customers. As Belcher points out, "the level of incentive and penalty available to Railtrack is really not large enough to influence a multi-billion-pound-turnover company". Both Railtrack and the TOCs now recognise that the original regime had a number of shortcomings and that compromises will be necessary to effect improvements.

Contracts with Suppliers

Railtrack's contracts with its suppliers have increasingly undergone substantial renegotiation since the end of the 1996–97 financial year as managers have attempted to simplify the maintenance and renewals structure. The 36 contracts awarded at the time of privatisation are to be slimmed down eventually to 15, with incentives linked more directly to train performance. The new contracts, to be tendered up to 2001, are intended to reduce the current £600 million annual maintenance budget by 10 per cent over a 5-year period during which it is likely that suppliers will have to cope with a significant increase in traffic.

Investment and Network Development

John Edmonds described in detail Railtrack's Asset Maintenance Plan (AMP) accounting system and how it led many incorrectly to believe that, during and initially after privatisation, the company had fallen behind the Regulator's expectations for investment in the network. He also noted that the general perception that Railtrack was behind on its investment programme led to increasing public concern that the Regulator should have tougher powers to be able to enforce Railtrack to invest in the network.

Swift had been reasonably content with Railtrack's investment performance in its first months as a private company, but by 1997 he had revised his opinion and formed the view that it had "got greedy" (see Chapter 9). Whilst he acknowledged that Railtrack was investing more than his 1994–95 review of track-access charges had anticipated they should, it was becoming obvious that both his original calculations and the company's investment plans were simply too conservative given the sharp growth in traffic which had occurred.

Swift had also become suspicious that Railtrack was hiding behind its accounting procedure. A source from the Office of the Rail Regulator (ORR) commented that some of its staff thought that Railtrack lacked private-sector management experience and were therefore unwilling or unable to take risks. Executives who had spent their lives working for the publicly owned railway, the insider suggested, were having difficulty adjusting to the new operational environment and the associated investment obligations. This was not only the case with regard to large, commercially driven investments; partnership schemes have also fallen through because Railtrack was incapable of co-ordinating them properly. Such occurrences are rather worrying when it is remembered that a number of Railtrack's planned network developments depend on partnership funding (see Chapter 3).

The ORR, as noted in the previous chapter, modified Railtrack's licence and introduced a new element, Condition 7, which had the effect of bringing about much more detailed information on its investment plans and targets. But despite this change, Railtrack and the Rail Regulator were involved in little more than shadow boxing for 2 years. Although Swift continued to accuse Railtrack of being too vague about its spending plans, he took no enforcement action to prompt a change of approach by the company (see Chapter 9). The mood changed drastically in March 1999, when the most comprehensive audit of Railtrack's activities to date was published. The report, commissioned by Swift before the expiry of his contract in late 1998 and written by Booz-Allen & Hamilton, the international management consultants, immediately increased pressure on Railtrack to set out its targets, alongside detailed proposals for their achievement. The authors were clear that "Railtrack's physical activity in renewing assets has been below expectations."[6] While rail renewals had exceeded initial targets, renewals of other track components had not been sufficient. Railtrack had failed to deliver signalling schemes anticipated at the start of its 5-year control period, which began in 1996, and had fallen behind in its plans to clear its inherited backlog of station maintenance by 2001.

The report came as regulatory pressure on Railtrack was growing. In the interim period between the departure of Swift and the appointment of Tom Winsor, acting Rail Regulator Chris Bolt issued a warning that Railtrack would be treated as a "boring utility", with the tight regulation such a body required, unless it began to take some risks on investment. The stakes were raised again when Winsor, a high-flying lawyer with an almost obsessive interest in railway regulation, took office in July 1999. For several years before taking on the job, Winsor had been increasingly outspoken about Railtrack's failure to invest sufficiently or to take risks to enhance the network. His chance now came to act and he wasted little time in taking the regulatory stick to Railtrack.

We have already seen that he issued clear warnings through an enforcement order that Railtrack would face fines of up to £52 million if it failed to reduce train delays. Winsor also returned to one of the core issues highlighted by the Booz-Allen & Hamilton report when he demanded an immediate explanation over the increase in the number of broken rails. Furthermore, he has recently issued a second enforcement order requiring Railtrack to provide more information about its plans for the upgrade of the West Coast Main Line (WCML).

The WCML upgrade has become one of the most time-consuming issues for the Rail Regulator – and understandably so, as the long-overlooked route was

Table 4.1 Current and projected journey times on the West Coast Main Line. Source: Virgin Trains.

London to	Summer 1999	June 2002	June 2005
Birmingham New Street	1 hr 39 min	1 hr 20 min	1 hr 10 min
Manchester	2 hr 30 min	2 hr 00 min	1 hr 50 min
Liverpool	2 hr 45 min	2 hr 00 min	1 hr 50 min
Glasgow	5 hr 15 min	4 hr 05 min	3 hr 55 min
Edinburgh	N/A	4 hr 10 min	4 hr 00 min

pivotal to any hopes of increasing rail traffic through some of the most heavily populated areas of Britain. It was also symbolically important for a railway industry anxious to have a glamorous example of how the privatised network could develop. Under a deal proposed between Virgin Trains and Railtrack, the key route would be given a £2.1 billion (recent estimates suggest this figure has nearly trebled, to £5.8 billion) upgrade by 2005, enabling tilting trains to run at up to 140 mph on fast tracks, while local services occupied slower lines. Virgin would replace its entire electric train fleet to significantly reduce journey times on the WCML (see Table 4.1). The package, which became known as Passenger Upgrade Two (PUG 2) was a considerable improvement on the original "PUG 1" proposal of providing only 125 mph capability.

After drawn-out negotiations with Virgin and Railtrack, Swift made clear that, if he were to approve the deal, Virgin would have to improve existing services between London and North Wales, Edinburgh and Glasgow. Crucially, in response to concerns from other passenger companies and freight operators that their interests were being overlooked by the PUG 2 proposals, Swift also demanded that Railtrack must provide additional capacity to allow extra services. He pointed out that the "renewal and upgrade of the West Coast Main Line is long overdue ... [but] the proposals must be sensitive to the needs of the railway as a whole," and insisted that Railtrack should create an additional 42 train paths a day on the heavily congested stretch of the route between north London and Rugby. Satisfied that Railtrack and Virgin would comply with his demands, Swift sanctioned the deal and preparations for "PUG 2" have now begun in earnest.

Notwithstanding Swift's efforts, many TOCs felt squeezed out by the deal. One such operator was Silverlink, which runs north London commuter services and trains from the Midlands over a congested stretch of the WCML. Silverlink's frustration at being forced on to the slower lines was coupled with fears that Railtrack would not offer the 42 train paths Swift had demanded, so it drew up plans to introduce its own high-speed trains that would be able to use the fast lines. Charles Belcher, Silverlink's Managing Director, said:

We had to find a way around the capacity problem and ensure that we could offer a consistent service. What Railtrack don't understand is that you must have that consistent service to attract new passengers. Passengers that have one good day followed by a bad day will only remember the bad one.

A series of articles in the rail press alleged that Railtrack was falling behind schedule in drawing up its plans for PUG 2. The company fervently denied that it was dragging its feet, although eventually it conceded that there needed to be substantial changes to its plans in order to meet all operators' needs. Instead of a highly advanced train-control system to allow more frequent services to use the fast lines, Railtrack shifted towards a scheme which would include fundamental infrastructure changes, including doubling the number of lines in places. In November 1999, Winsor ran out of patience with Railtrack over the WCML plans. He noted:

> *Railtrack declined to give the undertakings I consider necessary for it to comply with its licence obligations, and accordingly, I am obliged to initiate enforcement action. The proposed enforcement order is designed to end uncertainty about the future of this strategically important line by ensuring that Railtrack meets the commitments it made.*[7]

Railtrack was ordered to set out clear plans for providing the extra capacity, as well as answering key questions over its plans for signalling which also appeared to be running aground. At the time of writing, Railtrack's final response to the Regulator was still awaited.

In addition to the freight issues raised by PUG 2, the ORR has been forced to exert pressure on Railtrack regarding a significant disagreement between the infrastructure company and freight operators about the investment required to facilitate the latter's network-wide growth aspirations (see Chapter 8). English Welsh and Scottish Railway (EWS) has invested heavily to underpin its plans to treble its business over the next 10 years but Railtrack does not believe such growth is possible and is reluctant to provide additional capacity for trains it does not think will run.

Both Swift and Winsor have made it clear to Railtrack that its policies in respect of freight were not matters of discretion but rather matters of obligation, and that the company should ensure that its policies conform to those of risk-taking entrepreneurs such as EWS. The ORR took the view that, when substantial commercial risks were being borne by the freight operators and Railtrack was simply supplying the paths, Railtrack should not refuse to provide capacity because of its more pessimistic views about EWS's future prospects. In September 1997, Swift made a public statement intended to make clear to Railtrack that its attempts to block the expansion of freight would not be acceptable:

> *In respect of Railtrack my objectives are to ensure that it supplies rail freight with enough capacity efficiently, effectively and at the right price, to allow it to thrive, and to ensure that Railtrack's broader investment and property management actions contribute to the development of rail freight.*[8]

Railtrack made efforts to improve the punctuality of freight trains, but remained sceptical about projections of freight growth. In its 1999 Network Management Statement, the company acknowledged that more investment was needed but said much of the recent growth in freight had been in distance rather than tonnage. Its position did not impress Winsor, who hardened Swift's earlier pronouncements and demanded that Railtrack give freight operators detailed information about its plans to meet their projections. He said that it was "unacceptable that Railtrack should not have commenced adequate planning to allow it to implement capacity enhancements which may be required from 2005." Again, this issue awaits resolution.

Railtrack's Recent Performance

An assessment even of Railtrack's recent performance must acknowledge the sheer scale of the upheaval that beset the industry in the wake of privatisation. While critics of the privatised system have little sympathy for those companies – such as Railtrack – which have made very healthy profits, rail managers were also thrown into an economic and political maelstrom of which few had any experience and from which it will take time to recover. It is also important to note that the systems put in place at the time of Railtrack's flotation were devised against the background of the government's desire to sell the whole of the railway industry as quickly as possible and these are still in something of a state of flux. Mistakes, under such circumstances, were inevitable.

Although Railtrack still presides over a safe network, the current regime has been criticised and, at the very least, ministers should have been aware that every accident following privatisation would in some way have been linked to the sale by critics. Railtrack appears to be in a position where, despite the contrary reality, the public *perceives* that safety standards on its network have begun to slip. In terms of track-access agreements, the inflexible way in which they were drawn up has meant that there is practically no incentive for Railtrack to invest heavily to relieve congestion caused by increased train movements. This point is all too often forgotten by TOCs and commentators when criticising the company for failing to relieve bottlenecks. The current review of track-access charges being undertaken by the Regulator should go some way to resolving this dilemma.

Yet Railtrack cannot be entirely absolved of blame because of ministerial mistakes. There has been irritation that the company has not responded to Regulators' demands to drive up standards as quickly as had been hoped. Jim Steer, Managing Director of the consultants Steer Davies Gleave, voiced the feelings of many within the industry over Railtrack's apparent invulnerability, at least prior to Tom Winsor's appointment as Rail Regulator:

> *You can bash the TOCs, you can make the trains more reliable, increase the number of services, buy new trains, improve the Passenger Service Requirements and so on. You've got an agency of government who, if they crack the whip, the TOCs have to jump, even if they think it's unfair. You cannot [seem to] do that with Railtrack.*

While Railtrack's stance in resisting some of the TOCs' demands may have been commercially astute, it failed to recognise the political damage that would accrue from the public perception that it was a highly profitable but risk-averse monopoly. Although the company's year-on-year investment has without exception exceeded the Regulator's initial expectations, it could not seem to take on board that those expectations were quickly seen by most – including the Regulator – to be inadequate in the light of rapid traffic growth. The company's executives who dismiss such claims point to the revenue-sharing deal brokered with Virgin Trains on the West Coast Main Line and now also to a similar potential contract to upgrade the East Coast Main Line with Great North Eastern Railway. But even on the high profile and ambitious WCML project, Virgin managers have voiced their frustration over the lack of urgency attached to the scheme by Railtrack's original management team.

Railtrack is in a pivotal position. The pressure on the railway industry to succeed where it has been seen to fail will only intensify as the need to alleviate congestion and pollution becomes more acute. If once there was political dispute over the need for an efficient rail network, there is now almost universal agreement that, with road-traffic growth unsustainable, railways offer potential salvation for an affluent, but densely populated country. Even those Labour ministers implacably opposed to railway privatisation quickly realised Railtrack's importance but the company took too long to present itself as a willing and able partner of the new government.

On a positive note, there are signs that Railtrack is belatedly recognising the full extent of its role – Gerald Corbett recently admitted to the BBC that its £27 billion investment proposal outlined in the 1999 Network Management Statement is not enough – and the company is responding positively to pressure from the Rail Regulator. It does make clear, however, that a significant increase in infrastructure investment cannot be entirely commercially funded and additional public money may well be needed to realise some of the projects on TOCs' wish lists. In its infancy, as its systems bedded in, Railtrack was cautious; more recently it "got greedy." But its belated realisation that its parsimony was not politically acceptable may yet prove a turning point for the railways.

Notes

1. Nigel Harris, editor of *Rail*, noted that the term "SPADs" has entered common parlance and that this is symptomatic of the amount of concern over rail safety. As he points out, it is not often that a railway-industry term becomes widely used or understood by the public.
2. *Rail* **368**, 20 October–2 November 1999.
3. Association of Train Operating Companies. *More Passengers Means More Trains for Winter Timetable*, News release, 24 September 1999.
4. *Rail Professional*, August 1999.
5. *Rail* **371**, 1–14 December 1999.
6. *The Times*, 14 April 1999.
7. Office of the Rail Regulator. Press notice. 25 November 1999.
8. Office of the Rail Regulator. *Regulatory Objectives for Rail Freight*, ORR, 1997.

5. Trains: The Rolling-stock Companies

John Prideaux

The government's decision to privatise British Rail (BR) in a vertically segregated form raised three major questions about the trains: Who should own them? Who would use them? And who would look after them? The question of who would build them was already decided as they had been bought in a free market for some time, but the answers to the other questions would determine who would influence the design and specification of new trains in the future.

Different solutions were adopted for freight and passenger trains. This reflected the different approaches taken to operating those two parts of the industry. The three trainload freight companies (which eventually became EWS, Railfreight Distribution and Freightliner) were sold outright, but the position of the passenger railway was very different: passenger-train operating companies (TOCs) were to be franchised for a fixed term of between 5 and 15 years. The outcome was that rolling stock in the freight business – other than some which was already leased – passed directly to the new freight companies, whereas in the passenger business it passed to three specially created rolling-stock companies (Roscos). These companies would own the rolling stock for the whole of its 30–40 year life, the equivalent of up to five franchise terms.

The Roscos were the first major sale in the railway-privatisation process. Their sale was controversial and attracted criticism associated with railway privatisation in general as much as the particular structure adopted for train ownership. As companies, they employ relatively few people and they lack a public face. Their role and their contribution is less obvious than that of a TOC, Railtrack or a train manufacturer. This chapter deals with the process of establishing the Roscos, their sale and their performance in the private sector. The chapter concludes by reviewing the major issues raised by train ownership in the privatised railway.

The Initial Decisions

The decision to adopt a leasing structure for passenger rolling stock reflected trends in the transport industry in general and answered a long-standing criticism that public-sector spending restrictions had inhibited investment in rolling stock. The need for leasing was actually identified by ministers and officials prior to the

1992 general election and confirmed as policy shortly thereafter. There were three main reasons underpinning the decision. First, separating train ownership from operations would drastically reduce the barriers to entry facing a potential franchisee by limiting the amount of capital needed to acquire a TOC. Secondly, it was recognised that franchises could be let for periods much shorter than the life of assets, allowing regular competitive tendering for TOCs.[1] Thirdly, there was a belief that, because privatised rolling-stock companies would be outwith the public-sector funding requirements, they would be free to invest. The concept of passenger-train leasing was included in the White Paper, *New Opportunities for the Railways*, although no decisions had yet been taken regarding the precise mechanics of how it would work.

In the Autumn of 1992, the government began consulting on the options for train ownership. There were various suggestions. The trains could be sold, as is, to existing leasing companies; they could be sold with the benefit of leases in place or they could be transferred to public-sector leasing companies with the view to a future sale to the private sector. It quickly became apparent that ministers favoured the last of these options. On 25 November 1992, the Transport Select Committee of the House of Commons took evidence on rolling-stock leasing, notably from Babcock & Brown, the international leasing consultants, to establish how a public-sector leasing company structure might work. The government held seminars for invited experts which focused on technical details and the process of debate and discussion came to a conclusion on 29 April 1993 when Roger Freeman announced that three public-sector rolling-stock companies would be formed and that BR's rolling stock would be transferred to them on 1 April 1994. After a competitive tendering process, Hambros were appointed by BR to advise them on how to structure the new companies and the leases they would administer.

It was obvious to those in Hambros that, whatever their judgement, the Treasury's desire to promote competition in the rolling-stock leasing market would strongly influence proceedings. The decision had already been taken by ministers to divide BR's rolling-stock fleet among three new companies, the minimum number of substantial players deemed necessary to liberalise the market. Although the Treasury would have liked more, it accepted the Department of Transport's (DoT's) argument that to create too many Roscos may have rendered the new companies unsaleable. As a senior Hambros adviser points out:

> *When we first appeared on the scene, the hypothesis was already that there would be three. Selling three businesses in parallel was always going to be difficult and selling four would have been, one imagined, more difficult. Selling two perhaps would have been less difficult but, on the other hand, two couldn't have created the conditions for competition.*

Larry Shore, in charge of rolling-stock restructuring for the British Railways Board (BRB), noted that "three was a sort of a magic number really. The Treasury promoted competition [and] there were three of all sorts of things, like freight companies and so on. The only snag was that there was no previous experience of leasing passenger rolling stock."

The initial preference within BR was for the three companies to reflect the identity of the existing business sectors, InterCity, Network SouthEast and Regional Railways. This was quickly ruled out, however, on the grounds that it would not promote competition. Moreover, the numbers of vehicles allocated to the companies would have differed widely, with the ex-Network SouthEast company having by far the largest number. The Treasury's preference was to divide every type of rolling stock into three, but this was problematic because it would have meant replicating numerous functions in all three companies and subdividing some very small classes of stock. The outcome of the discussion was that one large class of vehicles (Class 423) was divided between the three companies, the remaining large classes were divided between two companies and the smaller classes were allocated to one or other of the companies. Porterbrook, for example, leased its Class 423 units to Network South Central, Eversholt's went to South West Trains and Angel's to South Eastern. The structure gave each Rosco a wide range of customers and gave most TOCs a relationship with at least two Roscos.

The form of leasing chosen was operating leasing. In operating leasing, each period of hire is significantly shorter than the life of the asset. The owner of the rolling stock takes residual-value risk – that is, the risk on both the likelihood of whether that asset will be relet at the end of any lease and the price at which it will be possible to relet the asset. This was different from previous passenger-railway rolling-stock practice in Britain or Europe where finance leasing had been adopted.[2] Such leases involve the lessor being fully paid out by the original lessee over a fixed initial lease term and effectively transfer ownership from lessor to lessee. The decision to adopt an operating lease structure inevitably meant the Roscos would become the predominant owners of passenger trains in the UK.

The leases between the Roscos and the TOCs followed a standard form, known as the Master Operating Lease Agreement (MOLA). These were the product of a remarkably long-winded debate between lawyers representing the putative Roscos, TOC representatives and ministers which involved the examination of commercial principles and obligations attached to lessor–lessee relationships and then transferring this experience to an unknown situation. The BRB adjudicated on any differences. One official looks back in admiration at the work carried out: "I think they did a fantastic job in making something out of virtually nothing. It has certainly been fit for the purpose of getting the process working."

Each contract leased specific vehicles from one Rosco to one TOC and took the form of a supplement to the MOLA and these were largely complete by December 1994. The leases were split between short term and full-length leases. The full-length leases ran to 31 March 2004, except in the case of the seven TOCs initially earmarked for "fast-track" franchising (see Chapter 6) when they expired on 31 March 2002. Some 70 per cent of the fleet ended up on full-length leases. OPRAF required that 15 per cent of the fleet should be on short leases (either 4 or 6 years with scope to extend) and the remaining 15 per cent represented vehicles that would be life-expired by 2004.

Separate pricing structures were adopted in the leases for capital and operating costs, with each component accounting for around 50 per cent of the total rent. Most of the non-capital rents are absorbed by operating costs in a typical year. Profit before interest and tax (the usually quoted measure) is therefore largely capital rents less depreciation. As the depreciation allowances transferred from BR were much less than the value of the capital rents, profit before interest and tax would be high compared with most commercial companies (52 per cent for Porterbrook is often quoted). This is more a matter of arithmetic than a measure of underlying profitability. Capital-lease charges were based on a finance-lease model, covering the cost of financing a modern equivalent vehicle over its life. Non-capital lease charges cover expenditure on heavy maintenance and other ongoing costs to keep the vehicles serviceable throughout their life. A BR team prepared estimates of the likely costs associated with maintenance, derived from historical data with allowances built in for ageing, corrosion and other potential liabilities. These forecast costs were discounted to April 1994 and then turned into an annuity payout covering the vehicle life. As an inducement to efficiency, an arbitrary 3 per cent real reduction per annum in this charge was then imposed throughout the initial lease period and was passed on to the TOCs. As the initial leases generally ran for up to 10 years this implied a compound reduction of over 30 per cent by the end of the period. There was no precedent for such an efficiency gain and this decision was to have a substantial effect on what bidders were prepared to offer for the Roscos.

A historic cost regime was considered, but this would have led to low capital charges in some cases which, apart from reducing the proceeds from the sale of the Roscos, would also have meant that it would have been difficult to justify investment in new rolling stock. As a member of the Hambros team put it:

> We started off from the concept that if we used historical costs, there would be a real disincentive to invest. Nobody would ever buy new trains. Equally, going the other way and saying, "we'll charge you everything as if it was a new train," would just enormously inflate the cost of the industry and it just wasn't fair.

Following substantial debate, an indifference pricing regime was adopted. The purpose of such a regime was to adjust capital rent to the point where a user of the rolling stock was theoretically indifferent about using new and older vehicles. New vehicles are assumed to have an advantage in terms of revenue-generating potential as well as advantages in fuel consumption and lower maintenance costs. Thus by comparing the repayment costs on the capital of the new vehicle and deducting the benefits acquired from using such a vehicle, the equivalent price for older rolling stock could be derived.

This carefully considered process generated rents which seemed too high – and which could have caused embarrassment once the Roscos had been sold but the TOCs remained in BR ownership. The leases were therefore re-priced and, overall, BR and the government reduced the capital rents – and asset values – by about 30 per cent before the Roscos were offered for sale. At the time, this was seen by the major manufacturers as a barrier to hopes of any large orders for new rolling stock. As we will see, however, the Roscos and manufacturers have in practice driven down the costs of using new stock.

This whole process took some 5 months to complete. Not only was there a lot to do, but progress was hampered by persistent indecision at government level. As Shore recalls:

> *[The] railwaymen ... were used to making decisions. When we came across civil servants who wanted to put off making decisions or would come back and change their mind, we were tearing our hair out. We had to make sure it was all minuted by the lawyers so that we knew when a decision was taken it stayed in place at the next meeting.*

There were other issues which needed resolving before the sale process could begin and key among these were the arrangements for looking after the trains. Responsibility for maintenance could rest entirely with either the rolling-stock company or the train-operating company, or it could be divided. Hambros looked at aircraft-operating leases as a precedent but, after some debate, decided to replicate BR's existing system. The responsibility for heavy maintenance, which had previously been arranged through the headquarters of the business sectors, passed to the rolling-stock companies, whereas cleaning, servicing and light maintenance duties, formerly undertaken by the individual profit centres, were assigned to the TOCs.

There were a number of reasons put forward at the time to support the retention of this historic division of responsibility. Most importantly, it was argued that if TOCs became responsible for heavy maintenance, they would be under commercial pressure to reduce or defer it, particularly towards the end of the franchise. Heavy maintenance is costly and would have exceeded most TOCs' ability to pay. As regular buyers of heavy maintenance, Roscos would achieve economies of scale which TOCs could not. In addition, heavy maintenance cycles are relatively long and may not have coincided with franchise periods. Some franchisees might thus have escaped heavy maintenance expenditure altogether while others would have been heavily burdened. On the other hand, if the Roscos had assumed responsibility for all maintenance – rather than just heavy maintenance – the level of costs under a TOC's control would have been substantially reduced and franchisees' scope for efficiency gains would fall proportionately. These considerations, plus the fact that an existing division was well established, resulted in BR's arrangements being maintained.

A senior government adviser to the sale recalled that the division of maintenance responsibility was taken without too much fuss:

> *It was going to be difficult for the TOCs to actually finance the [heavy maintenance] and all the rest of it, so you had to find some way to split it in the middle and that was the natural break. So in fact the decision, after quite a*

lot of discussion early on, was taken reasonably quickly and reasonably simply that that was where the natural break was.

With the benefit of hindsight, however, others now think that the issue was decided too quickly and should have been given more consideration. According to Euan Cameron, formerly of BR's privatisation unit and now Prism Rail's Group Operations Director:

> *The division between heavy and light maintenance was artificial and was based on the way that things had been done under BR. It was a useful starting point but it did not take TOCs long to find that there were more cost-effective ways to run the system by taking on some of the work themselves.*

As will be seen below, the system introduced for privatisation has evolved over time, to the benefit of both TOCs and Roscos.

The Sale Process

According to ministers at the time, it was always the intention that the Roscos should be sold early in the privatisation process. Not only was there an existing market for buying and then leasing capital assets in the transport sector, but it would also be easier to franchise the TOCs if the Roscos were seen by potential bidders as enabling, not complicating, factors in the privatisation as a whole. Yet this version of events is somewhat at variance with the evidence produced by officials at subsequent formal enquiries. For example, it came to light that the decision to sell the Roscos before the TOCs was not made before June 1994, in a joint submission to the Prime Minister by the Chancellor of the Exchequer and the Secretary of State for Transport.[3] Certainly, those then involved in rail privatisation at the working level expected that the companies would be allowed to trade in the public sector for 2 or 3 years and, consequently, that at least some TOCs would be franchised before the Roscos were sold. In reality, as with so many other aspects of rail privatisation, it is likely that ministers were unsure as to what the likely order of events would be.

Hambros were again appointed as advisers, this time by the DoT to manage the sale process, and issued an Information Memorandum in May 1995. At this stage the three rolling-stock companies were still owned by BR, although they became directly owned government companies in August 1995 prior to final offers being made. The Roscos were the first major part of BR to be offered for sale and, when they were sold, it was not at all clear that all the TOCs or Railtrack could be sold before the general election, due no later than spring 1997.

The Information Memorandum was sent to 78 interested parties in May 1995. Nine companies made indicative bids in July 1995 (eight of these were short-listed) and four made final bids on 29 September 1995. The groups involved in the final stage of bidding consisted of three management buyouts (MBOs), one from each of the rolling-stock companies, and five external consortia. Of the external consortia, IAF withdrew early and three more, CVC Partners, GE Capital and Natwest/GATX, withdrew at a late stage in the process.[4] Prior to the preparation of the Information Memorandum, the government, through Hambros, had approached 340 organisations. Most of the main international financial organisations were actively pursued and invited to bid, but only one finally chose to do so. It is clear that the reduction from this initial impressive number to those prepared to bid was drastic.

The only external consortium actually to submit a final bid was GRSH, a Consortium consisting of Babcock & Brown, John Prideaux and his associates and Nomura International. Babcock & Brown, with an international reputation in leasing, and John Prideaux and his associates, who brought industry and management experience, had decided at an early stage in the process to act together but they found it difficult to generate interest from financial institutions – even though some 25 were interviewed. Eventually three institutions joined Babcock & Brown and John Prideaux and his associates to submit an indicative bid (Nomura International, US Leasing (Ford) and Royal Bank of Scotland) but this consortium dissolved when it became apparent that there were differences between Nomura and US Leasing on the appropriate form of funding. Ultimately only Nomura was prepared to participate as a principal in a consortium as it saw the contractual capital rental stream as a novel opportunity for securitisation.

The government had decided that the companies should be sold to separate owners as a way of promoting competition, but that its selection of bidders would optimise total proceeds: ministers would take the highest *overall* amount on offer even if this meant that they did not accept the highest offer for each individual Rosco. The GRSH bid was substantially higher than the MBO bid for either Angel or Porterbrook, so the government was effectively forced to decide which of the MBOs represented worse value for money. The difference between the MBO and GRSH's offer was greatest in the case of Angel and so GRSH was awarded this company accordingly. GRSH eventually paid £136 million (24 per cent) more than the MBO had offered (see Figure 5.1).

The position on Eversholt was unclear. The final bidding schedule was extended by 2 weeks, as the government had decided during September to include 41 "Networker Express" trains, then being built under an existing lease arrangement, within the sale. The rentals due to the lessors of the Networker Express trains substantially exceeded the rents at which they would be let to the two train operators involved. Moreover, these trains had no safety case (see Chapter 3) and it was unclear when they might be able to enter service. Further complicating matters, the lease structure negotiated for these trains was completely different to that set out in the MOLA on which bidders had completed very substantial due diligence by that stage. Inevitably, this reduced the value of any external bids for Eversholt by a substantial amount.

Neither the MBO nor GRSH's bid for Eversholt was compliant. Both parties had sought to place the Networker Express trains in separate companies, thus insulating the risks associated with those trains from the rest of the portfolio. GRSH bid an extra £117.5 million for Eversholt without Networker Express – that is, each Networker Express vehicle was valued at approximately minus

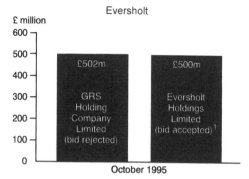

Notes: 1. Bid price shown excludes £18.3 million interest adjustments payable on completion
2. Bid price shown excludes up to £80 million for late payment dependent on Networker Express performance.

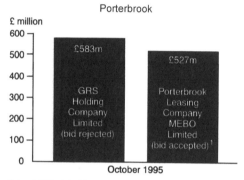

Note: 1. Bid price shown excludes up to £1.3 million interest adjustments payable on completion
The bid accepted by the Department was 10 per cent less than the highest in October 1995.

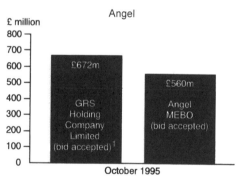

Note: 1. Bid price shown excludes £18.3 million interest adjustments payable on completion
The Department accepted the highest bid in October 1995.

Figure 5.1   Bids received, accepted and rejected for the Roscos: Eversholt (top), Porterbrook (middle) and Angel (bottom). After National Audit Office. *Privatisation of the Rolling Stock Leading Companies,* The Stationery Office, 1998. The figures are reproduced with the permission of the Controller of HMSO on behalf of the National Audit Office.

£720,000. Forward Trust's view (with the benefit of hindsight) is that BR had put in place expensive financing arrangements for trains which were expensive in capital cost and had expensive all-in maintenance arrangements. Angel Train Contracts subsequently estimated the loss of value due to including Networker Express in the sale at £60 million and the Eversholt MBO at £50 million with the benefit of the greater knowledge of these trains (and especially of the progress with the safety case) which was available to the management team.[5] By any measure, including these trains in the sale at a very late stage cost the government dearly.

The bidding costs faced by external entities were quite substantial. It is unlikely that any of the serious bidders committed less than £1 million to the bidding process and in many cases the actual cost would have been an order of magnitude higher. These bidding costs were a substantial potential loss and withdrawal at a late stage is not a decision any group would have taken lightly. A key difference between GRSH and the other consortia was that GRSH was deliberately structured to include industry, management and leasing experience, as well as financial innovation and substance and also that the consortium had taken specific advice on political risk. The view taken by the consortium was that any incoming government would put the interests of the railways first and would not want to undermine either train availability or the willingness of the private sector to invest in new trains.[6] For whatever reason, when it came to the crunch, GRSH was the only substantial outside party which would take the risk.

Against this background, Roger Mountford, the Managing Director of Hambros, describes the final efforts to ensure maximum returns for the government:

We were very conscious that, in trade sales, immediately exclusivity is granted to the highest bidder, power in the negotiation can shift to the purchaser. Accordingly, we required that each sale and purchase agreement be negotiated, and finance committed, prior to exclusivity being granted. As a result, definitive sale and purchase agreements, with as few as possible conditions to be fulfilled before completion, were signed within 3 weeks of exclusivity being granted.

Sale agreements were signed on 8 November 1995. By this point, the government had extracted virtually all the cash in the companies. There were delays in completing the sale, primarily because the European Commission took longer than expected to accept that the sales did not breach European legislation. Nevertheless, the sale of Angel and Porterbrook was completed in January 1996 and that of Eversholt, delayed by the Networker Express saga, was finished by February 1996. The direct proceeds of the sales were approximately £1.8 billion with a further £800 million extracted as cash.

The Rolling-stock Companies in Private Ownership

Since privatisation at the beginning of 1996, the rolling-stock supply market has developed rapidly. All three rolling-stock companies have invested heavily in

Figure 5.2   EWS Class 66, the first of a large order of diesel locomotives placed with Angel Train Contracts. Source: Angel Train Contracts.

new trains, as well as taking actions to improve their existing fleets. In addition all three existing companies were sold to new owners between August 1996 and December 1997 and a fourth rolling-stock company, GL Railease (the NatWest/GATX venture which withdrew from the initial bidding process), has entered the market to supply new trains to Virgin CrossCountry. The Roscos have also become involved in the freight sector, with Porterbrook buying and leasing back existing Freightliner equipment, Eversholt (now trading as HSBC Rail) acquiring over 300 wagons and Angel buying all of EWS's new locomotives (Figure 5.2). Since the general election in May 1997, however, there have been a series of parliamentary and government reviews, directed both at the proceeds realised from the sale and at the operation of the rolling-stock market.[7]

In the 3 years up to July 1999 the rolling-stock companies purchased over £2 billion worth of new rolling stock. Most of this investment was, of course, to be used by the TOCs who have committed themselves to procuring significant amounts of new rolling stock both as a part of, and in addition to, their franchise agreements. Indeed the safety approval process makes it almost impossible for a Rosco to buy trains without an initial operator. This is a very large investment programme (some 20 per cent of the total train fleet) and considerably in excess both of the normal replacement level of around 250 new vehicles a year and of anything put forward by BR in its later years (see Tables 5.1 and 5.2). In addition, there has been a substantial investment to improve the existing fleet. Angel and Porterbrook had each invested around £80 million and HSBC Rail £70 million by

Table 5.1 BR's last vehicle orders (delivered1993–1997 inclusive).
Source: Industry sources.

Class number	Total vehicles ordered	Total cost (£ million)
165/0	2	1.4
165/1	16	11.2
166/0	63	52.5
323/0	126	104.4
365/5	164	163.1
465/0	200	165.7
465/1	188	155.8
465/2	198	160.3
466/0	86	75.1
Total ordered by BR	**1,043**	**889.5**

Table 5.2 Post privatisation vehicle orders (1996–99 inclusive).
Source: Industry sources.

Class number/TOC	Lessor	Total vehicles	Total cost (£ million)
168/0 Chiltern	Porterbrook	20	18
170/0 National Express Group/	Porterbrook	179	164.5
Porterbrook/Anglia			
333 Northern Spirit	Angel Train Contracts	48	55
334 ScotRail	HSBC Rail	120	100
357 c2c	Porterbrook	176	130
357Connex	HSBC Rail	120	93
458/0 South West Trains	Porterbrook	120	90
460/0 Gatwick Express	Porterbrook	64	45
Class 66 Loco EWS	Angel Train Contracts	250	320
Class 67 Loco EWS	Angel Train Contracts	30	45
ATT (West Coast Main Line) Virgin	Angel Train Contracts	477	593
CrossCountry DMU Virgin	GL Railease	348	348
Total		**1,952**	**2,001.5**

Other orders:

332 Heathrow Express	BAA plc	56	68.8
180 First Great Western	Angel preferred bidder	40	36
180 First Great Western	Financing under discussion	32	32
375 Connex South Eastern	Financing under discussion	90	72
375 Connex South Central	Financing under discussion	120	99
175 First North Western	Angel preferred bidder	70	63
Total		**408**	**370.8**

Total ordered post-privatisation   2,360   2,372.3
[of which: Angel 915 vehicles (£112m); Porterbrook 559 (£448m); GL Railease 348 (£345m); HSBC (£193m); others 298 (£272m).]

July 1999. This amount comprises improvements to the trains over and above the cost of heavy maintenance such as the refurbishment of the GNER High Speed Train (HST) fleet and technical developments such as engine replacement or fitting automatic sanding devices.

The Roscos are also marketing trains to the TOCs at prices below both international norms and those achieved by BR. This is for two main reasons. First, the capital cost of new trains has been reduced, so that vehicles which were costing £1 million each in the later years of BR have been purchased for between £700,000–£900,000 (although prices may now be recovering). Secondly, lease rates have been remarkably reduced. The international norm for operating lease capital rents (that is, without any maintenance costs included) in equivalent markets such as aircraft leasing is of the order of 1–1.2 per cent of the capital cost per month. Costs recently bid into the UK rolling-stock market have been at very much lower levels, typically around 0.6–0.8 per cent a month. Taking those two factors together, the overall cost to an operator of acquiring the use of a new train has reduced to around 75 per cent of the equivalent cost pre-privatisation.[8]

To date, there is limited experience in re-leasing existing stock. However, a number of leases have been extended, most notably the Angel Networkers (Class 465/466) which are now leased to 2011. The short leases arranged under the original contracts expired in March 2000 but few negotiations had taken place at the time of writing. Those that had indicated that there was some movement in terms. In addition, a small number of off-lease vehicles have been leased to new operators, for example, Angel's Class 508 Electrical Multiple Units to Connex South Eastern. Forward Trust have also agreed new leases with new operators for Class 423 vehicles.

There is a general perception that there are very few spare vehicles available but this is not strictly true. While the most attractive vehicles are not surprisingly on long lease, a number of reasonably modern vehicles remain available. These include more Class 508 Electrical Units and Porterbrook Class 141 Diesel Multiple Units. In addition, there is always scope to pursue the traditional railway approach to traffic growth by retaining older trains for a few more years. Some of these have been put on the market but train operators in general appear anxious to maximise the use of their existing vehicles rather than increase their lease charges.

Despite the positive aspects of privatising the passenger rolling-stock companies, their performance in the private sector has generated much controversy. Issues surrounding the operation of the rolling-stock market and the effect of maintenance on train performance are important and will be discussed later. But of key importance to many commentators has been the level of the proceeds realised by the sale of the Roscos. This issue received exhaustive public attention in a report by the National Audit Office (NAO) and a hearing of the Public Accounts Committee (PAC) – the most senior Committee in the House of Commons.[9] The PAC hearing was described by the Committee Chairman as "a very long, probably record length, hearing." It certainly felt so to those on the receiving end.

On-Sale Proceeds

Porterbrook was the first of the three original Roscos to be sold, in August 1996. The purchaser was Stagecoach Holdings, who had come into the initial sale process at a late stage as major backers with an option to buy out the unsuccessful Angel management team. Stagecoach paid approximately £300 million more for Porterbrook than the MBO team, an enormous increase even allowing for the fact that the MBO had not been the highest bidder. Stagecoach explained their different approach by indicating that between November 1995 and August 1996 the Stagecoach share price had doubled. In addition, GRSH had demonstrated how securitisation of the contracted capital-lease rentals could produce very cost-effective funding. These factors allowed Stagecoach to bid £826 million for Porterbrook which had been sold for £528 million in November 1995. The Porterbrook MBO team sold because they were offered a price which realised in less than 1 year their hoped-for gains over 3.

The sale, not surprisingly, attracted a lot of comment. The NAO report was subsequently to make specific reference to the "very substantial gains for the institutional and individual equity investors." It continued to note that, whereas financial institutions generally looked for a return of between 25 per cent and 40 per cent a year on their investment, "the percentage gains made by the equity investors in the Porterbrook and Eversholt management/employee buyout teams exceed these figures; also, their gains are very large in money terms, compared to those of most management buyouts."

But the sale also altered attitudes in the other companies overnight. The view of one major investor changed from "we paid a lot of money for this company," to "good mutual investment." The other management buyout, Eversholt, was sold to HSBC in February 1997. The premium was £208 million (£726 million compared with the initial £518 million). The rapid growth in management efficiency within Angel led the GRSH consortium to market the company towards the end of 1997. There were a number of potential bidders and Angel was sold to the Royal Bank of Scotland on 17 December 1997 and was now valued at £1.1 billion, some 58 per cent higher than the £696 million originally paid by GRSH. The distribution of profit was in proportion to the original spread of equity in the company and every member of staff benefited. Both Porterbrook and Eversholt followed normal MBO financing structures, with most of the financing being provided by debt and with the management (and staff) holding a significant proportion of the ordinary equity. The sales in a very short period of time led to very substantial gains to the equity holders, whether these were venture capitalists or the management themselves.

Much of the controversy centred not on the absolute gain made by the investors but particularly how individual managers benefited. The PAC argued that the profits made by a small number of former BR Managers risked discrediting privatisation as a whole. In particular, this is a criticism directed at the MBOs, although commentators found it difficult to distinguish between benefits received by the incumbent managers at Porterbrook and Eversholt and those received by principals in the external bid to acquire Angel. Perversely, the fact that individuals in many of the institutions backing the bids made very large gains attracted little (if any) comment.

The NAO report concentrated on the key question of whether the government obtained value from selling the Roscos. After all, the companies had been sold on for £900 million more than the £1.8 billion originally received and the NAO estimated that the value of the companies in continuing public ownership would have been £700 million more than ministers actually realised.[10]

In the then government's favour, the Roscos were the first major sale of railway privatisation. Ministers had been forced to accept that selling them before the TOCs were franchised would cost proceeds – bidders would not know the calibre or creditworthiness of franchisees, nor even the length of the franchises. Early estimates, prepared for the DoT, put the possible loss of proceeds between £100 million and £300 million. In one sense, it is difficult not to sympathise with the DoT's difficulty in valuing the companies in an entirely new market, or to disagree with the comment of the Permanent Secretary in front of the PAC: "Whatever went first, whether it was TOCs, Railtrack or Roscos, was going to bear the risks." But a major criticism by the NAO, repeated by the PAC, was that the government did not update its initial valuation of the companies which had been taken some time before they were sold – and therefore lost the opportunity to benchmark the bids they eventually received.

The popular impression is that the Roscos were sold far too cheaply. Different observers attribute this to City cowardice, government incompetence or Labour Party mischief in different measure. For example, Bob Breakwell (MD of First Great Eastern) asserts:

> *The great scandal was that the City turned its back on the Roscos. One always assumes that the City has a sophisticated understanding and would weigh up the risk and reward. In fact they simply did not do that, and the loss has been the taxpayers'.*

Before accepting such a popular view too glibly, it is worth considering what commentators thought at the time, which factors might have depressed value and how the companies performed compared with the relevant financial index.

Informed comment at the time of the sale was divided. Whilst some commentators were not impressed by the level of proceeds obtained, others reckoned ministers had not done a bad job. Roger Ford, editor of *Rail Privatisation News* (now *Rail Business Intelligence*), commented that "this has to be a good deal for the taxpayer. We have got rid of a fleet of trains, two-thirds of which are geriatric, for not a bad price." *The Independent* also noted that "the price achieved for the Roscos does not look at all bad."[11] The Public Accounts Committee spent some time seeking to establish whether the government could have taken steps to increase the sales proceeds and the evidence gathered suggested that there were three ways in which this might have been done.

First, there were a number of procedural matters which were handled in a way which raised bidders' concerns. The Networker Express saga has been discussed above. It appears that including these trains within the sale, and within the final

2 weeks, probably cost some £50–£75 million. In addition, the government refused to give normal commercial warranties, although there is no evidence from the events after the sale that any such warranties would have been called. It may well be that the decision not to give warranties, a standard UK government practice at the time, cost a further £50–£75 million. It could reasonably be argued that such procedural matters will have cost of the order of £100–£150 million, or 5 to 8 per cent of the eventual sale proceeds.

Secondly, the impact on the prices bid of the decision to pass large maintenance savings contractually to the train-operating companies has almost certainly been understated by commentators. The 3 per cent per annum efficiency gain produced accumulated savings of £430 million to train-operating companies in their non-capital rental charges.[12] Bidders had no evidence that these savings would be achieved; the track record of the rail industry did not support the promise of large efficiency gains of this nature. Without appropriate evidence, bidders heavily discounted the scope for such gains in the prices they bid. The government wanted to promote efficiency and may have recovered any lost proceeds through the later TOC franchises. However, the effect on Rosco proceeds of the RPI-minus-3-per-cent clause will have been to reduce proceeds by £200 million or more (i.e. over 10 per cent of sale proceeds). Like the procedural matters discussed above, the government placed risks on bidders which they were not prepared to carry – and paid for it.

Thirdly, the sale was conducted against strident opposition from the Labour Party, then in opposition but with the opinion polls indicating that they were likely to form the next government. The PAC report, written after Labour's win at the general election, recognised "that market sentiment in general towards rail privatisation was adverse," but played the effect down. The NAO report was remarkably silent on this level of opposition, so much so that I commented at the time that "not to mention it . . . does seem somewhat like Hamlet with the Ghost edited out."

Press reports at the time make clear the Labour Party's position. Clare Short, the then shadow transport spokesman, warned that "anyone contemplating bidding for any part of the rail network should know that there will be no gravy train for fat cats out of this one and that Labour intends that the rail system should remain in public ownership." Brian Wilson, referring to NatWest's decision to withdraw from the bidding process, said "I warmly welcome this decision by NatWest which I am sure other key investors will follow. Labour's message is that they should stay clear of this high risk and totally unwanted privatisation."[13] Roger Freeman recalls clearly that such comments "caused real panic" among potential bidders and the NAO reported that all the parties who withdrew from the bidding process cited the uncertainty about the outcome of rail privatisation as their main reason for doing so.

Overall it does seem likely that this sense of uncertainty, driven largely by the level of political opposition, helped discourage numerous potential bidders from participating in the Rosco sales. In my evidence to the PAC, I suggested that the withdrawal of these more substantial bidders had allowed the management buy-outs through, costing £150–£250 million. Certainly Sandy Anderson was clear

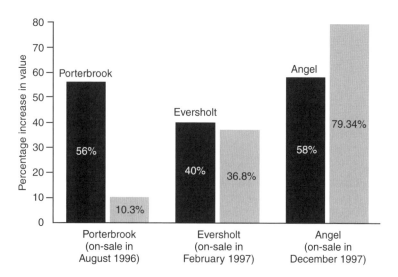

Figure 5.3 Increase in Roscos' value from November 1995 to their onward sales, set against the corresponding increase in the Financial Times UK Banks Index. It is this index, and *not* the Financial Times Transport Share Index, which is relevant because other transport leasing companies are quoted there.

that his MBO would not have stood much chance against a larger number of major bidders. He was later to quip: "If anyone says to me, why was I able to get Porterbrook so cheaply, I say I'd like to thank the Labour Party."[14]

There is no doubt that sale proceeds could have been increased. Attention to procedural matters might have recovered an extra 8 per cent, a less demanding imposed efficiency gain 10–12 per cent and a more favourable political climate at least as much again. There are clearly lessons to be learnt for future sales. But, curiously, despite this and the very large gains made by individual investors, the overall increase in value does not seem excessive when compared with gains in the market overall between the original sale and when the company was sold on. The increase in value came at a time when the market for UK financial stocks rose sharply (and leasing companies are classed as financial stocks). Porterbrook sold very early and substantially beat the market. Eversholt was also ahead, although only just. By the time that Angel was sold, the market had risen 79 per cent against a 58-per-cent increase in the value of the company (see Figure 5.3). All in all, this hardly supports the allegation of City cowardice – indeed it suggests that risks and rewards were weighed up quite well in the market of the time.

The Rolling-stock Market

The rolling-stock companies are perceived as suppliers to the railway industry, rather than an integral part of it. For this reason, they stand outside the formal regulatory framework. However, freedom from regulation is qualified, as all their customers are regulated by the Office of Passenger Rail Franchising (OPRAF) and the Office of the Rail Regulator (ORR) and are required by the Health and Safety Executive to hold a safety case for the operation of all the rolling stock which the Roscos own (see Chapter 3). Regulation is further imposed through the direct agreement entered into by the Roscos and OPRAF prior to their sale. Amongst the important provisions in this agreement is one preventing Roscos from scrapping any rolling stock without OPRAF's agreement, or from selling or leasing it outside the former BR operations. OPRAF also reserves the right, through its regulation of the TOCs, to agree the terms of all new leases. So although the Roscos are not formally regulated, their actions are nevertheless constrained more than would be the case for some commercial companies.

The position of the Roscos outwith the formal regulated structure was initially controversial. Following the election of the Labour government in May 1997, the Rail Regulator carried out a full review into the rolling-stock companies in early 1998. The review was prompted in part by concerns that the Roscos – despite the significant investment programme outlined above – were charging too much and not sufficiently willing to invest in improvements required by TOCs.

The review concluded that, despite the TOCs' concerns, there was no evidence of market abuse, or any barriers to entry within the market – as evidenced by the emergence of the fourth Rosco, GL Railease – and that, accordingly, a free market existed for the acquisition of new trains. The Regulator recommended that the Competition Act would be a sufficient basis for any regulation and that it could usefully be supplemented by a Code of Practice specific to the rolling-stock market. This Code of Practice was substantially agreed between the companies and the Rail Regulator by the end of 1998, OPRAF then agreed arrangements by which they could take a call option on all existing stock at the end of its initial franchise period.

There is a basic contradiction between the views of the capital market on the one hand and views held by a number of government supporters and of commentators on the other. The market is clear that more regulation would increase its risks and that it would therefore reduce the willingness of the market to make funds available for new investment and increase the price at which any funds made available would be offered. Outside commentators, in contrast, think that regulation would boost investment although they have yet to explain how this might happen. In reality, the Roscos have become more responsive to TOCs and their owners without the need for regulation because their continued existence will depend to a large extent on securing new orders and this can only be done by keeping happy the current franchise owners.

Maintenance and Train Performance

Expenditure on heavy maintenance dominates the Roscos' operating costs. With the capital rentals securitised in the case of Angel (and of Porterbrook after its sale to Stagecoach), Roscos' financial performance depends crucially on their ability to manage maintenance costs effectively, including the contractual 3 per cent per annum real reduction in costs passed on to the TOCs. Light maintenance costs are similarly important to TOCs. Of the costs under a TOC's direct control, they typically amount to 15–20 per cent. Given that rolling stock is associated with 20–25 per cent of train delays on average, the quality of train maintenance is important both for the financial and physical performance of the railways.

To deliver the required level of maintenance-cost reductions without compromising performance or safety was the major challenge. The data available to Rosco bidders was also poor. Even where computer systems existed, they were not interactive. It was therefore extremely difficult to establish how changes in the maintenance regime or prices would affect cashflows. Over the 3 years since privatisation, however, the Roscos have put in place a series of new maintenance contracts, both with specialised companies such as Alstom, Adtranz or Railcare and also with TOCs acting as heavy-maintenance suppliers in their own rights. Bob Breakwell says that this latter arrangement can be very positive: "The costs [of heavy maintenance] are huge, but what quickly developed was a win–win situation with Roscos subcontracting some of the maintenance work to TOCs, which benefited both, rather than use heavy-maintenance contractors."

Heavy maintenance is an occasional activity. It is easy to inspect trains after heavy maintenance to establish whether it is deficient in any respect. It is much more difficult to control light maintenance. Light maintenance, as indicated above, forms a substantial part of variable train-operating costs and most bidders for train-operating companies anticipated making substantial reductions (often 30 per cent) in light maintenance. Whilst some of these have been managed without adverse affects, in other cases it has proved difficult to maintain standards. Typically, TOCs reduced the levels of management involved in light maintenance. In some instances, spares have been bought competitively instead of from the original manufacturer. In the worst cases, experienced depot managers and supervisors were removed, and the better qualified staff left of their own accord. Component control collapsed so that, for example, the wrong electronic control cards were fitted to trains. Not surprisingly, reliability suffered.

Very often manufacturers or Roscos have been blamed for shortcomings actually due to the use of cheap spares and/or inadequate maintenance practices by the TOCs. It is interesting that most of the arrangements for maintaining new rolling-stock now place the responsibility for maintenance, even at depot level, either on the manufacturer, or on some consortium involving the manufacturer. In some cases the rolling-stock companies have written maintenance contracts with the manufacturer which go far beyond the timescale of the initial lease. While there are major exceptions, emerging good practice is increasingly moving maintenance responsibility to the owner rather than the user of the train. That said, however, there are also franchisees, such as Stagecoach, that have taken greater responsibility for maintaining leased stock. Either way, the evolving changes to the original arrangements are likely to become more varied as new contracts are agreed and franchises let.

At privatisation, there was no established structure for Roscos and TOCs to collaborate to improve train performance. Train operators were not required to, and in some cases did not, provide Roscos with any information about the reliability of their trains. This has changed and there have been examples of major initiatives by train operators and Roscos jointly to improve performance. Examples of these are South West Trains with Angel on the Class 442 electrical multiple units (up from 20,000 miles per technical breakdown to 60,000 now), the initiatives between Angel and First North Western to resolve outstanding problems with Class 142s, and Forward Trust's work with GNER on improving the InterCity 225 fleet.

The relationship between the Roscos and their TOC customers has been sensitive. Most of the staff involved on both sides – used to the command and control ethos of BR – found it difficult to adjust to a contractual relationship. TOCs wanted improvements to their trains – but without having to pay for these improvements within their franchise period. Roscos have been hurt by the effects of poor light maintenance – and have committed resources to improving reliability even where they felt that the responsibility lay with the TOC. Euan Cameron believes that the relationships between Roscos and TOCs are improving as the industry matures:

It took the Roscos 2 years to settle down and find out what they were supposed to be doing and to decide what they wanted. The TOCs didn't realise they had a bargaining position, particularly if they were looking at extending leases. The next set of franchises will give people the chance to mature but we are finding that there is a better relationship. We don't have to beat the door down ... It has had to evolve according to each TOC and Rosco and the relationship varies. But where it has succeeded has been where there has been real investment. It all comes down to investment and, because there was just no capital to invest under BR, people are wanting that investment to come quickly. In some cases, that hasn't happened.

Overall, the division of responsibilities between light and heavy maintenance under the MOLA was reasonable – although it is now, rightly, evolving – but the MOLA did not contain enough safeguards to ensure that light maintenance was sufficiently well done. An effective way of preventing a hard-pressed TOC from downgrading the way in which trains are serviced and maintained at depot level is the major remaining unresolved problem with passenger trains in the privatised railway. New contracts show considerable variation, but in general show a tendency to transfer more responsibility for maintenance to rolling-stock owners and their heavy-maintenance contractors.

Conclusion

The privatisation of the Roscos represented the sale of about half the assets of the railway industry and was inevitably a difficult and complex operation. Any government would have found it hard to complete this sale successfully. By the same token, however, it was inevitable that the Opposition would oppose and it is hardly surprising that there were aspects of the sale which proved controversial. The sale of the Roscos was the first major step in rail privatisation and it therefore attracted criticism associated with rail privatisation as a whole as much as controversy associated with the sale of the trains.

The government might have secured higher prices for the Roscos when they were originally sold if only by making a number of procedural changes. A key lesson for any future privatisation is that placing risks on bidders which they are not prepared to carry will inevitably reduce proceeds. In addition, strong political opposition at the time from the Labour Party discouraged bidders and reduced proceeds. Overall, the increase in value of the rolling-stock companies, from their sale by government to their onward sale to new owners, was not out of line with the movement in the relevant indices of stock-exchange performance.

Train provision is a part of the industry which, 3 years after privatisation, is performing well. Existing trains have been, or are being, substantially improved. The Roscos have shown that they are willing to order new trains even when the initial lease period is very short. The famine in new train orders has turned into a feast. The prices at which new trains have been put into the market are also lower than those achieved by the nationalised industry. These low prices are based on a market view that trains will last for 30–40 years and that prices will increase over time to compensate for inflation. The rolling-stock companies are also now moving substantially into the freight market. There have been regulatory reviews and these have resulted in a voluntary agreement to complement the Competition Act and to resolve doubts within OPRAF about the strength of their position at re-franchising. The remaining outstanding question concerns the adequacy of the arrangements for light maintenance and particularly whether these provide sufficient safeguards to ensure that the trains are looked after sufficiently well by the TOCs at depot level.

Looking forward, the SSRA proposals for franchise extensions have introduced new uncertainty into the industry. Without such uncertainty, perhaps 1,000 more new vehicles would have been on order by the end of 1999.[15] Manufacturers will have to consider redundancies in 2000 and will have to restructure to regain profitability. At the same time, the Roscos and their backers may well prove to be more nervous of investing in an industry where government is willing to change the balance of power to their detriment. If political pressure for new trains means that mid-life trains sit idle, then the market will no longer assume 30–40 years' profitable life and prices will rise sharply. The feast could revert to famine. It will be interesting to see whether the large efficiency gains achieved since privatisation will be maintained – or whether the costs to the operator of leasing or owning trains increases substantially.

Acknowledgements

A lot of people have helped compile this chapter. In particular, I am grateful to Larry Shore, Roger Mountford, Allan Baker, George Lynn, Shirley Galvin, Peter Rigby, John Vale, Sandy Anderson, Tim Gilbert, Keith Howard, Noel Quinn, Andrew Jukes, Tim Evans, Jennifer Dunstan, Iain Houston and Sir George Young.

Notes

1. This argument remains valid irrespective of whether franchises are for 5, 10 or 15 years. The risks are taken by the rolling-stock owner for several franchise periods.
2. Forty-one "Networker Express" trains had been leased by BR for £150 million prior to privatisation.
3. Public Accounts Committee. *Privatisation of the Rolling Stock Leasing Companies*, 65th report, Session 1997–98.
4. GE Capital and Natwest/GATX only withdrew in the 48 hours prior to the final bids being submitted. Other bidders were unaware of this and, had Hambros not managed to maintain competitive tension, the bids received would undoubtedly have been reduced.
5. Public Accounts Committee, op. cit.
6. This was also the view of some TOC bidders – see Chapter 7.
7. National Audit Office. *Privatisation of the Rolling Stock Leasing Companies*, The Stationery Office, 1998; Public Accounts Committee, op. cit; Office of the Rail Regulator. *Review of the rolling stock market*, ORR, 1998.
8. Forward Trust estimate of an EMU.
9. National Audit Office, op. cit.; Public Accounts Committee, op. cit.
10. Public Accounts Committee, op. cit.
11. *The Times*, 10 October 1995; *The Independent*, 10 November 1995.
12. National Audit Office, op. cit.
13. *The Guardian*, 24 October 1995; *The Daily Telegraph*, 20 November 1995.
14. Quoted in Wolmar, C. *Stagecoach: A Classic Rags to Riches Tale from the Frontiers of Capitalism*, Orion Business Books.
15. Oxford Economic Research Associates. *Britain's Railways – the Way Ahead*, Seminar held on 3 December 1999.

6. Creating the Passenger Rail Franchises

Christian Wolmar

The White Paper, *New Opportunities for the Railways*, was a sparse document setting out in just twenty-one pages the momentous changes which the government envisaged for the railway. The document gave a broad outline of the new structure of the railways, including setting out for the first time the way in which passenger services were to be franchised out to private operators.

There were a bare nine paragraphs on franchising and, in many respects, the document was more of a Green – consultation – paper than a firm basis for legislation. Numerous important facets of the document and associated ministerial statements differed sharply from the final model, in particular over such fundamentals as the level of competition, the number of franchises, network benefits such as interavailable ticketing, vertical integration and the length of franchises. In launching the document, for example, John MacGregor, the transport secretary, said there would be no blueprint for a franchise as this would be determined by the private sector. He also intimated that there was to be no guarantee that the existing network would be retained in its present form and angered critics by refusing to rule out closures.[1] MacGregor was later forced to renege on both of these statements. The document did, however, say that franchisees would have obligations regarding "minimum frequencies, the quality of service to be provided in terms of punctuality and reliability, maximum fares, etc." In the event, the obligations would, over the following years of political debate, become rather more onerous than the document suggested.

In order to understand the development of franchising policy over the next 5 years, it is essential to bear in mind two factors which underlay all the actions of ministers and officials implementing the policy: the ferocity and depth of opposition to the franchising process (and, as other chapters have indicated, rail privatisation in general) from the outset and the imperative of speed as it was realised that the task had to be completed by the early summer of 1997, the last possible date for a general election. The hostility came not only from predictable sources such as the trade unions and the Labour Party, but also from leading Conservatives and some potential bidders for franchises and did much to shape the eventual model that was adopted. The need for speed was mostly a result of the indecision over the choice of model but, in any case, to privatise an industry as complex as rail within the lifetime of a single Parliament would always have been a demanding task. Roger Freeman describes how, in the preparatory period, "we had literally daily meetings" consisting of the senior officials and ministers: "It was like a millennium clock which counts down the days. We had that clock at the back of our minds aimed at the last possible election date." This chapter and the following chapter (Chapter 7) tell the story of how the British passenger railway was franchised and what the initial outcomes of the franchising process have been.

The Concept of Franchising

As Chapter 1 shows, the lengthy debate over the type of privatisation model to be used left little time for a blueprint to be developed before vertical separation was formally adopted by MacGregor. This gave officials no time to prepare draft legislation before the 1992 general election which would have allowed the swift introduction of a Bill. A speedier and earlier legislative process would have had important political consequences as privatisation would have been bedded down by the time of the 1997 election, allowing the Conservatives to benefit from any of its perceived success. Instead, as will be seen in Chapter 7, there were events such as the South West Trains debacle – which led to thousands of trains being cancelled because too many experienced drivers had been allowed to take re-dundancy – to ensure there were absolutely no political gains to be had from rail privatisation. Another consequence was that, throughout the parliamentary process, there was a feeling that the legislation was being pushed through on the hoof.

With the arrival of MacGregor at the Department of Transport (DoT) following the surprise 1992 election victory, the climate changed immediately and instead of delay and obfuscation, there was an impetus to push through the privatisation of the railways with the realisation that enough had to be privatised within the lifetime of the parliament to ensure that the process was irreversible. A lot of work was done very quickly to ensure that the White Paper could be published before the summer recess and this was followed in the autumn by a more detailed consultation document, *The Franchising of Passenger Rail Services*. The details of franchising, however, remained sketchy. There was basic information about franchise administration and ministers had agreed the key point, which was later to be the subject of a court case, that successful bidders would be expected to provide a level of service at least comparable with that of BR. The document, however, still left open the notion that franchisees might take on vertically integrated franchises and there were still no details about their size or length.[2] This lack of detail prompted Andrew MacKinlay, a Labour member of the Transport Select Committee to say:

> *If you look at the franchising document, if I can use that term, I strain to find anything new in that, anything additionally revealing in substance to that which was in the White Paper ... I cannot see any substance in terms of beef being put on the issue.*[3]

There was, in a sense, still all to play for. As Roger Salmon, the first Franchising Director, put it, "at the time of my appointment, rail privatisation was seriously ill thought out, though the government did have some ideological and, believe it or not, idealistic views about what they were trying to achieve."

Franchising was a concept more associated with McDonalds and Wimpy than with transport and the only comparable model in the transport sector was the bus industry (see Chapter 1). London Transport (LT) already operated franchising, which involves tendering out services on the basis of giving exclusive contracts to the winning bidder to run a particular route. However, this was very different from the model set out in the franchising document because, at the time, the revenue risk was taken by LT rather than the operator. Contracts were let on the basis of "gross cost tendering", by which all fares revenue was handed over to LT and the operator received a set level of payment to run the service. In contrast, the rail franchising document said: "the franchisee will bear both operating cost and revenue risk." Outside London, however, there was another useful comparator, the provision of non-commercial – often called tendered – bus services. As Jim Steer, of Steer Davies Gleave which advised the government on this issue, pointed out, "this has two relevant characteristics. First, there is competitive tendering for revenue support and, secondly, there is an ongoing threat of open-access operators with the potential to undermine the economics of the supported service." These contracts also normally involve the operator taking revenue risk, unlike in London.

Freeman recalls how he went round the country assessing whether there was likely to be any interest in passenger rail franchising, visiting the bus companies which were starting to consolidate after the sale of the subsidiaries of the National Bus Company as well as other transport companies such as ferry operators and airlines. He also travelled to Japan, Germany and the US to assess whether the franchise concept was viable but says that only by late summer 1992 – i.e. after the publication of the White Paper – were ministers able to form the "distinct view that it would work, that it wouldn't be a gigantic flop" and this gave them enough confidence to maintain the breakneck speed at which privatisation was being implemented. The Railways Bill was therefore presented to Parliament soon after the publication of the franchising document even though many key decisions about the model had still to be made. While the government was convinced that services would be operated privately – though even here, John MacGregor, in launching the White Paper had expressed doubts about whether all franchises would be picked up by the private sector and appeared to leave the door open for BR to retain some lines – it was still envisaged at this stage that the track authority, which was never named in the Bill, would remain for the time being in the public sector (see Chapter 3).

Creating OPRAF

Despite the lack of clarity over exactly what constituted a franchise and how services would be delivered, it was obvious that a Franchising Director needed

Figure 6.1 Roger Salmon, former Franchising Director.
Source: Shadow Strategic Rail Authority.

to be appointed quickly to carry the process forward. Advertisements were posted in the national press but there was some confusion within the DoT about what kind of person was needed in the role. There was no previous experience to guide ministers because the Franchising Director did not fit the mould of previous privatised-industry regulators. Whereas the utilities had each been sold with one regulator, the rail industry was, of course, to have two (see below and Chapter 9).

The man eventually chosen for the job, from a rather thin list of applicants made even smaller by the government's vetoing of any rail-industry insiders, was Roger Salmon, a merchant banker who had been approached on the Department's behalf by headhunters (Figure 6.1). Salmon, a forceful character with a famously short fuse, had no experience of the rail industry but had been an adviser to the government on its water-privatisation programme and had already worked with Sir Patrick Brown, the permanent secretary at the DoT.

To say that Salmon was breaking new ground is a massive understatement. There was no previous model to follow and there were even problems about how to get him on board. Until the Railways Bill had passed through Parliament, OPRAF did not officially exist. He was employed initially as a special adviser, a rather unusual arrangement normally reserved for political appointees whose job disappears if their minister is sacked. This rather alarmed Salmon who read in the draft appointment letter that "if the minister changes, you resign automatically." Salmon asked "what is this contract about?" but was told not to worry. As he puts it, "it was a half-baked way of doing things."

Salmon set up shop initially in the Department and began what had to be a steep learning curve. He immediately experienced the clash in cultures between the private and public sectors:

There was an incident that demonstrated the difference in culture and background between government and merchant banking. About a month into the job, from talking to a lot of railway people, I recognised that one of the big issues was performance and that this would be heavily dependent on co-ordination between the track authority and the operators. The question was, how did you get good performance in the railway when everyone was going to be playing their own games and everyone was going to blame each other? So I produced a six-page-long discussion paper, with the first version of a performance regime, which as far as I know was the first time anyone had talked about performance regimes. I sent it round to a couple of people in the Treasury, the DoT, BR and the Number 10 policy unit – and I got told off by a very senior civil servant who said I should not send papers out to anyone without circulating them internally first.

OPRAF's status had to be sorted out. There were three possibilities. It could have been an agency, which effectively would have meant the director would have been a servant of the minister; or an independent statutory authority to which the Secretary of State gives instructions and guidance; or a quango. The Department had decided on the notion of an independent statutory authority, which meant the staff were civil servants. Unusually, Salmon was to be the sole accounting officer, not jointly with Sir Patrick Brown, which gave him much more independence because he could take decisions quickly and without having to review them in as much detail with the DoT.

While Salmon was happy to have this amount of freedom, in common with many others involved in the process he was critical of the arrangements between the two regulators:

They [ministers] decided quite late ... that they were going to have two regulators rather than one which had been the original thought [see Chapter 9]. They recognised the conflict between regulating competition and the economics of Railtrack on the one hand, and having someone who is spending real government money and needs direction on the other. One thought was to have one officer with direction in respect of some roles, but not in respect of others, but their final choice, which was a good one, was to split it. But the split was messy. It was crazy having two people both with overlapping responsibility for regulation on behalf of passengers. For example, ticket retail is the responsibility of the Rail Regulator, while regulation of ticketing and fares is actually split and in some respects joint. Thank God John Swift and I got on pretty well together because our statutory duties were seriously in conflict.

Indeed, the roles are somewhat blurred. The Franchising Director negotiates the terms of the contracts and polices them in relation to the agreed service levels (the passenger-service requirement) ensuring, for example, that the franchisees stick to their commitments on first and last trains and minimum frequencies. One of the roles of the Regulator is also to monitor the franchisees, but in relation to other requirements – such as ensuring that they do not discriminate against other

Table 6.1 Regulating franchises: the roles of the Rail Regulator and Franchising Director. Source: Welsby, J. (1998) "What next in UK railways?" in Beesley, M. (ed.) *Regulating Utilities: Understanding the Issues*, Institute of Economic Affairs, London. With permission.

	ORR	*OPRAF*
Fares regulation		✓
National railway timetable	✓	
Disabled access	✓	
Telephone enquiry bureau	✓	(✓)
Impartial retailing	✓	(✓)
Routeing guide	✓	(✓)
Through ticketing	(✓)	✓
Multi-model ticketing		✓
Discount cards	(✓)	✓
Interavailability		✓
Information at stations	✓	✓
Timetable connections		✓
Passenger's charter		✓
Complaints handling	✓	(✓)

Parentheses around ticks indicate secondary responsibility.

operators when selling tickets and that they meet performance targets on the National Rail Enquiry Service (NRES) – the Regulator has sole jurisdiction. On some issues, such as fare levels, the Franchising Director had to consult with the Regulator before deciding any franchise terms, which again results in a blurring of their respective roles. Information at stations is the responsibility of both regulators, while on other issues such as the telephone enquiry bureau, the routeing guide and the handling of complaints, the Rail Regulator has the primary responsibility but OPRAF also has a secondary role. John Welsby, the former chairman of BR, has attempted to classify the roles of both Regulators with regard to the franchisees (see Table 6.1), but he now notes: "it would not surprise me if the principals involved were to disagree with this classification."

Salmon's first task was to set up OPRAF from scratch. He immediately brought in an organisational consultant, which was rather unusual for the civil service, and the tender was won by a small firm called PJR, run by Penny Jones, with whom Salmon had worked before. She helped design the structure of the organisation, as well as its working methods and recruitment process. Salmon was clear about what he wanted:

There were clearly two phases to the job: the first was to create the contractual structure for the industry and the second was to sell the franchises. What I wanted was a team that worked well together, because there were going to be a lot of interdependencies. I knew there were going to be frequently changing priorities and changing workloads, so my initial concept was to have something very flexible where everyone knew what was going on. People would start to work on policy areas and progressively move over to selling franchises, the same people doing both. As no one had ever sold railway franchises before, no one had those skills, so we had to teach ourselves and we needed to build it up with a combination of railway expertise, civil-service expertise, merchant-banking type of expertise and pull it all together. We had to have teams that were small and able to make decisions fast and coherently, which is what happened.

In addition, OPRAF had to be capable of planning for the long-term management of the services after the sell-off was complete. As Salmon puts it, "we not only had to make something that was sellable, we had to design something that was manageable once we had sold it." Salmon's obsession with the structure and ways of working of the organisation – his "touchy–feely approach," as one sceptic put it – attracted criticism from some civil servants who saw it as a diversion of time and energy, but Salmon is unapologetic, saying that he was right to put a lot of energy into creating a robust organisation as demonstrated by the fact that it successfully franchised all the companies in time and its staff were never the source of a leak during the whole process. Chris Stokes, who was Salmon's first recruit from BR where he had been Director of Planning and Marketing for Network SouthEast and who was later Deputy Franchising Director, largely backs up Salmon's approach:

My sympathies were 75 per cent with Roger in that we clearly needed to get the structure right which involved providing sufficient certainty to franchisees to be able to start sales and achieve value from them. At one time, we had twelve sales at various stages going simultaneously, and that was because we had a robust product. However, the 25 per cent was that I think Roger had locked himself in a bit too strongly to his organisational vision.

Recruitment proved slow because, until the Railways Bill received Royal Assent, Salmon could only obtain secondees from the Civil Service and BR. Therefore by late autumn 1993, when finally OPRAF moved to offices in Old Queen Street just off Parliament Square, he only had ten staff when he had hoped to have thirty. By May 1995, when OPRAF began to let the franchises (and after a further move to offices on the South Bank), there were still only sixty, much fewer than the 175 envisaged in the legislation and the most OPRAF ever had was around 140.

The Political Climate and the Passage of the Bill

During the period in which Salmon was finding his feet and creating his embryonic organisation, there were still major doubts as to whether he would ever be allowed to franchise out the railway. The Railways Bill did not have an easy passage through either of the Houses of Parliament and, with such a small majority in the Commons, ministers struggled to push it through. Opposition came from unexpected quarters. Lord Ridley, the former Transport Secretary, an ideologue on the right of the party, questioned the feasibility of the concept of rail privatisation, saying, "I do not believe it is possible to privatise the railways. Nor does the government."[4]

In Parliament, MacGregor and Freeman kept the lid on the opposition with a series of meetings with backbenchers to address their concerns. Freeman recalls:

> *In the House of Commons, it [the opposition within the Tory ranks] involved considerable effort by the Secretary of State and by me in committee to make sure that we were dealing reasonably with criticisms. I spent a considerable amount of my time reassuring individual Tory MPs. The policy we adopted was not to use strong-arm tactics, but to reason with critics and explain to them that their fears of massive fare increase or cessation of service were unfounded. That's why minimum service requirements, caps on fares and the moderation of competition were developed.*

Freeman says that it was the House of Lords which gave them most grief:

> *The Lords' opposition was altogether of a different scale because it largely came from the Conservative benches. They felt it was a privatisation too far, that it was unnecessary and they couldn't quite see the benefits. It was led principally by John Peyton, the former transport minister. Their Lordships were not capable of gentle persuasion. Once they had adopted a particular view, they tended to sustain that.*

Such behind-the-scenes efforts did not stop the Commons Transport Committee, chaired by an old Tory railway buff adamantly opposed to privatisation, Robert Adley, from not only conducting an inquiry into privatisation but also taking the unusual step of publishing its interim findings before its enquiry had finished in order to stimulate opposition. The interim report, published in January 1993, was as critical as it was possible for a committee with a Tory majority to be and got straight to the heart of a major flaw in the franchising proposals, namely the possible conflict between open access and franchising.[5] It identified one of the key unanswered questions as "whether the concept of franchising, as defined by the government (i.e. the contracting out to railway operating companies of the management of different geographical pieces of the railway jigsaw) is compatible with the principle of open access for passenger services; or whether passenger franchises would, in practice, need to be exclusive in all but a few limited parts of the network." Some Tory members of his committee were so embarrassed by the report's contents that they attempted to dissociate themselves from it, but Adley himself made sure that the report attracted attention by calling rail privatisation "poll tax on wheels" and "an impending disaster" at the launch of the document. As will be seen below, just as this interim report was being published, John MacGregor conceded publicly that open access and franchising were incompatible by announcing that franchisees would at least initially have exclusive rights to the rails.

The final report, published in April 1993, reiterated and expanded on the criticisms of the earlier report and raised the fundamental point that the government had not set out what role it saw for the railways in its wider conception of transport policy.[6] The Committee also recommended that franchise terms should be as long as possible in order to create the best climate for investment. The MPs further expressed fears about fare rises, picking up on evidence by a pressure group, Platform, which suggested that some train fares might treble after BR was privatised.[7] The Committee recommended that fares should be regulated and tied to the retail price index (RPI), a suggestion that was eventually accepted by the government with dramatic consequences since fares control has been an important factor in the increase in passenger numbers on the railways (see Chapter 7). On network benefits, particularly interavailability of tickets, through ticketing and the preservation of railcards, the Committee was wary of the government's suggestion that there should be voluntary agreements between operators and recommended that the new franchisees should be required to provide these benefits, another point which the government was eventually forced to concede. The issues of fares, network benefits and franchise length are also discussed in more detail later in this chapter.

The opposition to privatisation was also fuelled by the fear that it would lead to closures and reductions in services. Jim Steer was one of the first people to realise that unless there were dramatic cutbacks or significant fare increases, the level of subsidy would have to rise markedly. None of the early documents gave any figures on subsidy and, as Steer puts it, "the government was trying to keep its options open on both fares and the 'margins of the network.' " Eventually, the government conceded on both these points and accepted that a rise in subsidy levels and stringent closure regulations were necessary in order to help pave the way for privatisation.

Adley's death in the summer of 1993 removed the linchpin of the Tory parliamentary opposition to rail privatisation and this subsequently waned, although in the House of Lords, Lord Peyton managed to force the government into accepting BR's right to bid for franchises. However, ministers felt that an in-house bid would drastically reduce interest from the private sector (see Chapter 7) and cleverly granted this concession only subject to the discretion of the Franchising Director. Much to BR's fury Roger Salmon subsequently denied BR the right to bid in all the early franchises and thereafter BR gave up. The episode was probably the closest that the Bill came to foundering because the amendment was batted back and forth between the Commons and the Lords, but Freeman is clear about who won the fight: "The substance of the point was not conceded. BR did not have the unconditional right to bid. It was subject to the discretion of the Franchising Director." This was a clever sleight of hand because, although on this particular point Salmon did not have to take government guidance – the decision was entirely his – ministers knew that he was personally opposed to allowing in BR for the same reasons as they were. The rebels, for all their bluster, had won nothing.

There was also a lot of lobbying from potential franchisees who had decided to criticise the model publicly in an attempt to influence the process. For example,

James Sherwood of Sea Containers suggested running the South West Trains franchise as an integrated railway, a theme also picked up by Stagecoach which, even after the legislation finally went through in November 1993, was still pushing for vertical franchises. Brian Souter, Stagecoach's executive chairman, said in July 1994: "We are still interested but we have learnt that we will need firm control of the infrastructure and firm warranties on all BR figures."[8] Souter had got something of a bloody nose when, in May 1992, he launched the first private passenger service to run on BR rails for nearly half a century which consisted of a couple of coaches tacked onto overnight-sleeper trains between Scotland and London. The operation was a commercial disaster, not least because BR overcharged for access to its tracks, and the service was withdrawn after a year. As Richard Branson of Virgin had also failed in an attempt to introduce a private service on the network (he had proposed five daily services from London King's Cross to Scotland) because of what he saw as BR's excessive demand for use of the track, the feeling in the private sector, which remained extremely wary of the rail industry, was that nothing short of a vertically integrated privatisation would work in practice.

BR, according to several of the leading players, was making life difficult for those seeking to press on with the privatisation process. BR's then Chairman, Sir Bob Reid, predicted in a radio interview just before Christmas 1992 that there would be cuts in services, problems over safety and extra costs as a result of privatisation.[9] While falling short of outright condemnation of the sell-off, Sir Bob only grudgingly accepted that the proposals were workable "if you are prepared to pay the [short-term] price and believe [long-term] cost savings are going to come out of the process".

Reid had been sceptical about the proposals right from the outset. As a former chairman of Shell UK, he had compared the two businesses, arguing, according to John Welsby, at the time BR's Chief Executive, that "you could sell upstream, as it does not matter who produces the oil, but you don't sell the Shell filling stations." Consequently, Sir Bob argued throughout the process for a "thin franchise" type of privatisation which meant, essentially, to outsource everything except the passenger operations. Welsby believes this was a misreading of the political situation because "the one thing the government needed was for passengers to be getting something that had 'NOT-BR' written all over it and to the public it didn't matter what was upstream. In this sense, it was a dialogue of the deaf right from a very early stage."

Welsby denies strenuously that BR was attempting to sabotage the privatisation process and argues that it was the government's refusal to involve BR in the process which caused difficulties:

That [the accusation that BR tried to sabotage process] is absolute nonsense. There is nobody who was a stronger advocate of privatisation than myself, simply because government is the worst shareholder I could possibly imagine working for. The concept of privatisation was very good, but they didn't understand the nature of the markets they were dealing with, how to produce train services or what the implications of their decisions were. They had taken no advice from anybody who knew anything about it and the consequence was one of frustration.

But despite Welsby's denials, there is a widespread feeling among the civil servants who drove forward the process of privatisation that BR was, at least in the initial stages, being difficult. Salmon feels BR managers were ambivalent, sometimes going out of their way to be helpful, but at other times making silly gestures such as "making all but one of the BR secondees in OPRAF redundant in the middle of the franchising process." Stokes feels Welsby was "passively obstructive" throughout the entire process.

The strength and breadth of opposition to rail privatisation coloured the whole process. The media picked up on the opposition and even loyal Tory newspapers such as the *Daily Telegraph* and the *Daily Mail* ran articles highly critical of the process. Insiders like Salmon felt embattled: "The media had the government on the run because the policy wasn't originally well thought through. There were lots of possible holes in it and the media criticised it as if every hole was then going to be left there for ever more and was going to be a disaster." He also argues that the torrent of criticism in the media had another important effect on the process:

The media criticism had a dramatic effect on the way that decisions got made. It meant the timetable became the single most important issue, by a big margin, and it locked the government into policy in a way it may not have if the coverage had been a bit more balanced. OPRAF was developing very detailed policies and, later, sales-proposal decisions and it was typically a matter of saying to the Secretary of State, "this is what we are proposing to do, are you happy?" So the government had few of the normal terribly elaborate consultation procedures. On sales decisions, we would consult with the DoT and the Treasury and, typically within 1 week of our preliminary decision, we would come back for a final decision which had been endorsed. That was very fast for government-contract awards.

OPRAF versus the DoT

According to John O'Brien, Salmon's Chief Operating Officer and, later, his successor, the Railways Act essentially gave the Franchising Director "two principal roles. The first one is to follow the Objectives, Instructions and Guidance [OIG] issued by the Secretary of State and the second, the short version of it, is to get the best value for money for everything he does [see Chapter 2]." Between the move to independent premises in November 1993 and the issuing of the first invitations to tender in May 1995, Salmon came under increasing pressure from the DoT to press on with the launch of the first franchise in order that the politicians could point to progress on what was now a flagship policy. In July 1994, Brian Mawhinney, a man noted for his aggressive approach to his colleagues and civil servants (one former senior official still has on his office wall a leaving present which was a framed picture of Mawhinney with his suit ruined by paint from demonstrators) took over as Secretary of State for Transport from the more affable John MacGregor and relations between the Department and

OPRAF, which had already been strained, became overtly hostile. The relationship between Salmon and the Department had been difficult right from the beginning when, 2 days after his appointment, he had a ferocious behind-the-scenes row with senior Department officials over OPRAF's independence. Salmon asked what his objectives were to be. A senior official responded, "you will do what you are told." Salmon replied, "No, I will do what is set out in my OIG." When the OIG were issued in March 1994, set out in thirty-nine paragraphs, they were framed in such a way as to ensure that many of the key decisions remained with the Secretary of State.[10]

The lack of obvious progress during 1994 was deeply disappointing to ministers because it gave them nothing with which to counter the public hostility to privatisation. In an effort to push the process forward, in March 1994 John MacGregor, had, in issuing the OIG, committed the government to have 51 per cent of the railway franchised out by April 1996. He was covering up for the fact that an original target of starting the process later in 1994 was unachievable. Seven franchises had already been working in shadow form since October 1993 (ScotRail, Gatwick Express, InterCity East Coast, South West Trains, London, Tilbury and Southend Rail, Great Western and Island Line) and six of these – the tiny Island Line was dropped because of complexities arising from the fact it was to be vertically integrated – were now to be let by the end of 1995 rather than during 1994 and early 1995 as promised earlier. The new timetable was a rash promise, made in public despite objections by Salmon who says the target was "pulled out of the air by John Major at a meeting." The specific nature of the objective was to cause endless trouble as it gave the hostile press an easy benchmark to judge the progress – or lack of it – of the privatisation process.

Salmon and his growing team were working incredibly hard during this period sorting out the contracts that were to form the basis of the franchise agreements. Salmon says:

> *Officials did not understand that if you went out selling these businesses before you had defined the contractual structure, you were going to get a bloody nose and you were going to get lousy value and it was quite possible you would never sell it at all. You would get the sort of thing that we saw . . . frequently with the Private Finance Initiative [a scheme designed to attract private-sector capital to fund public-sector projects]. You do a deal, and then you work out the fine print and you get ripped off, or in this particular case you probably would never close the deal at all.*

There were also delays being caused by factors outside Salmon's control as certain franchise-related tasks were the responsibility of other agencies, such as BR or the Department. Until April 1994, BR was mainly concerned with separating out Railtrack, and Salmon says:

> *There was little we could sign off on our own. The franchise agreement was about the only one. The interoperator agreements all needed a lot of BR input and BR refused to do anything until after April 1, 1994. The access agreements between*

Railtrack and the operators were crucial. These were the subject of protracted and often unpleasant negotiation between Railtrack and BR, with the DoT as umpire on the performance regimes, the Rail Regulator as umpire on all other matters and OPRAF involved as a key interested party. When the decision was made to privatise Railtrack, it meant that all these agreements needed to be settled, rather than just those relevant to the franchises being let.

Even after Railtrack was separated out, there was a lot for Salmon to sort out:

There were incredibly complex agreements, particularly the Ticketing and Settlement Agreement. How do you have competition on price while having interavailable tickets? We were working terribly hard doing our part of it and driving forward OPRAF's input into all these very complex agreements on track access, rolling stock, interoperator arrangements, staff travel, railcards, as well as ticketing and settlement. The performance regime got changed halfway through which didn't help. Railtrack was being bloody minded, as was BR, and the only people who could arbitrate were at the DoT but they did not want to because their expertise is in policy and telling people to do things. The obvious person to blame [for the franchising process falling behind schedule] was me, but I did not have authority over Railtrack and BR.

Salmon remains adamant that resisting the pressure from both politicians and officials for swift results was the right thing to do. As he wrote in a management paper on the setting up of OPRAF:

There were numerous pressures on the Franchising Director during the early stages of the process to cut corners so as to sell the first franchises faster. Particularly, this could have involved recruiting weak people or people who did not fit into the requisite culture, allowing poor contracts to be settled and commencing sales before the sale proposition was clear. The statutory status gave the Franchising Director a good position from which to resist the pressure for the long-term benefit of the programme.

Further delays were caused by the decision to privatise Railtrack during the franchising process instead of afterwards and to sell the rolling-stock companies by the end of 1995 (see Chapters 3 and 5) and, given all this, Salmon argues that the government should never have publicly set a target in the OIG which was always unlikely to be achievable: "The Treasury thought that it would put more pressure on. And once they knew we could not make it, they should have said so and the problem would have gone away." Chris Stokes backs up Salmon's argument:

If we had gone faster and half-baked with some of the earlier franchises, then we would have actually probably taken longer overall because we would have had a long process with major uncertainties on basic issues. We would have got

*conditional final bids which would have ended up diverting us from the next
tranche of franchises.*

Tension between OPRAF and the Department culminated in the latter commissioning a report into the operation of the former and this was written by
Christopher Clarke of Samuel Montagu in May 1995. There had been a furious
exchange of letters between Salmon and Sir Patrick Brown and the only way to
defuse the row was to bring in an outside body. Salmon saw the commissioning
of the Clarke report as an attempt to get rid of him but in the event the report
proved useful to OPRAF. Although Clarke recommended that OPRAF sorted
out a more coherent structure, he also wanted to see Salmon being given more
senior staff and the DoT taking a more active role in ensuring progress. Salmon
was reasonably satisfied: "We did then get a lot more staff which didn't help get
to 51 per cent by April 1996, but sure as hell helped to get 100 per cent by April
1997."

Resolving Policy Issues

The Contradiction of Competition

Chapter 1 showed that some in the government, particularly ministers and
officials within the Treasury, saw the promotion of competition between train
operators as the *raison d'être* of the track-authority model of rail privatisation. It
also pointed out that doubts about the appropriateness of liberalising BR's
markets had emerged even before the White Paper was published. Yet, remarkably, there seemed great reluctance from ministers to ditch the concept of open
access. Both MacGregor and Freeman defended the policy in speeches and
MacGregor, giving evidence to the Transport Select Committee, said that monopolistic, publicly owned transportation systems "could not hold a candle to the
market and competition as the best ways of determining what the travelling public
want."[11] This, of course, was rather overlooking the fact that BR already operated in stiff competition with other transport modes.

The contradiction between franchising and open access should have been
glaringly apparent. Certainly, Steve Norris, a junior transport minister at the
time, understood the point very quickly:

*From a business standpoint, it was clear that no franchise for train operations
could be let unless there were guarantees about where the potential revenue came
from. If there were the prospect that any other operator could come along and
cherry-pick the best bits, you've destroyed the basis on which you can make the bid.*

Norris also makes the point that total open access would have required much
higher levels of subsidy. By now it was likely that Train Operating Companies
(TOCs) would consist of a varied portfolio of routes, some lucrative and some in
need of subsidy, and the intention – though it was not something that was

shouted from the rooftops – was that there would be an element of cross-subsidy within franchises. An outsider running a few trains at lucrative times would clearly destroy the whole financial structure of a franchise.

Despite the fact that this analysis was widely understood throughout the industry, ministers were slow – at least in public – to recognise the inevitable and accept the need for moderation of competition. The first sign of a ministerial climbdown came in a speech by MacGregor in response to both the Transport Committee's interim report and, more significantly, the findings of a consultation process which had asked potential franchisees for their views on open access. In addition to the barrage of criticism about the concept from the Committee and other observers, MacGregor had been told by would-be bidders that on-rail competition would deter almost all private-sector interest in rail privatisation and, faced with the prospect of the policy running aground if the government maintained its commitment to market liberalisation, he told a railfreight conference in January 1993: "if some franchises have to be exclusive in whole or in part, then they will be made so."[12]

The Moderation of Competition (MoC) rules ultimately adopted were designed by the Regulator (see Chapter 9), John Swift QC, but were of key interest to Salmon because, in removing the threat of "cherry-picking", they would make his task of selling the franchises much easier. Swift effectively ruled out most on-rail competition by allowing franchisees to protect their core markets from open-access operations until 1999. The policy still allowed competition on some duplicated routes around the network (e.g. London to Birmingham, Southend, Reading, Exeter, Leeds and Edinburgh) and did not address the possibility of competition developing between TOCs through dedicated ticketing (see below). However, it was a total emasculation of the concept of open-access unfettered competition.

Moderating competition, while eminently sensible, made rather a nonsense of a key aspect of the track-authority model. If there was not to be much competition between TOCs, why devise an industry structure to facilitate it in every nook and cranny of the network? The enforced U-turn on competition policy perhaps demonstrates more clearly than anything else the lack of thought which went into devising the track-authority model. However, with the breakneck speed at which the process was now unfolding, there was no opportunity to resolve such paradoxes. As one senior government adviser put it, "if we had tried to change the model halfway through, people at BR who were opposed to privatisation would have seen it as the cavalry coming to rescue them."

Passenger-Service Requirements

Given the thinness of the hymn sheet from which Salmon was working, it is hardly surprising that he took some time to sort out the series of other controversial issues on which major decisions had to be made before the franchising process could begin. The most fundamental was over the level of service, what was initially called the Minimum Service Requirement but, in a shrewd political move, was later renamed the Passenger Service Requirement (PSR). Here, too, there was an inherent contradiction. The OIG issued to Salmon in March 1994 required him to be flexible in the allocation of franchises, leaving "maximum scope for the initiative of franchisees, imposing requirements no more burdensome than are required to achieve your objectives." Yet, on the other hand, ministers, under pressure from the rail lobby, had also written into the OIG that for the initial letting of franchises, the Franchising Director's "specification of minimum service levels for railway passengers is to be based on that provided by BR immediately prior to franchising." As Salmon puts it, "the political direction was wonderfully ambiguous. I was told you must allow everything to change over time, you must allow flexibility and market incentives, but they've got to be based on the existing timetable."

Developing the PSRs was, indeed, a politically contentious task and it was dogged by this contradiction between having a market-based system and the desire not to change too much too quickly. OPRAF eventually developed a model by which loss-making services were largely protected but which gave flexibility on profitable ones. Typically, the PSRs consisted of between 75 per cent and 95 per cent of the existing timetable but on some InterCity services only 50 per cent of trains were specified.

The announcement of the PSRs caused a political uproar. The first information about them was released at a press conference by Salmon in December 1994 where he outlined plans for InterCity routes and he said that, for example, services such as London to Birmingham, where there was a half-hourly frequency, operators would only be required to run one train per hour. Salmon dismissed suggestions that this would lead to cuts in services because operators would find it cheaper to run fewer trains. He said: "I am confident it will be commercially worthwhile for operators to run more trains than the minimum."[13]

Passenger groups and the Labour opposition were not assuaged by Salmon's attempt to dismiss their fears and the proposals came under fierce attack. Worse for Salmon, they rallied around a specific cause, the cuts proposed for the sleeper services between London and Scotland. These included the ending of the overnight Fort William service which became known, in the ensuing furore, as the "Deerstalker Express", a term coined by the *Daily Telegraph*'s transport correspondent which greatly endeared the story to the media. Salmon had announced that he would continue to subsidise services to Edinburgh, Glasgow, Aberdeen and Inverness, but that the Fort William and Carlisle sleeper services were "disproportionately uneconomic" (Figure 6.2).

Although with hindsight, the sleeper controversy appears to be a row that was unnecessary because the level of savings – losses were estimated at £2.5 million per year – was minute compared with the political fallout, Salmon explains that he was forced into making a decision over the Scottish sleeper services because BR had, in any case, planned cutbacks: "BR had to be planning their services for the following May and the basic decision was whether BR had to take it out of the timetable or not." Welsby, at BR, pressed Salmon for a decision. There was also a tactical motive behind Salmon's singling out of the sleeper services which, according to his calculations, cost £450 in

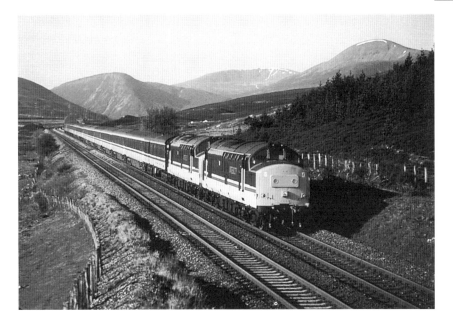

Figure 6.2 Scottish sleeper service in British Rail livery. Source: Milepost 92$\frac{1}{2}$.

subsidy per passenger – a figure that was to be much disputed – making them the most expensive trains on the network:

> *One of the signals I wanted to give the Treasury and everyone else was that we were going to run this thing with some sort of coherent and sensible basis, and my thinking at the time was that if we conceded to the Scottish lobby over Fort William, how could we ever say no to anyone else wanting their local service?*

Politically, though, it was a mistake and, embarrassingly, after a prolonged and very high-profile row, BR's attempt to scrap the service was deemed to be illegal at a court hearing because the Fort William service was the only passenger service on a tiny piece of line around Glasgow and therefore a full closure procedure would be required. BR retreated and Salmon quietly coughed up the extra subsidy, though the process did help develop a cheaper way of providing the service (which involved train splitting), saving some money.

The row over PSRs intensified when, in May, full details were issued at a press conference by Mawhinney and Salmon of the first three franchise PSRs – South West Trains, Great Western, and London, Tilbury and Southend. The press again picked up on the point that not all services would be specified in the PSRs and raised the issue of massive cuts. The government was so rattled that Mawhinney was even criticised in the Cabinet over the issue, but Salmon insists there was no alternative and that it would have been a mistake to specify the whole existing timetable:

If I had locked in the existing timetable, it would have been very difficult to change anything else. For example, if you are using all your rolling stock as some operators were and you don't have any spare capacity, you can't put on a new service over there unless you take one off here. Or say peak demand falls and you've put on extra trains in the peak and you no longer need them, you've still got to run them. That would have been very expensive and we would have had to pay a lot more in subsidy for a service which would have had less flexibility. Moreover, we would have had a service which did not begin to resemble the original idea behind privatisation, which was to deliver something that was driven by the market.

Salmon feels that some of this opposition was a result of rail privatisation being caught up in the wider political climate: "The real problem was actually the unpopularity of the government as a whole and rail privatisation just sort of ran with it. There was never balanced coverage. It was always going to be a story but the fact that it had such long legs and ran so fast for so long had a lot to do with a government that had lost all credibility."

Far from allowing the government to shut down lines more easily, the PSR system in fact guarantees services on loss-making routes for the length of the franchise and, to pre-empt opposition on this issue, ministers ensured the Railways Act made closure proceedings lengthier and more complicated than before. BR had sometimes been guilty of "closure by stealth" tactics, whereby the frequency of services was progressively reduced until passengers, discouraged by a sparse and inconvenient timetable, deserted the route, making it so uneconomic that it could be put forward for closure. One of the effects of the privatisation process was certainly that the shape of the railway became more difficult to change.

Fares and Network Benefits

The regulation of fares was the responsibility of the Franchising Director whose duty, as set out in the Railways Act and the OIG, was to ensure that they were reasonable where, in his view, the "interests of persons who use, or are likely to use, franchised services so require." In fact, this inelegantly phrased part of the legislation, which was a hasty late addition to the Railways Act, gave the Franchising Director sole responsibility for setting the fares policy. Salmon feels this was an unintended effect of the legislation, as neither the Regulator nor ministers had the power to give him instructions on fares.

The original plan was to devise a system that allowed the market to do its job and to be as unobtrusive as possible. The intention was to regulate fares only in areas where the train operator had an effective monopoly over other transport modes or where services were uneconomic – such as those on London commuter services and in rural areas. These had to be protected as pure market policy could have resulted in monopoly abuse, in the case of commuter services, or excessive demands for subsidy in rural areas because of what Salmon calls "ransom potential". But ministers were keen to make privatisation more palatable and keeping fares down was an obvious way of doing so. Salmon recalls:

> *I presented a package to Mawhinney and I told him if he wanted lower fare rises, count me in, that was great. He went to see Kenneth Clarke [the Chancellor of the Exchequer] and, slightly to the surprise of the Treasury officials, they did a deal, which was RPI for 3 years and RPI minus 1 per cent for the following 4.*

There were some problems with the arrangement. LT, which had long been forced to operate a policy of above-inflation fares increases in order to pay its way, had not been consulted and because of the widespread use of Travelcards in the London area, the policy had a very strong impact on its financial position. Fortunately, LT did not protest when Salmon was, belatedly, allowed to inform the chairman, Peter Ford, on the day before the announcement. Moreover, it was initially unclear whether the policy was really to be set in stone for 7 years and Salmon needed assurance that he could write the fares scheme into the franchise agreements without provisions for variation. Ministers quickly acquiesced to this demand.

The practicalities of working out the policy were complex. Mawhinney asked Salmon to devise a scheme whereby at least three fares, rather than just season-ticket prices, were controlled throughout Britain. Salmon was given very little time in which to do this: "My team and some BR experts set to work on this. It was politically hypersensitive but we produced it within a week." But the matter was not settled so quickly. Salmon recalls: "Mawhinney saw this and said: 'That's not what I meant at all, I want three fares *in addition* to the season ticket.'" In other words, the Secretary of State wanted a total of four different fares regulated between destinations. Salmon did not want to do that because controlling three fares and season tickets meant locking up a significant proportion of the system, giving operators little control over their sources of revenue. He was aware that any further restrictions on the franchise agreements may have deterred potential franchisees: "Remember, this was April 1995 and we still did not actually know if we would have any bidders." Indeed, when the policy was eventually announced in May 1995,[14] several potential bidders were critical. One told *The Independent*: "The cap on fares does not mean we are not interested, but in our business plan we had looked at increasing fares in real terms over the next few years. Now we won't be able to do that and, as a result, we face extra risk and therefore we will require more subsidy."[15] In the same article, Stagecoach was quoted as saying that the fares regime would make bidders "more cautious, since it will act as a constraint on their freedom."

Of course, to some extent these bidders were simply doing a bit of negotiating in public, but clearly the fares policy did have a subsidy implication and, as will be seen in Chapter 7, it also had an impact on passenger growth. The fares regulation should have been a positive policy initiative for the government, as it offered passengers a tangible reward from privatisation. However, most commentators and industry insiders failed to recognise its importance and the overall climate was so hostile to privatisation that the potential impact of the policy was missed. Like LT, BR had been forced to meet an increasing proportion of its operating costs through fare – rather than subsidy – increases and the implications of the fact that many above-inflation price hikes would be prevented under the new franchise system were ignored. Even ministers did not realise just how far-reaching the change would be at the time, although Sir George Young, Mawhinney's replacement, made a number of speeches on the subject later. The new fares policy was to be one of the most significant outcomes of the privatisation process because, for the first time in a generation, the price of rail travel would become relatively cheaper in relation to car use given the continued application of the fuel-tax escalator.[16]

The government also had to compromise its original position on network benefits, particularly by restricting the right of operators to set their own fares and guaranteeing the continuation of some railcards (such as those allowing discounted travel for students, the elderly and the disabled). A fares free-for-all with big differences between operators on the same route would have meant that tickets may have been dedicated; that is, only available on trains run by the operator selling the ticket. Railcards not protected by regulation might have been phased out altogether. The government's original hope was that the market would provide an incentive for TOCs to both maintain railcards and voluntarily agree to issue and accept each other's tickets, but there was no guarantee that this would take place in practice. A predominance of dedicated tickets would have allowed some price competition between incumbent TOCs despite MoC because, as a result of the geography of the TOCs, many of BR's existing routes would be served by more than one TOC after privatisation.[17] Equally, however, if operators chose not to co-operate, the ability of rail to provide a "turn up and go" service – which was widely believed to account for a significant proportion of its business – could have been eroded.[18] Moreover, through journeys involving more than one operator could have become difficult to undertake if each leg of the journey required a separate ticket (see Chapter 1).

The Transport Select Committee reported consistent hostility towards the government's *laissez-faire* attitude to network benefits and ministers were forced to concede – again after they had canvassed the views of the private sector – that they would have to protect railcards and ticket interavailability. This concession effectively ruled out any remaining hopes harboured by the government of liberalising the market because both major sources of potential competition, open access and dedicated ticketing, would now be restricted by regulations. The Franchising Director ensured the continued interavailability of virtually all ticket types on all but one flow on the network (London Victoria to Gatwick Airport) through a policy of Compulsory Interavailability (CI). Under the system, a lead operator is defined and creates fares which other, secondary, operators must honour. Revenue is "pooled" and divided among operators by Operational Research Computer Allocation of Tickets to Services (ORCATS), a computerised allocation system, according to passenger miles travelled. ORCATS calculates passenger miles by taking into account factors such as timetabling and speed of journey and by making assumptions about passenger behaviour based on historical survey evidence. It is not a precise measure, but OPRAF decided this was preferable to having a highly complex system which would have required using high technology and would have increased the costs of allocating revenue. Operators are entitled to commission surveys to challenge ORCATS allocations if they wish, but this is only likely to be economic on heavy flows.

Lead operators are permitted to offer dedicated fares for four ticket types – first class, temporary (such as promotions), special (mostly for local user groups who negotiate deals with TOCs) and some advance purchase (typically fares sold on a wholesale basis for resale by airlines, educational establishments, holiday companies, etc.). The advantage for the operator is that these tickets bypass the ORCATS system and therefore the issuing TOC gets all the revenue. Secondary operators have more freedom, being allowed to set dedicated fares for all ticket types, the revenue from which also bypasses ORCATS. Since, by definition, the secondary operator runs fewer trains, such tickets will only appeal to a limited number of passengers. The vast majority of tickets sold have been interavailable, the biggest exception being the greater use of advance ticket sales over the telephone and the Internet since privatisation. This is an avenue open only to longer distance operators, however, as it is impractical to offer "short-hop" tickets – generally used for impulse trips – which must be booked at least one day in advance.

Overall responsibility for administering network benefits now lies with ATOC. Initially, there was an assumption that this should be the job of OPRAF but eventually it was felt that this would not provide sufficient commercial drive. When ATOC was created in October 1994, it was a subsidiary of BR since all the railway was still in public hands. The main function given to ATOC was to manage common national activities such as supplying information about most tickets and arranging the collection and redistribution of revenues allocated by ORCATS. About one-quarter of the total revenue of £3 billion has to be reallocated between companies. ATOC was also charged with establishing and administering NRES, which now provides a single, 24-hour local-charge call information number for timetable and fare enquiries.

Although ATOC is not a statutory body, it administers, on behalf of the TOCs, the various national railcard schemes – both compulsory ones such as the Young, Senior and Disabled persons' and the voluntary ones such as the Family, Network and Forces'. Various other functions which no one had quite worked out what to do with dropped into ATOC's lap such as timetabling-information procedures and a co-ordinated approach to lost property.

As the franchises were let, control of ATOC passed to the private sector. ATOC, of course, could not wield power in the same way that the head office of BR ruled the railways. Indeed, there was some reluctance by the new franchise owners to make use of it as they were wary of recreating a BR-type organisation. Initially, it quite deliberately had no public profile, but gradually the operators began to realise that it had a potentially useful role in representing the industry to the media and the public at large. As James Gordon, the first Director General of ATOC, put it,

when the TOCs first moved into the private sector, they established their freedom to make their own decisions. They sought to minimise the requirement for collective action or interference from their trade body – rather in the manner of teenagers leaving home. As the industry matured, the added value to their businesses of effective collaborative action became more apparent and ATOC began to achieve its full potential.

The Passenger's Charter and Performance Incentives

For some years, BR had operated a passenger's-charter regime which monitored train performance, particularly punctuality (how many trains arrive within a set number of minutes of the scheduled time) and reliability (the measure of the percentage of cancellations) but provided only limited financial incentives for the organisation to perform better. Moreover, if the targets were not met, only season-ticket holders rather than casual users of the network obtained any compensation. The BR targets were based on historic performance of the line so they varied between routes. Lines which traditionally performed badly had easier targets than those where delays and cancellations were less frequent.

As a requirement of their tenders, bidders were asked to submit their own charters. OPRAF wanted to force bidders to sign up to targets that were more onerous than BR's, but were mindful of the fact that tough new targets could impact detrimentally upon the number of tenders received for each franchise if would-be bidders perceived them as being unattainable. OPRAF's solution was to stipulate that, while all TOCs must operate at least to the standards set out in BR's charter, bidders could sign up to tougher regimes on a voluntary basis. The theory was that competition between bidders would compel them to offer a better quality service than BR, although no one could be sure that it would hold: even Salmon was unsure as to whether there would actually be private-sector interest in the TOCs. While most successful bids did include some uprating, this was often minor, relating only to one or two routes in the operator s network and the required improvement was relatively small (see Table 6.2). There is, of course, a lot of PR value attached to improving performance – and the figures attract considerable media interest when published – but, although OPRAF had an eye to the future, its attention was focused primarily on letting the franchises before the general election to be held by 1997.

The one area in which OPRAF did introduce a mandatory strengthening of the Passenger's Charter regulations was financial penalty regimes. Casual travellers would now be compensated for poor punctuality (typically 20 per cent of the cost of a journey would be refunded if the train was more than 1 hour late) and a suite of performance regimes relating to the subsidy paid by (or premia paid to) OPRAF were also introduced. These are in addition to the fault-based regimes operating between Railtrack and the TOCs outlined in Chapter 3. There are three systems for determining whether any penalties or payments should be made. The most significant is the Punctuality Incentive Payment (PIP) which applies to peak London services and regional and rural services. It measures lateness and cancellations and performance in every 4-week period is compared with the relevant benchmark figure. If average lateness is better than the benchmark, OPRAF

Table 6.2 A comparison of key commitments in the passenger's charters of BR and Wales and West. Sources: British Railways Board, *The British Rail Passenger's Charter*, BRB; Wales and West Passenger Trains Ltd, *Our Passenger's Charter*, Wales and West.

Criteria	BR (Regional)	Wales and West	Improvement?
Punctuality	90% of long-distance trains to arrive within 10 minutes of schedule.	90% of long-distance trains to arrive within 10 minutes of schedule. To improve to 92% by 1998.	Yes
Reliability	99% of services to run.	99% of services to run. To improve to 99.5% by 1998.	Yes
Compensation (one-off journeys)	20% of price paid for journey refunded if delayed for >1 hour.	20% of price paid for journey refunded if delayed for >1 hour. Increases to 50% refund for delays >2 hours.	Yes
Compensation (season tickets)	5% discount on monthly or longer season tickets if punctuality <87% or reliability <98% for preceding year. 10% discount if both punctuality and reliability below those thresholds.	5% discount for monthy season tickets if punctuality <87% for reliability <98% for preceding year. 10% discount if both punctuality and reliability below those thresholds. For annual season tickets, above discounts rise to 7% and 14% respectively.	Yes
Ticket office queueing	Maximum 5 minutes peak. Maximum 3 minutes off peak.	Maximum 5 minutes peak. Maximum 3 minutes off peak.	No
Information	Timetables at all stations. Notice of engineering work at affected stations. Notice in advance if advertised, on-board catering is cancelled.	Timetables at all stations. PA or freephone or information boards at all stations by 1999. 7 days' notice of engineering work at affected stations. Advance notice of cancellation of advertised, on-board catering service.	Yes
Disabled travellers	48 hours' notice for assistance at staffed stations.	24 hours' notice for assistance at staffed stations.	Yes

pays out extra subsidy and vice versa. There are, too, Short Formation Incentive Payments for operators running into London and some other cities. These operators must produce a plan on how to deliver capacity and failure to meet this plan results in penalties. The third system, Timetable Change Incentive Payments, penalises operators who change the timetable from the printed version.

Operators must also now carry out customer-satisfaction surveys on such matters as cleanliness, information provision, staff helpfulness and catering every 6 months and the results are published by OPRAF. Again, however, the results relate to benchmark figures set before privatisation for each individual TOC and, for this reason, they are not directly comparable across the network. To further complicate matters, neither the questionnaires nor the methodology used to undertake and analyse them are standardised. Although it is possible to identify general trends (e.g. whether trains are getting cleaner), OPRAF now admits that the current system contains flaws and is working to address them.

The Franchises Take Shape

The paucity of detail in the government's proposals on franchises as set out in the White Paper left OPRAF and its ministerial bosses to sort out several other important aspects of the agreements before the franchising process could start. The White Paper seemed deliberately to leave the details fuzzy because ministers were wedded to the idea that the market should determine the shape of the industry and it was such new territory that they were reluctant to rule out any options. But this plan was unlikely to work in reality: over-reliance on the wishes of the private sector might be impractical, especially if "cherry-picking" left the government with a disaggregated residue of unsaleable services. As Salmon was later to point out, in order to get the job done in time, he needed to be able to attract bids which were comparable with one another. It was also becoming clear that bidders wanted more specific propositions – the government's line of "flexibility" was being interpreted by some as a euphemism for the fact that, really, it had no idea what it wanted to do. So OPRAF had to ensure that the details such as the depth, size and length of franchises were established before the sales could begin.

Franchise depth should have been resolved with the publication of the White Paper. Although it gave little detail about most aspects of the new railway, it was clear that it would involve a vertical separation of infrastructure from operations. It came as something of a surprise, therefore, when *The Franchising of Passenger Rail Services* noted that some franchisees might "take on a 'vertically integrated' franchise covering the operation of track and signalling as well as trains" and also that the Railways Act made no mention of Railtrack. Certainly, these developments muddied the issue and, as we have seen, some potential bidders continued to press for BR to be sold in vertically integrated chunks.

The decision to allow a degree of vertical integration was not, in fact, influenced by the arguments of prospective franchisees, but pre-empted them and had been agreed as there were likely to be exceptional circumstances around the network where vertical separation was neither logical nor desirable.[19] In particular, ministers were thinking of the Island Line, a single track, 8-mile route on the Isle of Wight which was detached from the main network and was always unlikely, given its relatively large subsidy requirements, to attract open-access operations. Although some within the DoT had suggested that vertical integration might be considered on other more or less self-contained parts of the network (such as the LTS system) to take account of bidders' concerns, the government gambled – correctly as it turned out – that franchising would attract sufficient interest from the private sector without making such a concession. Other areas of policy had been more open to change, but to compromise on vertical separation would have resulted in a serious loss of face for ministers who would have effectively been admitting that the White Paper was even more flawed than the MoC debacle had revealed.

The size of franchises was settled relatively quietly despite some initial debate within the government. The original idea, according to Freeman, was to have around fifty TOCs in order to foster a lot of competition between bidders. Some of these might even have been mini-franchises, consisting of a line or two, like the "mom and pop" railways of the United States. However, as it became apparent that on-rail competition would be a non-starter, ministers' attention turned to BR's existing organisational structure. BR had been divided into nineteen profit centres as part of its Organising for Quality (O for Q) initiative that was completed just before the privatisation process started (see Chapter 2) and it was suggested by the DoT that these units should largely be retained. Not only would this save time as further, large-scale reorganisation would be unnecessary, but also track records for prospective bidders, who would need financial information about the businesses they were to buy, would be *relatively* straightforward to assemble. As Freeman recalls,

> *We knew how BR organised itself and that seemed a sensible number of TOCs both in terms of the speed in which you could generate interest and complete the franchising programme. So we ruled out half a dozen, we ruled out hundreds and the existing structure seemed to present a practical and sensible way forward.*

There was a little scope for breaking them up further, where it made operational sense, such as separating Thames and Chiltern, which operated out of different London termini. Other small chunks were separated out, such as Cardiff Valleys from Wales & West, Island Line from South West Trains and Merseyrail from Regional Railways North West. The InterCity Gatwick/Anglia and Midlands/CrossCountry profit centres were also split (see Table 2.1). Twenty-five TOCs were ultimately created and this number still allowed direct competition on a few duplicated routes (see above) but this was generally coincidental rather than planned. A senior Department official pointed out that the promotion of competition was "not at all, absolutely not at all" a consideration in determining the shape of the TOCs. The Treasury, while accepting that a smaller number of franchises would limit the potential for competition *in* the market, had been worried that it would also impact severely upon the amount of competition generated *for* the market. Their fears were allayed when a DoT official pointed out that, "after all, twenty-five was not an inconsiderable number" of auctions to hold. BR prepared the evidence on the division and OPRAF made the final decision, sticking largely to BR's suggestions. BR then split the twenty-five into two divisions, North and West with twelve and South and Eastern which had thirteen, in order to begin the massive preparation task.

The length of franchises was a more contentious issue. The Treasury, eager to stimulate competition, had wanted the shortest possible terms and had suggested 3 years. According to Freeman, the potential franchisees, on the other hand, had sought to get the maximum in order to create a framework for investment and had wanted at least 12 to 15 years and possibly even 20. BR, too, wanted longer. A senior civil servant recalled that the Treasury pressed for a low figure in order to get a compromise of around 7 years and, except where major investment in rolling stock was required, this was to become the standard length. Remarkably the Treasury was prepared to set aside its normal rules about making no commitments beyond its 3-year spending plan by guaranteeing franchise payments for the full term of the franchise, even those that were for 15 years. BR had never had the benefit of such long-term planning. The Treasury's reasoning was that the private companies were prepared to enter into the commitment to provide the required level of services for the duration of the franchise term and that if the company started making losses, it was their shareholders, not the taxpayer, who would suffer. If BR had been guaranteed its income for 7 years and found that the numbers did not add up, it would have gone back to the government to ask for more. In theory, this option is not open to the private franchisees, although, of course, if they go bust their successors are bound to ask for extra subsidy or reduced premia.

So the model of franchise that finally emerged from this lengthy preparatory period was of a rather thin and narrow construct. The franchisee would have virtually no assets since trains were leased from the rolling-stock companies and stations, track and signalling would belong to Railtrack (see Chapters 3 and 5). The total capital requirement for the franchisees, it was later decided, was 15 per cent of annual turnover – of which half had to be backed by cash or a corporate guarantee and the other half had to be represented by a part-bond issued by a bank – which would be forfeited if the contract were broken. Franchises merely consisted of a commitment to run a minimum level of services for a relatively short term – generally 7 years – but would take both the revenue and operational risks. The franchises were to be much more tightly regulated than originally envisaged and would be required to operate within a framework of network benefits which, according to the government's initial suggestions, were to have been the subject of only voluntary agreements.

With all these matters sorted out and the work having been done on the complex legal agreements between all the various parties, the marketing of franchises was ready to start. OPRAF had been preparing a detailed outline of the rail industry, the *Passenger Rail Industry Overview*, a document which, according to Salmon, was "massively expensive to produce" but which was vital in setting out exactly what was on offer.[20] The PRIO, as it became known, was published in May 1995 along with the launch of the first three Invitations to Tender (ITTs). At last, some 18 months late, the franchising process was underway.

Notes

1. *The Independent*, 15 July 1992.
2. DoT. *The Franchising of Passenger Rail Services*, 1992.
3. *House of Commons Papers*. Session 1992–1993, 246-i.
4. *Evening Standard*, 29 November 1992.
5. *House of Commons Papers*. Session 1992–1993, 375.
6. *House of Commons Papers*. Session 1992–1993, 246-i.
7. *The Independent*, 24 November 1992.
8. *Evening Standard*, 26 July 1994.
9. On *The World This Weekend*, 20 December 1992, reported in *The Independent*, 21 December 1992.
10. Office of Passenger Rail Franchising. *Annual Report* 1994–95, OPRAF, 1995.
11. *Hansard*, **213**, Cols 1161–2, 29 October 1992.
12. *The Independent*, 20 January 1993.
13. *The Independent*, 14 December 1994.
14. Unrestricted, standard-class return fares, certain single fares, saver fares and certain standard-class season-ticket fares including all weekly season tickets were included in the regulation. Fare increases were initially restricted to RPI but must now be RPI minus one. They are controlled by way of a "tariff basket", which means that the *overall* level of fares included in the regulation must not exceed the increase allowed. This leaves the operator some flexibility with respect to individual fares in the basket.
15. *The Independent*, 16 May 1995.
16. The fuel-tax escalator was introduced by the Conservatives and abandoned by Labour in 1999. It imposed a real-term increase on the cost of fuel for motorists of 6 per cent per year (initially 5 per cent). Labour's replacement is more ad hoc.
17. For example, London to Penzance InterCity services, operated by one company, would duplicate some Cardiff to Penzance regional services, operated by another, on the stretch between Taunton and Penzance. Office of the Rail Regulator. *Summary of Responses*, Unpublished information document (available in ORR library), 1994.
18. Curwen, P. "The end of the line for BR" in *Public Money and Management*, **17**, 1997.
19. Shaw, J. *Privatising Britain's Passenger Railway: Expectations and Outcomes of the 'Free' Market Approach*, Unpublished PhD thesis, University of Plymouth.
20. Office of Passenger Rail Franchising. *Passenger Rail Industry Overview*, OPRAF, 1996.

7. Selling the Passenger Railway

Christian Wolmar and Roger Ford

The franchising process finally began in May 1995. Roger Salmon explained that the bidding procedure would consist of five key stages. Companies interested in obtaining a TOC would first be asked to pre-qualify, in order that OPRAF could check whether they had the the financial backing and management competency to run one. Invitations to Tender (ITTs) would then be issued to those who had pre-qualified, inviting indicative bids. Third, OPRAF would produce a shortlist of bidders on the strength of the indicative bids and, fourth, a "preferred bidder" would be announced after final bids had been received from shortlisted companies. Finally, provided that contractual negotiations were successfully completed, the franchise would be awarded to the preferred bidder and private-sector operation would begin.[1]

OPRAF issued the first ITTs for three clutches of routes – South West Trains, London, Tilbury and Southend (LTS) and Great Western. The other early candidates for franchising had fallen by the wayside for one reason or another. ScotRail was made more complicated by the role of the Strathclyde Passenger Transport Executive which subsidises services in the Glasgow area; Gatwick Express needed new trains; Island Line was being vertically integrated and proving legally complex; and InterCity East Coast had run into problems over its performance regime. That left the three whose ITTs were put out in May 1995. Salmon was insistent that three of the most simple franchises were offered first, "to ensure they sold well."

The big unknown was the number of serious bidders OPRAF could expect. In 1993, the Department of Transport (DoT) had claimed over 150 expressions of interest to illustrate the enthusiasm for privatisation but the *Financial Times* managed to identify only sixteen, eleven of whom were eventually successful bidders.[2] In reality, this impressive total included a broad spectrum of what the motor trade calls "tyre kickers". These time-wasters ranged from train enthusiasts to consultants and bankers eager to gain access to whatever information was going. A better indicator was the result of the Franchising Director's pre-qualification exercise for the first franchises to be let. When applications closed on 17 March 1995, thirty-seven organisations had come forward, but this included the first eight MBO teams and British Rail (BR), so there were about twenty-eight outside serious bidders. Some of these were just coming along for the ride and played no further part in the process and there was an element of desperation about the way that ministers stressed that there was strong outside interest. While Secretary of State for Transport Dr Brian Mawhinney welcomed the response as a "vote of confidence in rail privatisation" and Salmon called it a "significant demonstration of private-sector interest in passenger franchising," the deadline for pre-qualification had to be extended for another month. Salmon recalls that, in reality, "we were short of bidders. There was the terror that there were not going to be enough bidders, like with the Roscos [see Chapter 5]. It might not have mattered having the same people run it, but you wouldn't have got a decent price. You finish up giving it away." As Steve Norris put it, "there were a lot of crossed fingers. We couldn't see why there shouldn't be a market, but there was a lot of uncertainty about the colour of the next government."

Salmon had, of course, ruled out from the initial process one sure-fire bidder, BR. Salmon said he felt "there would be a very dodgy market if the dominant incumbent had been bidding and there was a lack of transparency about their costs. It would have severely turned off other bidders." In effect, BR was to be ruled out completely from the process when Salmon later repeated his move for subsequent batches of franchises and, after being rejected for the first twelve, BR then gave up even asking. A judicial review into the ban upheld his decision and, according to Salmon, justified his move: "There were affidavits from the bidders like Stagecoach and the management teams from LTS and Great Western which said they would have been severely discouraged or might not have bid at all." John Welsby admits that a BR bid would have created difficulties because a nationalised industry borrows from the National Loans Fund, which gives it access to cheaper capital and also because it cannot go bust, both factors which might have represented unfair competition.

Those private companies who did decide to bid – some had seen potential benefits in owning a TOC despite the uncertainty which surrounded rail privatisation – were immediately daunted by the data rooms to which they were given access.[3] These rooms contained information on every conceivable aspect of the business, from past performance and passenger numbers, to details of all the agreements drawn up with the other new players in the industry such as the Roscos and Railtrack. The long form reports which had to be examined were 18 inches high. The lawyers had a field day, although some companies, like Stagecoach, did not bother with detailed due diligence, trusting, rightly, that the information being provided was largely correct.

The bidders were entering new territory. As Jim Steer, who advised several of them, put it, "nobody had done it before. You didn't know how OPRAF were going to deal with it, whether they would give little signals and hints or not." He says there was a general perception that Management Buy Out teams (MBOs) would have had an advantage because of their knowledge of their business:

You couldn't possibly read all the stuff. It was a fundamentally useless thing to do. So the trick was to decide what you wanted to know in the first place. What you were really looking for was whether the management is holding something up its sleeve and is it really using its assets properly?

Chris Garnett, Chief Executive of GNER, notes that, in giving this information, some managements were co-operative, others were not. He recalls visiting South West Trains and because they were doing a management buyout, the senior managers were just plain rude. There were difficulties, too, in getting regular, up-to-date management information: management were getting monthly accounts, but the information was not passed quickly on to bidders.

In the event, despite these perceived advantages, MBO teams would win only three franchises. The reality was that, although MBOs may have had their fingers on the pulse operationally, they were having difficulties raising finance from banks and venture capitalists who were nervous about rail privatisation. The financiers' advisers, who rarely had any inside knowledge of the industry, compounded the money men's fears – the Midland Main Line management team, for example, whose losing bid with commitments to run extra services was not dissimilar to NEG's successful one (see below), was forced to scale down its bid 24 hours before the deadline. Even where MBOs could get financial backing, it was often more expensive for them than for corporate bidders who could take advantage of an established credit history, initiate a stock-market flotation or even raid their own balance sheet to raise capital.

OPRAF tried hard to maintain a level playing field between MBO teams and external bidders and quickly took to task BR managers who were not co-operating with private-sector rivals. After Garnett had been treated shabbily at South West Trains, for example, he "complained formally to OPRAF and, next time, South West Trains were a lot more polite." Indeed, one of the most striking aspects of the franchising process is the fact that bidders were generally full of praise for the way OPRAF carried out its task. Many commented that Salmon and O'Brien ran an efficient and, importantly, discreet operation and Garnett, like almost everyone involved in the process on either side, singles out Patricia Hudson (who was the lead Director of Samuel Montagu advising OPRAF) as one of the great heroes of the process "as she seemed to be able to keep the Treasury and the DoT on one side and was very clear about what was possible and what was not."

The Sale of the Franchises

The sale of the franchises was to be the ultimate test of the organisation that Salmon had created and it passed with flying colours. Despite the initial fears about lack of bidders, all the franchises were sold before the general election and many were let on very favourable terms from the government's point of view. As this chapter will show, the later stages of the process were becoming very competitive, the amount of subsidy required by franchisees was falling greatly in proportion to what was being paid out at the start and, although subsidy remained the key award criterion, bidders were also forced to offer significant improvements in bid quality – such as the acquisition of new rolling stock – in an attempt to outgun rival bidders (see Table 2.3). Table 7.1 shows which bidders were shortlisted for which franchise during the process.

When the invitations to tender for batch one – Great Western, LTS and South West Trains – went out on 17 May 1995, Mawhinney said that privatisation was "well and truly underway, [providing] an opportunity for the private sector to create first-class business on our passenger railway". Potential franchisees were required to submit indicative bids by 10 July, giving 10 weeks to put together offers for an entirely novel type of business. Bids had to be for a 7-year franchise, but alternative non-compliant offers – for example, including new trains in exchange for a longer franchise period – would be considered. Roger Salmon says that "one of the key tasks was to educate bidders as to what the franchises were all about." Although, because of the difficulties OPRAF had experienced in putting the franchising proposition together (see Chapter 6), there were some initial problems – particularly as many procedures were not yet standardised – these were quickly sorted out and Salmon regards OPRAF's detailed liaison with bidders as "one of our major successes."

On 11 November, the list of preferred bidders was leaked to *The Independent*. The management team was selected for LTS, both the MBO (together with CGEA) and Stagecoach were down for South West Trains and Resurgence Railways had been chosen for Great Western. Resurgence was one of three surprise entrants to the bidding process, start-up companies which had been specially created to bid for franchises and which delighted ministers by showing that the bidding was attracting wider interest than originally feared. Resurgence was led by Mike Jones, a Thatcherite former BR freight manager, and Richard Morris, another old BR hand and now Safety Director of Eurotunnel. GB Railways was the creation of pro-private enterprise Canadian consultant Michael Schabas and Prism Developments had been set up by a group of second-tier bus-company owners advised by right-wing transport theorist and former BR junior manager Kenneth Irvine.[4] Both Prism and GB Railways won franchises and now operate five between them, but Resurgence quickly got into trouble. Because the banks were still unconvinced about rail privatisation, they refused at the last minute to confirm its funding. The company's plight was not helped by a *Financial Times* front-page report revealing that its Finance Director had headed up a double-glazing firm that went bust (OPRAF had investigated this, but was satisfied that he had acted properly). Without the necessary financial backing, Resurgence couldn't even capitalise the business and could therefore take no further part in the Great Western bid. Meanwhile, the MBO team had obtained backing from First Bus (now First Group) and venture capitalists 3i who each took up half of a 49 per cent minority shareholding and this joint venture became the preferred bidder. At the same time Stagecoach overtook a hyper-cautious CGEA, which, as a French company, was taking a pessimistic view on gambling on the British economy, to take the lead on South West Trains.

There was one more hurdle for Salmon to overcome before he could, at last, show the fruits of 2 years' labour: a court case launched by the Save Our Railways (SOR) campaign, a union-funded lobbying group opposed to privatisation, aimed at derailing the franchising process. SOR argued on a number of fronts at a

Table 7.1 Shortlisted bidders in the franchising process (TOCs listed in order of letting). After Cormack, J. and Pigott, N. 'The great railway sale is over', in The Railway Magazine, April, 1997.

	Nat Expr	S'coach	Prism	FirstGrp	MTL	Go-Ahead	CGEA Con.	Sea Con.	Virgin	GB Rail	Govia	Halcrow Cowie	Resurgence	GW Hold	M40	M(E)BO
South West Trains		Y					(N)[1]	N								(N)[1]
First Great Western	N		(Y)[2]				N	N					N	(Y)[2]		(Y)[2]
c2c		N	Y							N						N[3]
GNER	N	N					(N)[4]	Y		N						(N)[4]
Gatwick Express	Y		N													N
Midland Mainline	Y		N		N		N									(N)[5]
Connex SouthCentral	(N)[5]	N					N								(Y)[6]	(Y)[6]
Chiltern Railways	N	N		(N)[7]			Y									(N)[7]
Connex South Eastern		N	Y							N						N
Wales & West	N	N	Y													N
Cardiff Railway Co.		N	N			(Y)[8]						N				(Y)[8]
Thames Trains	Y								N					N	N	
Island Line		Y[9]														
Virgin CrossCountry	N	N	N				(N)[10]		Y				N			(N)[10]
First Great Eastern	N	N	Y							Y						
Anglia Railways	N		N	(N)[11]					N	N						(N)[11]
West Anglia Gt Northern		N	N		Y	N										
Merseyrail Electrics	N		N	Y			N							Y		
First North Western	N		N											N		
Silverlink	Y										(N)[12]					(N)[12]
Northern Spirit		N		Y	Y						Y[13]	(N)[14]				(N)[14]
Thameslink		N					N	N								
Central Trains	Y	N		(N)[15]						N	N					(N)[15]
Virgin West Coast		N	N					Y	Y							
ScotRail	Y	N						N			N					N

Key: Y = successful bidder; N = shortlisted bidder. Ys or Ns in parentheses indicate shared – or otherwise allied – bids.

Notes
1 MBO bid was in conjunction with CGEA.
2 Great Western Holdings was an MBO bid in conjunction with First Group and 3i.
3 MBO originally successful then revoked.
4 MBO bid in conjunction with CGEA.
5 MBO bid in conjunction with Stagecoach.
6 M40 Trains was an MBO bid in conjunction with Laing plc.
7 MBO bid in conjunction with First Group.
8 MBO bid in conjunction with Go-Ahead.
9 No shortlist published.
10 MBO in conjunction with CGEA.
11 MBO in conjunction with First Group.
12 MBO bid in conjunction with GoVia (see below).
13 GoVia is a partnership between Go-Ahead (65 per cent) and VIA GTI (35 per cent).
14 The MBO bid was in conjunction with Cowie.
15 The MBO bid was in conjunction with First Group.

judicial review into the process and actually won a pyrrhic victory in the Court of Appeal. The judges ruled that the PSRs had been set too low in relation to the existing rail timetable and therefore that the Franchising Director had not followed his Objectives, Instructions and Guidance (OIG) when setting them (see Chapter 6). Although this jeopardised the sale of later franchises, the judges ruled that batch one sales could go ahead because SOR's objections had not been tabled in time to prevent them. After fraught discussions during which ministers seriously considered pulling the whole process – a significant part of the rail privatisation exercise had effectively been declared illegal – Mawhinney's replacement, Sir George Young, eventually resolved the problem by announcing on the Monday following the court case that he would reword the OIG to permit the production of more lenient PSRs. Although the Government's move was really legal legerdemain – the content of the PSRs could, after all, remain unchanged – SOR was deterred from going to the House of Lords and the following day Salmon was able to announce the letting of the first franchise, South West Trains.

Stagecoach was declared the winner of South West Trains on 19 December 1995 and was given a 7-year deal which, in retrospect, has proved highly profitable but did involve a reduction in subsidy from the £63.3 million paid to BR in 1995–96 to £46.7 million in Stagecoach's last full year of operation (see Table 2.4). There were, however, few benefits for passengers. In the press release, OPRAF could only highlight improvements to the Passenger's Charter, a few bus links, station improvements and "improved customer information on stations."[5] It was hardly exciting, but at least the process was under way. And the presence of Stagecoach, a relatively large and growing transport company, had saved the day for the Government in demonstrating that at least one stock-exchange quoted company believed in the privatisation process despite all the anomalies and hiccups. There would have been great disappointment if only MBO teams had won: not only because one of the benefits of privatisation was always claimed to be the injection of new blood into the industry, but also because external bidders might have viewed the process as a fix and been discouraged from submitting further bids. Norris commented:

Brian Souter [Stagecoach's chairman] was in there early and you should not underestimate the extent to which he took a leap in the dark. Would the process even be completed by the general election and the inevitable Tory defeat? What would happen to his balance sheet if he had to spend 5 years in court fighting the new government through the European courts for compensation? But as the process went on, more and more people saw the potential. At first, they wondered how Souter could justify the figures, but then, as the process unfolded, they saw he was right.

By September 1996, the *Investor's Chronicle* was predicting profits of £50 million per year for the South West Trains franchise on modest assumptions of growth (in fact, in the year to the end of April 1999, South West Trains made £34.4 million, up from £6.3 million 2 years previously, very much in line with the predictions).[6] Such coverage did much to stimulate greater interest in the later franchises.

The day after announcing the Stagecoach franchise, Salmon confirmed that Great Western Holdings, the new name for the MBO/First Bus/3i consortium, and Enterprise Rail, the LTS MBO, had won Great Western and LTS respectively and would, like Stagecoach, each get 7-year franchises. Unlike the South West Trains deal, however, both would have the opportunity to win extensions if they met certain conditions: Great Western Holdings could have a 10-year franchise if it modified its existing fleet and/or bought new trains to increase service frequency and Enterprise Rail would be given a 15-year contract if it made commitments to replace existing slam-door trains on the original "Misery Line".

Even as there was good news to announce, the franchising process still refused to run smoothly for OPRAF. Just as the first privatised trains were about to run, events conspired to take the gloss out of the publicity launch. On 1 February 1996, 3 days before the LTS MBO was due to take over its franchise, a routine check by auditors uncovered an anomaly. LTS had been printing season tickets on ticket machines at Fenchurch Street for sale at Upminster. The effect was to reduce the proportion of ticket sales at Upminster, a shared station, and to increase them at Fenchurch Street, where a higher proportion of the revenue went to LTS.[7] It was a silly little scam operated by lower levels of management but Salmon, under pressure from Sir George Young, had no choice other than to postpone the handover. A week later, following an investigation by BR, the management team's bid was ruled out. The managing director and financial director of LTS were moved to other duties and OPRAF asked the three unsuccessful shortlisted bidders to retender for the franchise (see below).

Matters were made worse when it was discovered that the first train to operate under the privatised regime would, in fact, be a bus. The 1.50-am Great Western service of 4 February from Fishguard to Paddington was replaced, as a result of engineering works, by road transport to Cardiff. Reporters were accordingly directed to the first Stagecoach service, which was the 5.10 am from Twickenham to Waterloo, but this carried only nine genuine passengers. Stagecoach had laid on extra coaches, expecting plenty of trainspotters, but, generally hostile to privatisation, they failed to materialise, again leading to much ribaldry in the press.

The continued hostile reception for privatisation merely increased government pressure on Salmon to speed up the franchising programme. With the general election possibly just over a year away, the aim, emphasised in private to his ministers by John Major, was to achieve "irreversibility"; that is to say, the irrevocable break-up and sale of BR before polling day. Certainly the pace was hotting up as the OPRAF machine gained experience of the franchising process. Pre-qualification documents for the second and third batches of franchises – InterCity East Coast, Midland Main Line, Gatwick Express, Network SouthCentral, Chiltern Railways and South Eastern Trains – had been released by early October 1995 and batch four – Cardiff Railways and South Wales & West – was introduced to the market on 10 February 1996. Private-sector interest was by now increasing, with batch four attracting nineteen serious replies when the list closed 3 weeks later.

On 29 March, Sea Containers was announced as the preferred bidder for InterCity East Coast. Sea Containers, the international transport company, had really wanted Great Western and had also tried half-heartedly for South West Trains, but had just demonstrated the shoot-from-the-hip attitude that was to characterise its involvement in rail privatisation. In bidding for batch one, it had initially wanted control of the track and then sought 10-year franchises to under-pin investment. When this was rejected the group said that it was no longer interested in bidding for franchises on the current terms. Now it was back and triumphed. Chris Garnett explains:

> *Jim Sherwood [the head of Sea Containers] had travelled on the East Coast route and said, "this is great, this is the one we really ought to go for because the airlines are awful and this has got enormous potential." So, despite the fact we knew we could not get control of the track which created a difficult relationship with Railtrack, we felt that East Coast was so attractive that we decided to have one more go at it.*

Garnett also gives an insight into how much wheeler-dealing was going on behind the scenes as OPRAF sought to get the best possible deals. He says that the Sea Containers bid for InterCity East Coast changed radically from first-bid stage – to get on the shortlist – and the final bid. OPRAF told his team when shortlisting that they were "well off the pace." Sea Containers reduced its demand for subsidy bid at the last moment because the information on possible disruption by the construction of the Channel Tunnel Rail Link turned out to be not as bad as expected and it won very closely over the runners-up, Stagecoach.

In April OPRAF declared NEG the preferred bidder for both Midland Main Line and Gatwick Express, the latter being the only franchise which was to start off with a premium payment. The Midland Main Line bid offered a considerable enhancement of the service, a rare feature of the early franchises, with a much increased service on the line – for example, between London and Leicester, NEG committed itself to fifty-four trains per day compared with the thirty-two run by BR. The company would also be paying a premium of £10.5 million by 2006, compared with a subsidy in its first year of £16.1 million and would lease some new rolling stock, which enabled it to negotiate a 10-year franchise. The Gatwick Express franchise was let for a 15-year term, conditional upon NEG's replace-ment of the entire train fleet by mid-1999.[8]

Competition for Network SouthCentral was intense. The MBO team, in conjunction with Stagecoach, seemed to have the edge, but it was make or break time for CGEA. The bidding team was told by its French parent to win a franchise or else and, revising its previously pessimistic view of the British economy, made higher assumptions about post-privatisation revenue growth. CGEA's final bid was better than Stagecoach's effort and is now seen as a key moment in the privatisation process as it was significantly more aggressive than many had expected. Although much press comment focused on the fact that a

French company would be taking over a large chunk of the British railway, the gauntlet had been thrown down by CGEA – future franchising rounds would now be a lot more competitive.

The retendering process for LTS allows an interesting comparison between what the MBO would have received in subsidy and what Prism, who won the franchise nearly 5 months after the MBO bid was disqualified, obtained. The results clearly demonstrate how competition among bidders was beginning to hot up. Whereas in the first year both bids required around £28 million, Prism's subsidy declined to £12 million by year 15, making an average of £18.4 million over the life of the franchise. This compared with the £23.9 million Enterprise Rail would have received in year 15, an average of £26.1 million over the life of the franchise. Prism also promised more improvements, notably a station at West Ham, and specified the new stock it would lease.

On 10 April, Roger Salmon announced his resignation, having decided at the outset that he only wanted to stay long enough to ensure that the task was in hand. He was succeeded in November 1996 by his chief operating officer, John O'Brien, who, helped by his commercial background, saw through the sale of the final batches of franchises. Salmon had offered his resignation in December 1995, immediately after the sale of the first three franchises, suggesting he would go in October 1996, but was asked not to go public with his decision straightaway as, so soon into the process, this would have sent a negative message to bidders. He was subsequently forced to make an announcement in April by a legal obligation to disclose his position in the Railtrack prospectus. But Salmon could point to a successful start. While the target to franchise 51 per cent of the passenger railway by December 1995 had been missed, ministers had been forced to accept that this was inevitable and the franchising machine Salmon had created was really starting to deliver. A fortnight after the resignation announcement, pre-qualification documents for the next seven franchises were issued which meant that the sales process had now started for twenty out of the twenty-five franchises. By the time Salmon left in October, over half the TOCs had been let.

Pre-qualification documents for the final five franchises were issued on 11 June 1996. This last batch had been held back because it contained the most problems. InterCity West Coast was tied up with the long-deferred modernisation of the Anglo-Scottish route (see Chapter 4). Three of the other four operated trains in PTE areas and involved the largest subsidies (North London Railways was simply at the end of the queue for the southern franchises which BR could not process all together). InterCity West Coast was to be the most complex and difficult franchise to let. Potential franchisees were asked to bid for two options, both for 15-year terms. Option one assumed Railtrack's Core Investment Programme which would see £1.35 billion spent on the core investment programme to make good the backlog. Option two was based on an additional Passenger Upgrade ("PUG 1"), brokered with Railtrack by OPRAF, which would allow tilting trains to run at 125 mph.

In the event, Virgin was confirmed as preferred bidder for InterCity West Coast in February 1997, undercutting Sea Containers' subsidy profile by £1 billion over 15 years but Stagecoach's by barely £150 million. The franchise

Figure 7.1   ScotRail Class 158 at Wick Station, July 1999.
Source: National Railway Museum.

had seen a late entrant to franchise bidding in the form of the then Channel Tunnel Rail Link concessionaire London & Continental Railways (see Chapter 2). However, with so much riding on this franchise, where the privatised railway faced its biggest commercial, financial and technical challenge, the shortlist had concentrated on three big hitters with financial resources. Ministers had been keen to ensure that the highest investment choice for West Coast was made in order to show benefits of privatisation and Virgin's bid certainly delivered. It promised to replace virtually the entire rolling stock with a fleet of new tilting trains with services operated at 140 – rather than the envisaged 125 – mph on some of the route (the so-called "PUG 2"). Journey times between London and Birmingham would be reduced from 100 minutes to around 70, while London – Manchester would be under 2 hours (see Table 4.1). Moreover, a subsidy of £76.8 million in the first financial year would be transformed by 2011–12 to a remarkable premium payment of £220.3 million. Whilst clearly of benefit to the passenger railway, the PUG 1 and 2 deals are of concern to freight operators (see Chapter 8).

ScotRail had attracted five indicative bids, more than had been expected given the high political risk because of the PTE involvement (Figure 7.1). OPRAF had engaged in some arm twisting to get the numbers up and all five made the shortlist. The negotiations with the PTEs were carried out by John O'Brien and at various times looked like breaking down but his political masters wanted to make sure the railway-franchising process was completed by the election. O'Brien was more willing to make concessions to the PTEs in order to ensure the work was completed than Salmon who might have proved more obdurate. Several people involved in the privatisation process mentioned that without O'Brien, the target would never have been reached. He was helped by a change of heart within the Labour party. Andrew Smith had replaced Clare Short as shadow transport spokesman and he told the PTEs to stop trying to prevent the process being completed by the election and, instead, to ensure that all the franchises were let so that Labour did not inherit a messy half-privatised rail service. OPRAF was unaware of this and the Labour politicians who controlled the PTEs were canny enough to realise that they could obtain concessions in terms of increased and improved services in return for their co-operation and in the end they were bought off with generous deals.

The shortlists for the Regional Railways franchises in the final batch had shown there were no new bidders making a late entry into the market (see Table 7.1). Interestingly, despite a lack of new blood, there was keen interest in these last franchises as demonstrated by the sharp reductions in subsidy obtained by OPRAF. All three Regional Railways bids in the last batch also included commitments to acquire new rolling stock in a 7-year franchise period. The bids reflected in part the fact that bidders were now making highly optimistic assumptions about cost reductions, for on highly subsidised routes revenue is a less important factor in profitability. Indeed, in some areas, the local PTE took the revenue risk, leaving the operator simply to collect the fares on its behalf. On the North West franchise, subsidy was reduced from £100.3 million in the first year, to £69 million over 7 years, and on North East, the reduction was from £224.5 million to £145.6 million. The sharp subsidy reductions have, subsequently, made several of these late franchises loss-making because operators have found it difficult to reduce costs.

By April 1997, despite all the uncertainty which had surrounded rail privatisation, franchising was over. The last BR trains, the overnight sleepers between London and Scotland, ran on the night of 31 March signalling the end of just under half a century of nationalisation. The franchises had, by and large, passed effortlessly into the private sector. As Michael Schabas, whose GB Railways company won Anglia, put it, "we didn't have to do anything on the day we took over. The system just kept on running." However, Schabas was aware that the declining subsidy profile he had signed up to would keep him busy in the coming years: "If we hadn't done anything in the long run, of course, we would have started losing money."

Franchising the passenger railway was a remarkable achievement by OPRAF. By allowing its young and enthusiastic staff a relatively free hand in letting the franchises and making key decisions, OPRAF delivered on time. The machine created by Roger Salmon and then taken forward by John O'Brien had sold off the passenger railway in just 551 days, achieving "irreversibility" with weeks to spare before the general election. In addition to the compliments it has received from bidders (see above), OPRAF was formally praised by the National Audit Office (NAO) in a report into the letting of the first three franchises.[9] The NAO said that OPRAF had been "able to generate a good level of competition" in the letting of the first three franchises and had largely met its set objectives by securing value for money for the taxpayer despite the paucity of bidders. The significant decreases in subsidy paid to later franchisees would presumably have also met with NAO approval. The report did criticise OPRAF for having failed to set a budget for the costs of external advisers – which amounted to nearly £40 million in the period 1993–96 – and for not having put all this work out to tender. But these were small considerations for ministers. Had the Tories retained power, there would no doubt have been honours for these Stakhanovite heroes of Thatcher's privatisation revolution. But as railway privatisation failed to be the vote winner the Tories had originally expected, OPRAF's achievements were to be reviled rather than celebrated in the new Labour administration.

The Winners and Losers

In a sense, both the optimists and pessimists had been proved wrong. The pessimists' predictions that the railway franchises were unlettable were completely mistaken. There was genuine competition for all franchises – typically four serious bids if MBOs are included – and in the later stages subsidy levels were driven down quite hard thanks to the readiness of successful bidders to look at further franchises. However, the optimists' notion that there would be a wide spread of companies eager to run the railways was also wrong. Apart from bus companies and a few start-up outfits, there was very little interest from outside the industry and virtually none from big listed companies (see Table 7.2).

The most active bidder was Stagecoach, which bid for every franchise, taking the view that it would not spend an enormous amount of money on due diligence or detailed bids, but it nevertheless obtained fourteen shortlistings. However, this only translated into two franchises, South West Trains, the first, and the tiny Island Line, because of its conservative approach on assessment of future revenues. Despite this, it had still acquired franchise revenues (which includes subsidy) of £337 million, or 7.9 per cent of the national total. In contrast, National Express, which translated ten shortlistings into five franchises had revenues of £837.8 million, 19.5 per cent of the total, thanks to the heavily subsidised former Regional Railways businesses in its portfolio. Connex was second in terms of revenue, with its two big London franchises (from nine shortlistings) providing a total of £601 million franchise revenue (14 per cent) while Prism, with its twelve shortlistings yielding four franchises, had gained £397.7 million (9.3 per cent). All these were from the bus industry (CGEA has considerable bus interests in France), and it was the bus operators which dominated the process throughout, obtaining nearly three-quarters of the franchise revenue and eighteen of the twenty-five franchises. The biggest outsider was Virgin which, with its two franchises, obtained franchise revenues of £517 millon. Ultimately, at franchising, four big groups – National Express, Stagecoach, Connex and Virgin – controlled 54 per cent of the passenger franchise business by revenue. Stagecoach and Virgin have subsequently become partners on West Coast and CrossCountry, and First Group has taken over Great Western Holdings, which means that these five groups now control 70 per cent of franchise revenue.

Table 7.2 Profiles of winning bidders.

Connex Rail	Connex South Eastern Connex South Central	Connex Rail is a subsidiary of Compagnie Générale des Eaux (CGEA), itself part of the fast-expanding French Vivendi group, which has substantial media interests as well as a range of other transport operations, including freight and passenger rail and road services in France.
First Group	First Great Eastern First Great Western First North Western	Formed as First Bus – major bus operator with many British and international bus operations. Initially participated with the MBO team that won Great Western Trains and North West Trains (along with several other investors).
GB Railways Go Ahead	Anglia Railways Thames Trains Thameslink	Set up specifically to pursue rail franchises. Bus group with roots in North East, and also bus companies in London, Oxford and Brighton. Took over Victory Railway MBO that won Thames Trains. Shares the Thameslink franchise with the French Via GTI company.
Laing	Chiltern Railways	Major construction and engineering group. Bought control from the M40 Trains MBO team in 1999 – the last to retain its independence.
MTL Rail	Merseyrail Electrics Northern Spirit	Bus group based on Merseyside.
National Express Group	Central Trains Gatwick Express Midland Main Line ScotRail Silverlink	Major bus and coach operator with many British and foreign companies – also controls airports. In terms of number of franchises awarded, the most successful passenger rail operator.
Prism Rail	Cardiff Railway Co. c2c Wales & West West Anglia Great Northern	Formed by a team of bus-industry executive/managers specifically to bid for rail franchises.
Sea Containers	Great North Eastern Railway	Transport conglomerate with interests in sea transport, containers, ports and the leisure industry.
Stagecoach	South West Trains Island Line	Fast-expanding Scottish-based owner of numerous bus operations in Britain and overseas.
Virgin Rail	Virgin West Coast Virgin CrossCountry	Part of the diverse, high-profile Virgin Group. Both franchises were awarded for a 15-year period.

The dominance of these big groups resulted in the failure of the MBO teams to make much headway in the franchising process. Although they were shortlisted on eighteen occasions, they won only three TOCs. The MBO teams had suffered from a terrible workload during the franchising process. As John Welsby put it,

these guys were doing two jobs at the same time by ensuring that the trains were running, and producing all this information about the business for the bidders. And if they were trying to win it, they were doing three jobs. So they were working 18 hours a day, 7 days a week for 18 months or so.

That workload may finally have told on them in terms of the lack of success but, as we have already seen, the key factor was that the managers had difficulty getting finance and this had an impact on their bids, making them overly conservative in comparison with those of their rivals. Unfortunately for the MBO teams, OPRAF was not allowed to discriminate in their favour in financial terms as the government had done in earlier privatisations. When the bus companies were sold, for example, management teams were given some leeway whereby if their bid came within five percentage points of the "winning" submission, the deal would be theirs. Although this system had been designed to take account of the fact that the cost of capital was higher to MBOs than established corporate bidders, it was deeply unpopular with the latter and, presumably because it would act as yet another deterrent to potential franchisees, was left out of rail privatisation.

Interestingly, though, 3 years after franchising, most members of MBO teams – both winners and losers – were still running train-operating companies. The only difference was that the winners – Great Western in partnership with First Group, Chiltern in partnership with John Laing and Thames in partnership with Go-Ahead – had sold out to their partners and become "fat cats" in the process, providing yet more opportunity for the press to knock rail privatisation.

While the track-authority model of privatisation meant that the level of subsidy was significantly increased when the TOCs were franchised, OPRAF at least managed to ensure that the reduction of government support was sharp enough to bring it below old BR levels by 2001–02. While all the new franchisees signed up to a regime of declining subsidy, this varied both absolutely and in terms of the rate of decline. To put forward the most contrasting franchises, the subsidy for South West Trains drops from £63 million per year in 1997–98 to £37 million (at February 1998 prices) in 2003–04 with little investment commitment, while on InterCity West Coast, the change in the same period is from £76 million to the *payment* of a premium of £54 million along with the leasing of new rolling stock. Welsby estimates that the reduction in subsidy as a proportion of passenger revenue combined with the TOCs' own expenses varies by a factor of 25 between different companies. In other words, some operators have a gold mine, while others look as if they will struggle.

City analysts are unanimous in their view that the early franchises, in particular the first two, South West Trains and Great Western, were let on the most favourable terms to the operators, while the latter ones may pose problems for their owners. The annual financial improvements needed by TOCs to compensate

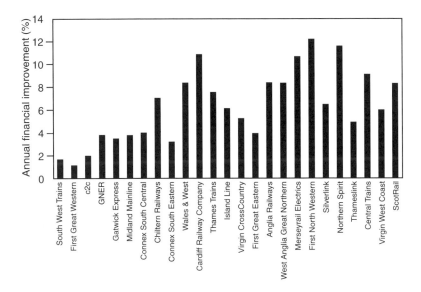

Figure 7.2   Annual financial improvements needed by TOCs in order of letting.
Source: Glover, J. 'The franchised railway', in *Modern Railways*, **54**, 1997.

for declining subsidies or increasing premium payments are shown in Figure 7.2. Although there is by no means a neat time/subsidy correlation, there is a significant increase in the financial improvements required after the first three TOCs were let. The impact of the Network SouthCentral deal can also be seen. The ambitious targets which many private-sector operators have set themselves mean that they will not only have to cut costs, but also increase revenues substantially if they are to remain financially viable – indeed, for some TOCs, the financial improvement required exceeds their ticket revenue at the beginning of the franchise.[10] Welsby argues that this variability "highlights the short-sightedness of refusing to allow BR to bid, if only as the benchmark against which to determine the desirability of allowing a particular franchise to proceed at that point in time." However, as the Government was in such a rush to complete the franchising process, even the knowledge that a bid was financially overambitious may have been unlikely to have stopped a sale.

Opinion is divided over the "costs" of rail privatisation. Transport experts Nigel Harris and Ernest Godward, in their book *The Privatisation of British Rail*, have argued that, even when sales revenues (from Railtrack, the Roscos and other rail businesses) and subsidy reductions are accounted for, the net cost of rail privatisation to the government could be as high as £5 billion after 15 years.[11] Clearly, such an outcome would be deeply disappointing to the Treasury given that a key expectation of the track-authority model of rail privatisation was that it would benefit the government financially (see Chapter 1). In contrast, however, the Railway Forum points out that the headline figures on the level of rail subsidy, in particular the oft-repeated statistic that it doubled after privatisation, are

misleading because, among other reasons, commentators fail to take proper
account of the money raised from asset sales.[12] Transport academic Peter
White lends some credibility to this view, suggesting that, if all TOCs meet
their subsidy-reduction targets, the state will see a net benefit of £240 million
by 2003–04.[13] White does make clear, however, that these calculations do not
include any efficiency savings that BR – or a successor privatised in a less complex
manner – may have made over the same period and that these could have
amounted to as much as £1.6 billion. Although including this figure in the
calculations is problematic because it deals with the counterfactual, it does suggest
that any savings the government makes out of the track-authority model of rail
privatisation may not start appearing for a very long time. The jury is still out.

After the Dust Settled

Any analysis of what has happened on the railway in the 3 years since rail
privatisation started is coloured – dominated even – by one remarkable fact:
the phenomenal and possibly unprecedented growth in the use of the railways.
This averaged around 7 per cent per annum, a staggering figure which is normally
associated with an immature industry rather than one that is over 150 years old
(see Figure 7.3). Perhaps inevitably, the level of growth witnessed by TOCs has
varied around the network (see Table 7.3). Some operators, especially InterCity
TOCs and those in the South East, have fared remarkably well. Those which serve
the London airports have also benefited from the recent growth in air travel.
OPRAF's figures for the year ended 31 March 1999 show that sharp rates of
growth were recorded by Gatwick Express (which grew by 21.5 per cent in that
period), West Anglia Great Northern (which covers Stansted), Thameslink (which

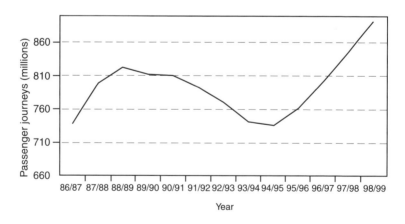

Figure 7.3   Aggregate patronage on the passenger network, 1986/87–1998/99.
Source: Department of the Environment, Transport and the Regions.
Transport Statistics Bulletin, Government Statistical Service.
Information provided by Transport Statistics.

Table 7.3 Growth in patronage, by TOC, around the network. Source: *Rail Magazine*, no. 368, July–August 1999. With permission.

Train operator	*1996–97* (millions)	*1997–98* (millions)	*Variance %* 96/97–97/98	*1998–99* (millions)	*Variance %* 97/98–98/99
Anglia Railways	5.40	5.99	10.93	6.80	13.52
c2c	21.30	23.70	11.27	24.70	4.22
Cardiff Railway Company	5.90	6.10	3.39	6.10	No change
Central Trains	30.50	32.40	6.63	34.50	6.48
Chiltern Railways	8.10	8.80	8.64	9.60	9.90
Connex South Central	86.00	93.00	8.14	98.30	5.70
Connex South Eastern	113.40	117.20	3.35	122.20	4.27
First Great Eastern	48.00	51.60	7.50	54.40	5.43
First Great Western	15.00	16.40	9.33	16.90	3.05
First North Western	25.10	27.00	7.57	27.60	2.22
Gatwick Express	3.70	3.70	No change	4.50	21.62
Great North Eastern Railway	11.90	13.70	15.13	13.90	1.46
Island Line	0.69	0.70	1.45	0.70	No change
Merseyrail Electrics	22.00	23.00	4.55	23.00	No change
Midland Mainline	5.80	6.30	8.62	6.80	7.94
Northern Spirit	39.00	42.00	7.69	43.70	4.05
ScotRail	53.40	56.70	6.18	59.00	4.06
Silverlink	28.00	30.70	9.60	34.30	11.73
South West Trains	110.65	118.20	6.82	122.90	3.98
Thames Trains	26.80	28.50	6.34	31.00	8.77
Thameslink	27.00	30.20	11.85	34.40	13.91
Wales & West	12.90	13.60	5.43	13.70	0.74
West Anglia Great Northern	50.50	52.80	4.55	55.70	5.49
Virgin CrossCountry	12.00	12.50	4.17	13.80	10.4
Virgin West Coast	13.20	14.99	13.56	15.90	6.07
Total	**776.24**	**829.76**	**6.90**	**874.40**	**5.38**

runs to Gatwick and Luton) and CrossCountry (whose growth rate had been relatively poor in 1997–98). Connex South Central claimed a 20-per-cent increase in passenger numbers using Gatwick. In contrast, regional operators running trains on less busy parts of the network – such as Wales & West and the Cardiff Railway Company – have performed less well and, given that some of these TOCs have rapidly declining subsidy profiles as they were among the last to be let by OPRAF, they might face financial difficulties before their franchises expire (indeed, both of the above have already started to lose money). Nevertheless, the high level of growth across much of the network is significant and any examination of the outcomes of franchising must start with an examination of why this growth has happened and the extent to which it is a result of privatisation.

Euan Cameron, who was managing director at Thameslink, the fastest growing operator, before moving to Prism in 1999, reckons there are three key elements which have contributed to the growth on the railways:

> *There is the natural buoyancy of the London economy which is helping the South East TOCs, and which also means people are feeling that they can spend some of their disposable income off-peak; there's government policy which is leading to a structural change in transport; and there's the marketing and flair of the private sector and those three make up the growth that has occurred.*

An economic boom is good news for many industries and rail is no exception. The industry experiences a double bonus, whereby more jobs in the major conurbations lead to an increasing number of rail commuters while the demand for leisure travel also rises.[14] But whereas BR's fortunes had always improved as the economy expanded, the rail-industry's performance has been better this time than in previous economic upturns, especially in the South East and on InterCity routes.

Some of the new government's rail policies, such as the creation of a Strategic Rail Authority (SRA) to replace OPRAF (see Chapter 10), have not yet become law and have therefore had little effect on the industry, but the state is making itself felt in other ways.[15] The cutback in the roads programme (now partially reversed) and the impact of the fuel-tax escalator (now abandoned) both helped to boost the fortunes of rail. With only a few new roads coming on stream and traffic continuing to grow at around 1–2 per cent per year, the bottlenecks are getting worse and motorists see little hope of improvement. Congestion on the roads has reached the point where many people will choose an alternative if there is one.

The effect of the fuel-tax escalator is being compounded by the regulation of many rail fares (see Chapter 6). This changed the longstanding policy of BR being forced to choke off extra demand for rail travel by raising ticket prices, and Chris Garnett, the chief executive of GNER, has no doubt that fare capping has stimulated growth:

> *It was a hell of an achievement by Brian Mawhinney to persuade the Treasury to accept fares capping and it is the real tiger by the tail in this whole system. Our analysis is that fares went up by 45 per cent ahead of inflation between 1980 and 1999, about 3 per cent per annum. Now we've got the vast majority of commuter fares capped, so the cost of coming into London or Leeds or any major conurbation by train is actually coming down in real terms and that's going to put enormous pressures on. It will push demand for commuter travel and, generally, demand for all rail travel.*

Garnett estimates that within 10 years, the real cost of rail travel will have gone down by 10 per cent.

It is difficult to assess the impact of Cameron's third reason, the flexibility and flair of the private sector. For a start, the current growth in passenger numbers began before privatisation (see Figure 7.3). Moreover, in some respects the private sector has been disappointing in failing to address customer issues such as cleanliness of trains and customer service. Such measures were left out of the original Passenger's Charters because there was the feeling that, in order to attract more passengers onto their trains, private operators would make sure that their trains were clean and their staff were plentiful, courteous and helpful as a matter of course. Some commentators now argue that TOCs will in future need to be more tightly regulated to address these issues (see Chapter 10).

On a more positive note, however, there is no doubt that some TOCs have been instrumental in enticing more passengers on to their services. The refurbishment of existing rolling stock and the purchase of brand-new trains has helped make train travel more attractive. Better marketing, particularly for off-peak deals, has also been a significant component of growth. Cameron stresses that much of this would not have happened under BR:

> BR was not a risk taker. It always had one eye on the PSBR, so it always had the eye to that because [any changes] had to have a neutral effect and, of course, neutrality takes a number of years to come to pass. If it meant a greater subsidy one year, it didn't happen. Now we can afford to take risks and if it takes 2 to 3 years to come to pass, it's worthwhile doing in the life cycle of the franchise.

Passenger numbers on some flows, especially busy ones targeted for special fares and improved services, have increased dramatically. Since privatisation, there has been a much greater emphasis by ex-InterCity companies like Virgin and GNER on selling advance pre-booked tickets. This has two advantages for operators – they can keep all the revenue since the ticket is only available for use on the company's own trains, allowing the ORCATS scheme to be bypassed (see Chapter 6), and they can predict demand, selling tickets at different prices. Virgin, for example, created some very good deals, such as £15 return from London to Birmingham and £20 to Liverpool and these have contributed to its 13.5-per-cent growth rate in its first full year of franchising. However, only limited numbers of these fares are available on any train, they are not sold for peak times and they have significantly increased the range of ticketing options available which can cause confusion among passengers. In addition, the company has increased its walk-on fares dramatically. A standard return to Manchester rose to £141 in September 1999, compared with £96 at privatisation 3 years previously. This prompted criticism that the company was moving away from rail's traditional role as a walk-on service – a key argument underpinning the maintenance of interavailable tickets – but Virgin has, rather predictably, denied this.

Other operators have introduced dedicated walk-on fares where the Compulsory Interavailability requirements allow (see Chapter 6). West Anglia Great Northern launched cheap tickets in March 1998 on the Peterborough–London route which resulted in a 17 per-cent increase within 3 months, and a 49 per-cent increase in its Peterborough fares revenue. Anglia, too, promoted a range of off-peak fares for its Norwich–London route and boosted the frequency of its between London and Ipswich services, where it operates in competition (but with a co-ordinated timetable) with Great Eastern. There are now four off-peak trains per hour as opposed to one previously.

New services are springing up all over the network – there has been an 8-per-cent rise in daily trains in the first 3 years of franchising. The economics of the new railway, with most costs fixed and Railtrack's access charges being low or nil at the margin (see Chapters 3 and 4), means that operating more trains is likely to be profitable once the existence of the services becomes known to the potential market. TOCs have been "sweating" their existing assets more than BR used to but, as Chapter 5 makes clear, many have also ordered new rolling stock either to replace life-expired trains (thus further increasing the availability and efficiency of their fleet) or to expand their asset base. As a result, TOCs are creating new services, such as Connex's Gatwick–Rugby trains introduced in 1997 which, within a year, were carrying over 100,000 people per month, and bolstering existing ones. Connex is also running 200 more trains per day on its south London "metro" routes than BR did, an increase of 14 per cent. While at first these were loss-making, by early 1999 the company reported that the revenue growth from them exceeded the cost growth and they had become profitable.

It is now easier for the TOCs to supply passengers with information about their new services and fares because of the creation of the National Rail Enquiry Service (NRES). Although this attracted criticism in the media when the Association of Train Operating Companies (ATOC), which is responsible for running the service on behalf of train operators, was fined in 1998 because the target of 90 per cent of calls being answered was not being met, there is no doubt that the use of a national number is a vast improvement on the haphazard service provided by BR.[16] While there are legitimate complaints that the operators, who are centrally based in a handful of call centres, do not have local knowledge, many more calls – now over 1 million per week – and a much higher proportion are being answered. As one operator, a former BR man, put it, "traditionally you did well if you answered 50 or 60 per cent. In fact, if there was any budgetary trouble, the first thing you did was to reduce the number of staff in your telephone-answering bureaux." Indeed, the huge number of calls to NRES and hits on the Railtrack website which gives timetable information (it is reckoned to be Britain's most used site) may be one hidden explanation for the growth on the network. Some TOCs have even begun to offer real-time information on their websites which provide up-to-date information on services and such innovations will undoubtedly attract more passengers.

Finally, there are some other more off-beat explanations for the growth which has undoubtedly taken some of the industry by surprise. George Muir, the director of ATOC, suggested that some of the growth may be a result of the vast amount of publicity given to the railways during the privatisation process. While he was not being entirely serious, the old adage that all publicity is good publicity may well have some truth in it. Another factor has been better revenue collection. Several companies in the London area have installed gates and in-creased the number of "revenue protection officers" on their trains. South

West Trains, for example, estimates that over one-third of its extra income in the first 3 years of privatisation came from better revenue protection. Since taking over the franchise, the company has quadrupled the number of revenue-protection officers to over 400. This has benefits for increased security on trains as well as bringing in extra income. A South West Trains executive, who formerly worked for BR, said "BR was just not interested in revenue. Every year we were asked to cut costs, and that was it. The BR Board was not interested in the fact that these cuts resulted in more people not paying their fares." It is certainly the case that some of the growth witnessed by TOCs is attributable merely to existing passengers being made to pay their fares.

Market Growth and Train Performance

Growth has been so rapid on certain parts of the network that it has exceeded that which even the most optimistic bidders had predicted. Chris Garnett, for example, said: "We went for 18 per cent in 7 years and people at the time said it was a brave bid, in the Civil Service definition of brave – bloody stupid. Now we are at 21-per-cent growth in 3 years." Euan Cameron makes the same point: "I don't think we went through all the implications. I don't think we understood the growth we were going to get. I've worked in this industry all my life and I didn't expect this to happen." It is perhaps no surprise, therefore, that there has been a downside and this has been most notable in terms of punctuality and reliability and a corresponding rise in passenger complaints.

After a very good first year of private-sector operation in which performance improved well above historic BR levels, the second and third years showed declines on a majority of routes. OPRAF's beaming smile positively shone through the press release announcing that, in the year to March 1997 (ignoring those which stayed the same), forty-six route groups showed improved reliability and fifty-four punctuality, while in only seven and two respectively did these measures worsen. Actually, for most TOCs this was the transfer period between public and private ownership but in any case the figures showed that privatisation had not caused the expected upheaval. Gatwick Express, crowed OPRAF, even had a 100-per-cent reliability figure during the latest 4-week period. However, the position soon deteriorated. The following year, the broken-down figures were 23–22 on reliability and 17–35 on punctuality, although figures on most route groups were still above those under BR. In the following year, the figures continued to deteriorate. On punctuality, 21 improved against 45 deteriorating, while on punctuality, the score was 27–48. The latest aggregate figures show that punctuality is still better than it was under BR whereas reliability is about the same (see Table 7.4).

There was also controversy over the increased use of 'void days", a regulatory loophole which allows operators to take a bad day's statistics out of the passenger's charter figures when some unforeseen event caused widespread disruption. Virgin, in particular, made heavy use of this declaring 137 void days on its three route groups in the year to the end of March 1999. Although void days were only supposed to be taken when the delay was caused by an event outside the

Table 7.4 Aggregate punctuality and reliability figures, 1992/93–1998/99. Source: Department of the Environment, Transport and the Regions. *Transport Statistics Bulletin*, Government Statistical Service. Information provided by Transport Statistics.

Date	Punctuality (all companies)	Reliability (all companies)
1992–93	89.7	98.7
1993–94	90.3	98.8
1994–95	89.6	98.7
1995–96	89.5	98.8
1996–97	92.5	99.1
1997–98	92.5	98.9
1998–99	91.5	98.8

operator's control, some companies took a very liberal interpretation, using events such as passengers interfering with doors or minor acts of vandalism to rule out particular days from their figures. OPRAF began to collate the number of void days in 1998 and, with the media also taking an interest, the numbers began to tail off.

The declining performance inevitably led to an increase in the number of complaints by passengers which topped a million in 1998–99, 700,000 of which were written. Just over half were concerned with train performance. Overall, this represented 122 complaints per million miles of travel, an increase on previous years. It was difficult to measure how much this reflected an actual deterioration in performance or other factors. Indeed, disappointment over the failure of the privatised railway to deliver the type of customer care which had been promised (or which passengers had believed they would get – potentially two different things) from privatisation was certainly a contributory factor. Moreover, just over half the complaints were on pre-printed forms and the TOCs certainly made it easier to complain than BR did.

In one sense, it is reasonable to say that the success of the railway has muddied the picture in terms of its performance and made it difficult to compare the results of the private sector's efforts with those of BR. As we saw in Chapter 4, Railtrack research suggests that, with the network in its current state, a 1 per-cent increase in the number of trains leads to a 2.5 per-cent rise in congestion-related delays and any assessment of the performance of the railway has to take the 8 per-cent increase in services into account. Railtrack was sold with the expectation that rail traffic would at best remain constant and the company argues that it was not prepared for such a large aggregate increase in demand.[17] On the other hand, however, Railtrack's position is rather undermined by the fact that others clearly saw the railway as a growth industry, particularly the train operators – as witnessed by the revenue assumptions which underpin their franchise bids. As John Welsby points out, someone should have kept a closer eye on the bidding process to ensure that the infrastructure would be able to accommodate the demands of the new franchisees and informed OPRAF accordingly:

You have a situation where all 25 franchisees are telling you that their financial performances are going to improve. [But] fares are controlled, so it can only be through an increase in traffic. Nobody did any work at all to see whether the aggregate of that growth of traffic could be fitted onto the network. The operators bid for that growth and now they are saying, "can we handle all this growth within the confines of the network?"

In fairness, Railtrack's performance has improved and the company has recently upped its growth forecasts. The problem is that it has not been fast enough to satisfy the TOCs or the Regulator, who in the summer of 1999 issued a formal warning to Railtrack that unless it rectified matters quickly it would receive a heavy fine (see Chapter 4).

The sheer weight of numbers of people now using the railway also puts a strain on the system. Euan Cameron says his experience at Thameslink demonstrated precisely how this affected performance:

Growth means more people travelling, more people travelling means greater overcrowding, greater overcrowding means your trains don't run to the same time because you've got greater station dwell time. It means poorer performance and the Government doesn't like poor performance.

While passengers travelling with some companies will see a reduction in over-crowding following the introduction of new rolling stock, others will be less fortunate and critics are blaming the structure of rail privatisation for this. As we saw in Chapter 6, companies are supposed not to breach overcrowding limits. TOCs breaking these limits are, in theory, in breach of their franchise agreements, but OPRAF, knowing that there was not much that could be done about it because of the shortage of platform capacity and rolling stock on the Thameslink route, did not take any enforcement action to begin with. Now this is no longer possible: all but two of the ten South East commuter TOCs were in breach of the limits in March 1999 as a result of the employment boom in London.

Under BR, of course, excess capacity was choked off by pushing up the price of tickets and waiting for an economic downturn. The case of Thameslink is interesting because it illustrates the difficulty the privatised industry, with its lack of strategic guidance (see Chapter 2), is having getting to grips with this problem. Thameslink experienced near or above double-figure growth for several years. As well as the economic boom, this growth was heightened because it was a newly developed service which was still gaining first-time customers and also because of a large number of housing developments near its stations. The company wanted to order extra trains when its existing ones became crowded but says it cannot do so without a franchise extension. Of course, establishing the Roscos was sup-posed to overcome such problems as they are supposed to take residual-value risk, but the issue is still unresolved and only a short-term solution – Thameslink is sub-leasing a limited number of units from other TOCs – has been found.

It is apparent from this and the Railtrack example cited above that the virtuous circle is not entirely virtuous. More passengers – which the Government wants and has set targets for – means more trains and still more passengers but, under present conditions, a deterioration in performance standards. John Prescott, the Deputy Prime Minister, criticised this strongly at the October 1998 Labour Party conference when he called the rail companies "a national disgrace." Railtrack and the Roscos' ability to meet the growing demands of the TOCs is, of course, fundamental to the long-term success of the industry and will be of key interest to the SRA when it comes formally into being. It is hoped that the Authority will be in a position to provide the strategic vision and guidance needed to help resolve such matters.

So unexpected growth has affected performance. But TOCs themselves must also take some of the blame for deteriorating levels of service. Some, for example, seem to have embarked upon over-ambitious cost-cutting exercises, shedding too many managers and staff too quickly. According to Chris Stokes: "They lost people who were good at running the trains and some of them did make cock-ups in terms of restructuring." The most famous was Stagecoach's blunder on South West Trains. In its efforts to reduce costs as it had in the bus industry, Stagecoach allowed too many drivers to claim redundancy leaving them short of experienced route-trained staff and thousands of trains had to be cancelled. This was in the spring of 1997 and the consequent media coverage helped ensure that the Tories would gain no political advantage from the privatisation of the railways, especially as Stagecoach escaped being fined by OPRAF – giving the impression of toothless regulation – because it managed to remedy the situation by a deadline set under the rules (which, as a result, were changed in 1999). In the second and third years of its franchise, South West Trains actually increased the number of staff and still managed to be highly profitable. Its costs went up by 11 per cent in the 2 years to 30 April 1999 but, as we have seen, it is making very comfortable profits. Whereas overall the twenty-five operators reduced the numbers they employed from 42,986 in March 1996 to 38,129 2 years later, several TOCs are now increasing them after realising, like Stagecoach, that performance was being affected by shortages.[18]

There were 11 breaches by TOCs of franchise agreements in the year to March 1998, but most of these were minor and resulted in little enforcement action. For example, Northern Spirit raised fares beyond what it was allowed to do, Connex South Eastern had wrongly discontinued discounted off-peak fares and several companies had failed to consult with OPRAF over proposed changes. The most serious punishment resulted from Great Western's three "call-ins" which followed a rise in cancellations. As a result, the company committed itself to spending £500,000 on new rolling-stock items and £500,000 on additional customer-information systems, which seemed pretty small beer in the light of the size of the company's overall revenues and subsidy.

OPRAF has used the change of ownership of franchises (which, so far, has been the sale of the management's share in management-won contracts) to get enhancements and promises of better performance. In 1998, John O'Brien claimed that £75 million of passenger benefits were obtained in this way when First Group bought out the remaining shares in Great Western Holdings which has three franchises. The most significant gains were a more specific performance regime and thirty-two new vehicles by 2001–12 for First Great Western, and replacement of all First Great Eastern's slam-door stock by the end of 2002. However, as some of these improvements may well have been introduced anyway given Great Western's need to expand in the face of growing demand (with a 10-year franchise, it would have seen itself as being in a position to invest in new stock), O'Brien's claim was rather optimistic.

There are also problems with the regulatory regimes designed to enhance performance which were established by OPRAF as the franchising process was being designed (although in a sense this is hardly surprising given the speed at which Salmon was forced to operate). There is a widespread view that the incentive schemes designed to discourage poor performance – both those be-tween the TOCs and Railtrack and those between the TOCs and OPRAF – have not been strong enough to make it worthwhile for Railtrack or the TOCs to concentrate as hard as they might on improving punctuality and reliability. Chris Stokes defends OPRAF's position and argues that, contrary to popular opinion, the schemes do work. He points out that, in his opinion, the incentives are already in the system:

> *Prism, for example, made a profit of half-a-million pounds in its latest half-yearly figures (1998–99) and they paid us, for all five franchises, £2 million for underperformance. That's not marginal. It's not the comparison with revenue you have to make, but the comparison with the profit line.*

Nevertheless, the absolute numbers are small in relation to overall income and for most franchises the figure was well under £1 million. In the year to July 1999, only four TOCs made payments – or received bonuses – of over £2 million (see Table 7.5). Stokes seems to argue that the devil is in the concept rather than the detail and that the industry is still learning how to cope with the track-authority structure: "I don't think there is anything intrinsically impossible about delivering good performance with a vertically separate structure but it's something the industry had to learn." Cameron admits that, "in the rail industry, you have to learn to do the same things, day after day, week after week. You have to get it right every day." So far, however, the industry does not seem to have managed to learn that lesson.

The increase in passengers has meant that the safeguards built into the system to protect the numbers and frequencies of trains – Passenger Service Requirements – have not been tested except in one or two cases. Prism's decision in the summer of 1999 to cut back some of its rural services in the West Country to the PSR minimum showed that PSRs were necessary on heavily subsidised routes and also suggested that on such lines all services had to be part of the PSR if the social function of the service was to be provided as intended. Devon County Council is enraged that only seven out of the eleven pre-privatisation daily services on the Barnstable–Exeter line were protected and has had to fork out a substantial sum to Prism to persuade it to run nine. Prism has come under heavy fire from rail-user groups for its actions and other TOCs would do well to learn that the public-relations impact of what they do may be more significant than the small

Table 7.5 Incentive payments and fines paid to/by TOCs, 1998–99.
Source: Office of Passenger Rail Franchising. Appendix 8,
Annual Report 1998–99. Reproduced with
permission from OPRAF.

Train operator	Incentive payment/fine
Anglia Railways	£302,000
c2c	£747,000
Cardiff Railway Company	−£1,423,000
Central Trains	−£1,651,000
Chiltern Railway	−£276,000
Connex South Central	£1,118,000
Connex South Eastern	−£1,629,000
First Great Eastern	£541,000
First Great Western	−£2,452,000
First North Western	£238,000
Gatwick Express	−
Great North Eastern Railway	−
Island Line	−£14,000
Merseyrail Electrics	−£114,000
Midland Mainline	−
Northern Spirit	£1,761,000
ScotRail	£6,280,000
Silverlink	−£199,000
South West Trains	−£3,933,000
Thames Trains	−£2,224,000
Thameslink	−£270,000
Wales & West	−£378,000
West Anglia Great Northern	−£452,000
Virgin CrossCountry	−
Virgin West Coast	−
Total	**−£4,028,000**

cash savings made from such gestures. On most other parts of the network, operators have found that the benefits of retaining existing services above the level of the PSR outweighs the cost savings of cutting them.

The End of the Beginning

Assessing the success of the great franchising experiment is not a task for the faint-hearted. There is, interestingly, little debate about the issue in the political arena. The Tories cannot associate themselves with an industry where complaints levels are at an all-time high and the media coverage is highly critical. Labour is loath to offer any praise to a system whose creation it fought to prevent. Railtrack is wary of boasting too much about its profits, a figure which, in any case, is hardly a measure of success on the railways. The train operators do not want to give the impression they are doing too well because this may compromise them in negotiations over new franchise terms. It is no wonder, then, that publicity of the railways has largely concentrated on negative factors.

The privatised railways have delivered massive passenger growth – or, at least, sustained the increase in passenger numbers which had begun before the franchising process. Only a proportion of the growth can be put down to privatisation as the state of the economy and other government policies have also contributed. But what of other criteria? Franchising was to deliver an improved railway in terms of a better deal for passengers, boost efficiency and investment, promote competition and reduce subsidy. Did it?

As yet there are no clear answers. Subsidy has increased since privatisation but, as Sir Alastair Morton, to be the inaugural chairman of the SRA, has stressed, this additional cash is for a limited period only. Indeed, in 2002–03 when eighteen of the twenty-five franchises will be nearing the end of their terms, subsidy will be some £300 million below the level paid to BR in its dying days. Whether Britain will have a cheaper railway – in the sense that rail privatisation will have made an overall net contribution to the Treasury – remains to be seen.

We have already seen that, according to Peter White, rail privatisation could result in a net gain to the Treasury by 2003–04 if we ignore any efficiency gains BR or a different successor may have made and if we assume that all TOCs meet their subsidy-reduction targets. But we have also seen that the financial prospect for some of the TOCs, particularly those let on very optimistic assumptions, is very poor towards the end of their terms. Figures for the twenty-five franchises, mainly for the year ended March 1997, showed that nine franchises made a loss – SouthCentral, South Eastern, Island Line, West Anglia Great Northern, Cardiff Valleys, Central, Northern Spirit, North West, ScotRail and Wales & West.[19] Many of these had taken substantial hits for restructuring costs which would not be repeated in the following year, however, and while the accounts must be published, they are somewhat opaque as they may disguise that fact that TOCs may be transferring profits to, or absorbing costs from, their parent companies. Most operators had managed to offset the loss of subsidy and make more profit than they did in the previous year thanks to the growth and the reduction in restructuring costs. On the other hand, very few franchises were making profits bigger than the amount by which subsidy would be reduced in the subsequent year which suggests that, apart from the few lucky early franchisees who receive generous subsidies, many of the operators will struggle towards the end of their terms if the number of passengers stops growing so fast.

OPRAF's overall figures for 1998–99 did offer some comfort with passenger use rising by 5.4 per cent in that year, compared with 6.9 per cent in 1997–98, only a small slowdown and a performance that remains impressive. However, among the worst loss-makers – First North Western, Northern Spirit, Cardiff Valleys and Wales and West – none showed significant growth in 1998–99: Northern Spirit, with 4 per cent, was the best while First North Western was just 2.2 and the two Prism franchises showed little change. The fact that First Group operates two profitable franchises as well as North Western, as does Prism, means that cross-subsidy will meet the losses and there is little threat of operators "handing in the keys" as suggested by Prescott at the 1998 Labour Party Conference (although MTL, which runs Northern Spirit, only has the small Merseyrail franchise to compensate for losses and the company's attempt to sell its rail businesses during 1998 foundered when it failed to obtain the required price).

Even if no franchises go under in this franchising round, private companies will be unwilling to continue sustaining heavy losses next time and operating subsidy may well have to increase notwithstanding Morton's comments. Moreover, given the acute capacity problems which are developing in some areas of the network – and the associated problems with punctuality and reliability which have arisen – government subsidy will be required for capital projects, too. Resolving capacity issues will be expensive and is bound to involve schemes which are commercially unattractive to Railtrack and the Roscos. If the government as a matter of policy wants still more people to use the railways, it will have to go into public/private partnership with these companies to alleviate congestion on the system.

For other criteria the picture is, as yet, equally inconclusive. There have certainly been improvements for passengers but these have often been at a cost. Some new services have been introduced and extra trains have been put on to certain routes but these are responsible in part for patchy performance. The incentive regimes, while clearly penalising some operators, are not, perhaps, as comprehensive or as stringent as they might be. Better marketing has helped to promote a wider range of discounted tickets, although this may cause confusion among some passengers. Moreover, unregulated tickets have often risen in price dramatically. Customer service, while being vastly improved on some TOCs, has not been the focus of many operators' energies. The poor standards on Virgin have, on numerous occasions, attracted spates of media publicity and embarrassed Richard Branson. Connex, too, was the butt of much poor publicity in the early stages and, overall, the customer surveys which the TOCs are required to fill out indicate few signs of improving service.

On efficiency, it really depends what you mean. Yes, some TOCs have cut staff numbers but this has, on occasion, had adverse results as Stagecoach and other operators have found to their cost. Most managers claim that they are now able to take decisions far more easily without having to negotiate the bureaucracy associated with BR. But if the railways are becoming more efficient, then it is no thanks to the one factor which the Tories originally viewed as fundamental in securing it: on-rail competition. Competition between TOCs was deliberately constrained because the free-market model put forward by those who drew up the plans for rail privatisation could not be implemented. There has been hardly any scope for on-rail competition and, while the rules are now being relaxed somewhat, there is little prospect of opening up the network because of the ongoing conflict between franchising and open access. Train operators will, as in the days of BR, be more interested in competing with other modes of transport rather than each other.

Investment in the railway is now a matter for numerous parties. Railtrack's role in infrastructure development is discussed in Chapters 3 and 4 and the purchase of new and refurbished rolling stock is covered in Chapter 5. TOCs are involved in – and in many cases drive – the investment decisions of Railtrack (through revenue-sharing schemes) and the Roscos (through orders for new and/or refurbished trains). In other aspects, many TOCs have invested only limited amounts. Constrained by the shortness of their franchise terms and having a paucity of demands made on them by OPRAF, little progress has been made in making the lot of the rail traveller more comfortable beyond increasing security measures and building customer "lounges" for first-class ticket holders in certain locations. That said, a key investment priority has been the appearance of improved information systems at stations around the network.

As one commentator notes, we are at the half-time stage, not the end of the match.[20] The Tories may consider themselves lucky in the sense that OPRAF was able to deliver an "irreversible" franchised railway before the 1997 general election. The rail operators have also started to deliver real improvements in certain areas. But rail policy was formulated and implemented on the hoof and problems in the system are revealing themselves. In addition to regulatory weaknesses, there is the growing perception that elements of the privatisation structure employed were created to cope with a declining market in a declining industry rather than the upturn in railway travel which has taken place. If the architects of rail privatisation had been confident in the future of rail, a different type of franchise may have been created. Garnett is clear that many of the difficulties since privatisation have their roots in pessimism:

> All these procedures which we signed up to as franchise operators are all written on the basis of the expected failure of the system. It's about how you cannot change the number of trains because the temptation was that we would decrease them. That's why we have fixed payments to Railtrack, that's why everything is locked in. It's all written about failure whereas most of the problems we've got are about how to deal with investment and success.

A degree of "tweaking" will be needed by the new government if the privatised railway is to improve its overall performance and continue attracting – and accommodating – ever-larger numbers of passengers. Further developments are in the offing – some of the franchises are being renegotiated as is Railtrack's access regime. A new Regulator, Tom Winsor, is taking a tougher line on Railtrack and the operators. The leasing arrangements between the Roscos and the TOCs will also undoubtedly develop. Only when these changes begin to bed in will we have some idea of the real economics of the new railway and whether franchising is a viable system of delivering an improving railway at a reduced cost.

The current Transport Bill, likely to become law in autumn 2000, will result in some tighter regulation and the creation of the SRA which open the way for changes in the structure of the industry. The lack of an overall plan and the absence of any attempt to co-ordinate an industry which, by its very nature, requires an integrated approach, was a fundamental weakness of the model created by the Tory Government. The envisaged ability of the SRA to take on this task will help determine the success of the new railway. There is considerable irony in the fact that it is a Labour government which is being called upon to make a success of the Tories' most radical and technically complex privatisation.

Acknowledgements

Chapters 6 and 7 were kindly supported by the Association of Train Operating Companies and for this we are extremely grateful. Thanks are also due to Roger Salmon, Steve Norris, John Welsby, Jim Steer, Chris Stokes, Euan Cameron, Christopher Garnett, Michael Schabas, James Gordon and others who must remain anonymous for granting interviews and offering comments on earlier drafts of both chapters.

Notes

1. National Audit Office. *The award of the First Three Passenger Rail Franchises*, The Stationery Office, 1996.
2. *Financial Times*, 21 July 1993.
3. These bidders presumed that, given the increasing political, economic and environmental concerns about traffic congestion and pollution, rail was likely to be a growth industry in the future regardless of the party in government. Indeed, one pointed out that he thought a private rail operator would be safer under Labour because he saw the Party as more pro-public transport than the Conservatives. A further consideration was the fact that, precisely because of the uncertainty surrounding rail privatisation, few bidders were likely to enter the process straightaway – they would assess the lie of the land before committing themselves – and this would mean less competition, and therefore a better deal, for those who went in at the outset.
4. Kenneth Irvine wrote *The Right Track*, the ASI paper which had advocated the track-authority model in 1987.
5. Office of Passenger Rail Franchising. *Franchise Director Awards First Passenger Rail Franchise*, News release, 19 December 1995.
6. *Investor's Chronicle*, 9 August 1996.
7. LTS had, in effect, been manipulating the ORCATS system (see Chapter 6).
8. The new Gatwick Express trains were introduced late. OPRAF fined the National Express Group around £500,000 as a consequence.
9. National Audit Office, op. cit.
10. Knowles, R. "Passenger rail privatization in Britain and its implications, especially in urban areas" in *Journal of Transport Geography*, 6, 1998.
11. Harris, N. and Godward, E. *The Privatisation of British Rail*, The Railway Consultancy Press, 1997.
12. The Railway Forum. *Financial Support to the Rail Industry, Before and After Privatisation*, April 1998.
13. White, P. "Rail privatization in Britain" in *Transport Reviews*, 15, 1998.
14. Nash, C and Preston, J. "Franchising rail services" in A. Harrison, (ed.) *From Hierarchy to Contract*. Transaction Books, 1993.

15. Having said that, the SRA is currently in shadow form and its chairman, Sir Alistair Morton, has used his position to make known his views on railway performance.
16. BR's information service was very fragmented and the number you called depended on what part of the country you were in and where you wanted to go. There were a total of eighty-three numbers nationwide.
17. SBC Warburg. *Railtrack Share Offer: Mini Prospectus*, 1996.
18. Shaoul, J. Unpublished report, Manchester Business School, 1999.
19. *Rail*, issues dated 16 December 1998, 30 December 1998 and 13 January 1999.
20. Preston, J., Whelan, G. and Wardman, M. "An analysis of the potential for on-track competition in the British passenger rail industry" in *Journal of Transport Economics and Policy*, **33**, 1999.

8. Selling the Freight Railway

Julia Clarke

The needs of the rail freight business were never prominent in the privatisation process but the prospect of change provided an opportunity to improve its fortunes. Following four decades of decline, few anticipated the revival in rail freight which has occurred since privatisation. In 1992 it was a question of fighting to have the needs of freight considered seriously in the context of a privatisation designed primarily with the passenger railway in mind. Against this background, this chapter will examine the privatisation of the rail freight sector. It briefly reviews how it was regarded by officials and ministers at the end of the BR era and what they expected the privatisation process to achieve, before exploring in more detail the sale process and the post-privatisation performance of the rail freight industry.

Rail Freight Before Privatisation

Freight by rail had been declining both relative to road haulage and in absolute terms for 40 years. Whereas in the 1950s over 40 per cent of all freight in the UK was moved by train, in the early 1990s this figure had dropped to around 6 per cent (see Figure 2.10). Many freight customers, particularly those not needing to ship extremely heavy or bulky items such as coal and steel, had long been of the view that road hauliers could service their needs better than train operators – the former were usually cheaper, quicker and more flexible – but rail's relative position was made worse in the 1980s and early 1990s when the government imposed strict financial targets on British Rail (BR). The closure of Speedlink, the wagonload network service launched only a few years earlier, was part of a process which sought to force all freight movements either into a profitable regular trainload format or off the railway altogether. Customers failing to deliver the volume needed to fill daily trains were faced with dramatic price increases, in at least one case of more than 200 per cent. Others were asked for unrealistically high volume guarantees or minimum annual payments.[1] Terminal operators were faced with service reductions or complete withdrawals of service and a number closed, others went into liquidation or withdrew entirely from the rail freight business. "Exit pricing" became a term used to describe the process whereby

Figure 8.1   Ed Burkhardt, former chairman of EWS. Source: EWS.

operationally inconvenient business was priced off the network with unreasonable price increases. John Welsby, Chief Executive of the British Railways Board (BRB) at the time, explained:

> *We were working to an objective which actually said 'make as much profit as you can out of this business', and that's what we did. If it came to profit versus growth, profit won. I don't see that as a criticism, that goes with the nature of the objective we were given and we were pretty damn good at it.*

Ed Burkhardt, former Chairman and Chief Executive of English, Welsh and Scottish Railway (EWS) – the private company which now operates most of Britain's freight trains – referred to the last few BR years in an open letter to his employees (Figure 8.1):

> *I would like to say some words about our customers. Like those I'm familiar with at home [in North America], EWS customers range from some of the sweetest and the most co-operative people you will ever meet to those meaner than a junk-yard dog. Most of their ideas of what a railway can do (or cannot do) for them were shaped from a lifetime of dealing with British Rail. That means we have a real task on our hands to change our act and, by so doing, to change our image to that of a truly customer-oriented organisation. BR poisoned the well*

everywhere it went. It ran off single-wagon shipments and made it impossible for anyone but the largest shippers to use rail. As an example, EWS has 100 customers, whilst Wisconsin Central, a smaller system has 670. Even among the remaining trainload customers, BR made enemies through unmitigated greed in pricing and forced customers to buy their own wagons and even their own locomotives. The result is well known, a steady decline towards oblivion [for its] rail market share.²

The architects of rail privatisation had hoped that their policy might help arrest the decline in both passenger and freight traffic on the railway but did not envisage any significant growth and therefore did not plan for a situation in which capacity would become constrained, substantial investment in the infrastructure would be required, new freight terminals, stations and associated facilities would need to be built and closed branch lines, tracks and diversionary routes reopened. As the chapter will show, all these issues have now come to the fore as the privately owned freight sector has instigated something of a rail renaissance by improving what is on offer to its customers. Nevertheless, many in the industry, including the Rail Freight Group (RFG), a lobbying organisation, were more optimistic than ministers and officials and saw privatisation as the only way to ensure any reasonable future for those wanting to use or provide rail freight facilities.

Moves Towards Privatisation

Ministers dabbled with the idea of allowing private-sector involvement in the rail freight industry before they announced the full-scale privatisation of BR in July 1992. In May 1991, the then Secretary of State for Transport, Malcolm Rifkind, declared himself "enthusiastically and unequivocally desiring to see far more traffic, both passengers and freight, travelling by the railways." Rifkind argued that BR should be subjected to some "on-rail" competition in order to help achieve this:

There is no reason why BR should retain a monopoly of rail freight services. We intend to allow anyone who wishes to provide rail services . . . and who can meet the necessary standards for safety and competence to be able to do so. They will no longer require BR's permission or be obliged to use their staff or rolling stock. Monopolies are no more acceptable on the railways than elsewhere.

Rifkind began preparing the ground quickly for open-access operation. In October 1991, Rifkind wrote to Sir Bob Reid, then Chairman of BR, asking him to extend the principles of the European Directive 91/440 (see Chapter 1) to domestic freight services on a voluntary basis. The letter noted that:

I have announced that we intend to introduce legislation to end BR's monopoly and open access to private operators of domestic freight and passenger services.

But we do not need to wait for that to start this process. I should therefore like the Board: first, to respond positively and sympathetically to any reasonable proposal from the private-sector to introduce new freight or passenger services; second, to charge private-sector operators fairly for the use of BR track and other facilities; third, to allow private operators to use their own locomotives if they so wish; and fourth, to allow private-sector operators to employ their own train crews, including drivers, as long as they have the proper qualifications for the work required of them.

Rifkind's announcement was supported by many in the freight lobby on the basis that more choice should result in a better service. Moreover, it had the potential to be a real shot in the arm for the rail freight sector:

Open access was seen as particularly desirable [for freight] since new entrants would by definition not be encumbered with the manning and operating practices developed over nearly half a century of public ownership and could be expected to inject "a breath of fresh air" into the industry, thus stimulating widespread efficiency gains through demonstration and emulation.[3]

Reid was known to be hostile to Rifkind's ideas – as chairman of BR, he resisted what he saw as attempts to undermine his organisation – and it was not widely expected that he would "play ball". Indeed, in response to Rifkind, Reid merely "noted the Government's intention to introduce legislation" and stated a willingness "to discuss within the framework of the Board's existing statutory and other obligations how your ideas may be taken forward."

No progress was made towards establishing a voluntary open-access regime. An attempt by Hunslet Barclay, a company which already had non-BR trains operating a weedkilling service on the network, to develop an open-access freight operation was thwarted and the company eventually dropped its plans. It was suggested to ministers at the time by the RFG (on the basis of evidence from individuals involved in the initiative) that undue pressure may have been brought to bear as Hunslet Barclay was part of the larger Hunslet Group which had significant interests in securing heavy-engineering contracts from BR. Other companies, including the ports of Felixstowe and Thamesport, who showed an early interest in open-access operations also failed to develop their plans and, in a confidential letter to Roger Freeman, then Minister of State for Public Transport, I wrote in my capacity as RFG Director that: "the government must recognise that the goodwill of BR in progressing towards privatisation is lacking."

As things turned out, of course, Rifkind's liberalisation plans were soon replaced by far more ambitious privatisation proposals. But it is important to note here that the early debate about the model of privatisation to be used was always dominated by passenger, not freight, issues. Although Rifkind seemed to believe in the prospects for sector growth through open access, others in government had no real expectations that freight would undergo a significant revival following privatisation. Freeman, who was partly responsible for developing the rail-privatisation proposals, explained:

I have to tell you that the focus of our early attention was on passenger railways. There is no sense in trying to give you any other impression. The political interest was what would benefit the passenger, what would the implications for the passenger be? Freight was very definitely a poor relation, certainly in terms of the intellectual analysis.

Suspecting that this was the case, the RFG emphasised the need for the freight industry to promote its interests through an effective lobbying campaign and debate was encouraged among key players about the favoured shape of the post-privatisation railway. In contrast to the views of commentators and BRB members, most of whom were also concerned mainly with the passenger railway, the freight lobby argued in favour of the track-authority model of rail privatisation for precisely the reason that others opposed it: ownership and management of the infrastructure would be taken away from *passenger* train operators and passed to an independent body who would deal with *all* train operators impartially. As Brian Wadsworth, a senior Department of Transport (DoT) official, pointed out:

Since the only workable vertically integrated models for railway organisation involved combining infrastructure control with dominant passenger operations, increasing pressure for a separate track authority emerged from those arguing the cause of rail freight. It was felt that a neutral, third-party control of infrastructure would be more conducive to the commercial and operational requirements of freight than would a series of vertically integrated, passenger only, railway operators.[4]

Another advantage of the track-authority model for the freight lobby was that it would easily allow the development of an open-access regime similar to that which Rifkind had originally advocated in 1991 and it was increasingly apparent that the freight lobby and the government shared a common purpose. In a speech to the Institution of Civil Engineers in March 1992, Freeman set out the Government's philosophy behind the forthcoming privatisation:

Railways can only play their part if they give passengers and freight customers the services they want. This requires responsive adaptable management with proper incentives to react to customers' needs. We believe that this, in turn, is best secured by introducing the stimulus of competition and the flexibility of the private sector in the operation of our railways. The outdated nationalised monopoly structure is simply no longer appropriate for the railways if they are to play their part in the modern economy.

This sentiment was reinforced when the White Paper was eventually published. Paragraph 46 noted:

Rail freight will be able to meet [its] challenges only if it is efficient and responsive to the demands of its customers. This is best achieved through introducing the management and financial freedom of private ownership.

The Government's policy is therefore to establish a competitive and privately owned rail freight industry in the course of this parliament. This offers the best prospect of attracting new freight to rail with the environmental benefits that will bring. The Government proposes to liberalise all rail freight operations and privatise BR's present rail freight operations. Together these policies will bring the disciplines of the market to bear equally on all rail freight operators, and give management the added freedom for innovation and investment available in the private sector.[5]

In addition to open access and privatisation of BR's freight operations, the White Paper contained other proposals of significance to freight, notably the establishment of a Rail Regulator who would oversee the licensing and access regime. A major consultancy study on track-access charges – i.e., the amount passenger and freight operators would have to pay Railtrack to run trains on its network – was announced and the continuation of "freight facilities grants" was assured. These grants were of great significance to the rail freight industry because they subsidised conversion to rail freight which involved high, and potentially prohibitive, capital costs (see below). Again, however, it should be noted that the interests of the freight sector were incidental rather than influential in ministers' thinking. As Freeman points out:

I am afraid freight did not register on the general political radar screen ... [as] the whole thing was driven by the passenger railway. In the wake of those policy decisions, one suddenly realised that this could be an opportunity for freight, but it wasn't freight driving the policy. We were concentrating on the implications for the passenger railway and the cost of running the passenger railway. We understand, however, the underlying environmental importance of shifting as much freight as possible on to the railways.

As we will see, the relative lack of ministerial attention to rail freight privatisation would impact upon policy decisions and affect the interests of rail freight both during and after the privatisation process.

Because the publication of the White Paper in July 1992 marked the end of the debate over which model of rail privatisation would be used, interest in the freight industry now shifted towards more specific issues such as the form and method of sale envisaged for BR's freight and parcels businesses, the structure of charges for freight access to the network, the extent to which competition on the rails would be encouraged and the interim arrangements for freight during the period that privatisation was taking place. The RFG highlighted these concerns on behalf of the industry in a presentation to Freeman and its subsequent *Policy Statement on Open Access*, both of which covered several key points including: support for the principle of on-rail competition and open access to "encourage use of the network by companies currently wedded exclusively to road haulage"; the need for equal opportunities between new entrants and BR's successor companies; the need for access charges to be simple, affordable and fairly applied; and the important point that care should be taken in the period before privatisation "to avoid irrecoverable loss of some types of traffic and alienation of potential private operators."[6] The Group was concerned that, because many observers – including freight customers – suspected (rightly) that the government's plans were at this stage incomplete, clients may have opted for the "safer" option of road haulage. As noted in the academic press:

With the railway industry experiencing such a fundamental and systematic transformation it is, of course, very difficult to predict the future with any certainty. With uncertainty therefore being the only certainty, perhaps the major impact of rail privatisation will be felt in further demand for road transport.[7]

The Group also welcomed the continuation of the Freight Grants Scheme and argued for further incentives for modal shift as well as emphasising that it was crucial for the government to ensure that future investment in the network be planned on a national strategic basis.[8] The White Paper had not adequately addressed this issue and it was unclear where such guidance would come from. The Labour administration's plans for a Strategic Rail Authority (SRA) (see below and Chapter 10) have been formulated in response to continuing demands from those who felt that the Conservatives never succeeded in providing for strategic future planning.

The *Policy Statement* was followed by the initiation of the Freight on Rail (FoR) campaign which aimed to influence the shape of the Railways Bill and subsequently to amend the Bill as necessary and to the extent possible in the interests of freight. The campaign, supported by the members of the RFG, endorsed the vertical separation of the industry in the face of a strong lobby, including the late Robert Adley MP, which continued to press for the vertical integration of passenger franchises (see Chapter 6).

The 1993 Railways Act

The Railways Bill, published in January 1993, added little detail to the White Paper as it was primarily enabling legislation allowing for the transfer of both the infrastructure and rail operations to the private sector (see Chapter 1). Its publication did, however, generate much frenzied activity and FoR began the task of analysing the Bill and proposing amendments. An early success for the freight lobby came in the adoption of an amendment to the Clause 4 duties of the Secretary of State and the Regulator. The original draft read:

Clause 4 – (1) The Secretary of State and the Regulator shall each have a duty to exercise the functions assigned or transferred to him under or by virtue of this Part in the manner which he considers best calculated ... (b) to promote the use of the railway network in Great Britain, and the development of that railway network, to the greatest extent that he considers economically practicable.[9]

An amendment moved at the suggestion of FoR by Peter Luff, MP, changed the sub-clause to:

(b) to promote the use of the railway network in Great Britain for the carriage of passengers and goods, *and the development of the railway network, to the greatest extent that he considers economically practicable [emphasis added].*[10]

Although this proved to be the only amendment on which FoR lobbied successfully, it has been valuable in the period since the Act was passed. The Regulator has on numerous occasions referred to this duty and it has been influential in many of his policy decisions regarding rail freight. For example, in the foreword to his policy statement *Framework for the Approval of Railtrack's Track Access Charges for Freight Services* the Regulator states:

> *Parliament has given me the function of approving individual access agreements between freight operators and Railtrack and it has imposed duties on me. In particular, Parliament has given me a specific duty to promote the carriage of freight by rail.*

One example where the Regulator arguably failed to take account of this duty occurred recently, however, when he approved the upgrading of the West Coast Main Line to benefit passenger operators, particularly Virgin, possibly at freight's expense. This issue is discussed in more detail below.

A further amendment proposed was the establishment of a statutory Freight Users' Consultative Committee, along the lines of the passenger CRUCC, but the government's view was that the freight industry was commercially driven and that customers would be able to look after their own interests through normal commercial negotiation and the regulatory mechanisms of the Act. FoR was also concerned that the Railways Act gave no protection against closure of freight facilities by Railtrack and it lobbied for amendments which would have required the infrastructure authority to notify the Regulator of any closure of facilities which would affect freight or might potentially affect future freight carryings. Tied up with this was the suggestion that Railtrack should offer for sale at nominal charge any facilities it no longer wished to maintain to private operators willing to keep the facilities available for operational use. While these ideas attracted some support from officials and were viewed sympathetically by ministers, they were rejected when tabled as an amendment.

At the second reading of the Bill in February 1993, John MacGregor announced three "new measures". Interestingly, his emphasis had shifted from the ideological commitment to competition towards an awareness of environmental matters. "Everyone agrees," he said, "that carrying freight by rail usually offers environmental advantages as compared with using lorries. But translating that sentiment into practice is another matter."[11] Accordingly:

> *We will enhance the existing freight facilities grants scheme. The scheme provides targeted financial assistance to capital projects which demonstrably help the environment by switching traffic from road to rail ... I propose to expand the scheme in three ways. Grants will be made available to private rail freight operators as well as customers and consignors; grants will cover all forms of*

capital expenditure and equipment, including locomotives and track and structures specifically needed for freight; and grant assessments will now include traffic taken off inter-urban main roads and motorways. Secondly, I propose to issue a consultation document containing proposals to encourage combined transport movements and to help keep down the number of lorries on our roads . . .[12] My third proposal involves a new principle . . . I propose to introduce a new grant, up to 100 per cent of the track charges if necessary, to contribute towards track charges for freight traffic which can be demonstrably proven otherwise to move from rail to road or could not be attracted to rail without it. This even means that, where the environmental and other benefits clearly justify it, access to the network can be made free at the point of use for freight operators.[13]

Rail Freight Grants had been available since 1974 under Section 8 of the Railways Act of that year. They were perpetuated under Section 139 of the new Act but MacGregor's "new measures" resulted in an altered wording to make them easier to obtain. Instead of having to demonstrate benefits to a particular locality the applicant now only need show that the transfer was in the public interest. This opened the way for an allowance to be made for the removal of lorries from all roads including motorways whereas previously grant had only been paid for traffic removed from specific roads such as those through National Parks and built up areas. This change was particularly important for the development of general-distribution traffic on rail and intermodal traffic which tends to move long distances but predominantly on the motorway network as it had previously had difficulty in attracting significant grant.

The new "Track Access Grant", ultimately set out in Section 140 of the Railways Act, allowed freight operators to apply to the government for a revenue grant toward the charges negotiated with Railtrack. It was designed to retain environmentally sensitive freight on rail even if the traffic could not support the avoidable cost of access to the infrastructure. In this way the government hoped to avoid the accusation and the actuality of freight being priced off the railway on to unsuitable roads as a result of the privatisation – a real prospect because Railtrack's access charges were expected to be high and ministers did not want the embarrassment of further freight traffic losses.

The Railways Act finally received Royal Assent on 5 November 1993. While it provided the legal framework by which the rail freight sector would be privatised, there was much left to resolve. The RFG made its view clear on this subject in a press release issued at the time which stated:

The private sector sees this [the passing of the Bill] as the beginning rather than the end of the privatisation process. The Railways Act leaves a great deal to the discretion of the Secretary of State, the Regulator and Railtrack. This discretion must be used to create genuine above-track competition and a truly cost effective, fairly priced infrastructure. The government must now follow through to its logical conclusion the liberalisation intended by the legislation, by . . . ensuring fair competition in the transition phase while parts of BR's freight remain in the public sector and encouraging new operators into the market by, for example, making available a proportion of ex-BR locomotives ... The opportunity to redress the balance between road and rail, in the long-term interests of the economy and the environment, must not be missed.

The New Operational Environment

Important decisions taken to mould the new operational environment for freight are reviewed elsewhere in the book. One of the most significant, the formulation of the track access and charging regime, is covered in Chapters 3 and 4. Attention here is focused on the creation of BR's successor companies and the initiation of the open-access regime in the freight industry. BR's freight sector had been divided into the profitable Trainload Freight and unprofitable Railfreight Distribution (RfD) and Rail Express Systems (RES). Trainload freight operated heavy-haul services in four main sectors: coal (mainly for power stations), metals (mainly ore and semi-finished steel), aggregates and petroleum products. RfD was developing the Channel Tunnel intermodal business, operated the deep-sea-port container business under the Freightliner brand and also managed the residual wagonload business following the closure of Speedlink (Figure 8.2). Rail Express Systems operated to fulfil a Royal Mail contract to move letters and parcels around the country.

Figure 8.2   Freightliner Class 92 locomotive on the West Coast Main Line, July 1996.
Source: Freightliner.

A key question faced by ministers was whether to sell the entire freight sector as it already existed or to split it up further before privatisation – as was happening with the passenger-train-operating companies – in an attempt to promote competition between the successor businesses. Although open access would in theory provide the scope for the introduction of new services, ministers were concerned that the barriers to entry would be insurmountable if no new split were effected because of the size of the incumbents.

In making its decision, the government relied in part upon a consultation with potential buyers of the freight business, but predominantly on a major study undertaken jointly for the DoT and the BRB by Mercer Management Consulting Limited. The study included an analysis of the trade-offs between the benefits of a more fragmented rail freight industry, generating efficiency improvements through greater competition, and the effects of fragmentation upon existing economies of scale. It identified that about one-third of all trainload traffic was both short distance and high volume. These parts of the business were inherently free-standing with dedicated resources and train crews for single flows or groups of flows. The remaining two-thirds, however, consisted of long-distance low-volume business. This relied on small pockets of resources and train crews distributed along the line of route. Dedicating resources to serve a single flow or customer of this type would have been very expensive and these types of flows were best served therefore in combination with each other. These characteristics, it was argued, both limited the number of units it was sensible to create and pointed to a geographic – rather than commodity or customer based – structure.

Anxious to promote competition, ministers took the decision to sell RES as a stand-alone unit and separate Freightliner from RfD in order to sell the two independently of one another. Trainload Freight was to be re-packaged as three regionally based companies – Loadhaul, Mainline and Transrail – on the basis that two was too few and four too many (see Figure 2.11). Critics of the government's proposals were quick to point out that fragmenting the rail freight business would destroy economies of scale and render the successor companies unsustainable because lower barriers to entry would allow a flood of open-access operators to undermine them. As a result of these factors, it was added, ministers would seriously compromise the proceeds they would raise from the freight sale. John Welsby recalls a famous row with Freeman over proposals to break the freight business up:

I had a meeting with Freeman about this when it first arose in which I was perhaps unwisely forceful and operated in the vernacular. The next thing I knew, it was in The Guardian *and it was full of phrases like "you're in a hole, stop digging" and "you're going to be presiding over a car-boot sale." The reality was that as far as the freight industry was concerned you needed a certain level of freight business in order to reach even take off. It's all very well for National Power to scream that we're [BR] a monopoly but, my God, they're a monopsony buyer as well and if you get yourself into a negotiation with them and they come out of it badly I don't have a lot of sympathy. We said to them [ministers] that the best solution was to have one [Trainload Freight] company; the next best, if you won't have one, is to have two and the worst of all worlds is to have three.*

A further problem was identified by operations managers. Although the new companies were to be of similar size in terms of resources, turnover and traffic mix, they would be quite different in terms of profitability. Graham Smith, who was planning manager for Trainload Freight from 1991–94, explained:

The north-east company, which became Loadhaul, had within it a number of very efficient trainload operations, particularly in the coal, steel and iron sectors which delivered exactly what the customer wanted on a conveyor-belt basis and was therefore a profitable business. Mainline, the South-East company, had a lot of mid-range flows, some good coal traffic in the Midlands, some aggregates traffic, and there were some other bits and pieces running at the margin. That was middle-of-the-range profitability. Then the west company, Transrail, although it had some good core business in South Wales and some power station coal, was also responsible for a lot of long thin straggly services which did not have enough substance or volume to them to make them really profitable.

The government defended its decision in the 1993 document, *Rail Freight Privatisation: The Government's Proposals.* Undeterred by the points critics had raised, it noted that the new structure would: "maximise competition on rail to the extent that is compatible with preserving essential continuity for existing services, meeting the needs of key customers to have security of supply and preserving the economies of scale which come from operating a substantial portfolio of business."[14] Although the companies were set up on a geographical basis, it was envisaged that they would compete with each other by making "incursions" into each other's core territory. At one time it was contemplated providing each company with out-bases in the form of train-crew depots in each other's areas but this was dropped on the grounds that it was impractical to manage lots of remote units hundreds of miles away from the core territory. As *Rail Freight Privatisation* pointed out, "of 11,600 track miles carrying trainload freight at present, more than half will carry trains operated by more than one company and nearly a quarter by all three."

Loadhaul, Mainline and Transrail were vested in December 1994 and began operating in shadow form leading to an expected privatisation the following year. The three companies quickly became engaged in a "phoney war" where, on the one hand, they were encouraged to start competing with one another but, on the other hand, they were prevented from doing so because overall control still remained with BR. An indignant article in the Mainline staff newspaper, *Newsline*, reported that:

Transrail is to open a train-crew depot at Willesden Brent Sidings – right in the heart of Mainline Freight territory. Control of Brent switched from Railfreight Distribution to Transrail in March despite strong objections from Mainline. A month later, Transrail announced it was setting up its own train-crew depot due to the poor quality of service received from RfD. It is disappointing that Transrail has seen fit to set up a new depot when there were other alternatives available to them. Mainline is happy to provide services for them and will continue to do so. I hope that, despite privatisation, we will not see other proposals of this type come forward.[15]

Whereas the government had decided against establishing a large number of depots in competitors' territory prior to the split, Transrail clearly saw advantages in setting up at least one. A key reason for this was its reintroduction of services for less-than-trainload consignments in the form of "Enterprise". This service made a virtue out of necessity by marrying essential long distance civil-engineering trains (which carried equipment and materials for the maintenance of Transrail's geographically extended area) and commercial freight opportunities. The resultant "network" initially consisted of two intersecting routes running south-west/north-east and north-west/south-east across the UK with an interchange point at Warrington. The service has continued to the present day and has grown into a national network service (see Figures 8.3 and 8.4).

Selling the Freight Businesses

A survey of rail freight customers carried out in June 1995 by the RFG recorded their experiences since the split of Trainload Freight into three companies. Notwithstanding the concerns of critics, the key findings were that customers had found a marked improvement in commercialism and, in a significant number of cases, much more attractive rates enabling them to put new flows on rail. On this basis the RFG supported the government's decision to split Trainload Freight and, in a letter to the DoT, noted that: "for medium-sized users, [the initiation of] open-access services will be a poor substitute for competition between three balanced rail freight operators with national scope." Whereas in 1991 the RFG had welcomed open access on the basis that some competition was better than none, it was now minded to ensure, in the light of the government's new proposals, that the rail freight market was liberalised as far as reasonably possible. The letter continued: "the availability of open access [alone] is insufficient to compensate for competition [between Loadhaul, Mainline and Transrail] since for the majority of freight customers it will be prohibitively expensive and in any case their operations would be below the minimum economic scale."

The RFG's interjection was prompted by rumours – which turned out to be true – that the government was considering reuniting Loadhaul, Mainline and Transrail because it was having difficulties finding bidders for the fledgling companies. Ministers were having to go to extraordinary lengths to drum up interest from the private sector. MacGregor's replacement as Secretary of State for Transport, Dr Brian Mawhinney, flew to Chicago in 1995 to meet Ed Burkhardt, President of the US-based rail operator Wisconsin Central. Burkhardt had established a reputation as a shrewd operator after transforming the fortunes of a relatively small Mid-Western rail freight company and

Figure 8.3   The Enterprise Network as originally established, including so-called rail "motorways". Source: English, Welsh and Scottish Railway. With permission from EWS.

Figure 8.4 The Enterprise Network in 1999. Source: English, Welsh and Scottish Railway. With permission from EWS.

subsequently expanding his operations by leading a consortium to purchase New Zealand's railways in 1993. Burkhardt had rejected initial approaches from the UK government because of the heavy emphasis on passenger services in Britain and, more importantly, what he viewed as the "crazy" privatisation structure of vertical separation, open access and splitting up Trainload Freight. Whereas many in UK rail freight supported the government's proposals because they promoted on-rail competition, Burkhardt was not impressed:

> *Nobody amongst the government or the consultants that put the structure together seemed to understand the point that this is a business that has quite an economy of scale. They thought that those three companies would compete vigorously with each other within a 6 per-cent market share. I didn't see that ... If you want a company that has a low enough unit-cost base to actually provide competition with the lorries you have to have a pretty strong, sizeable company, not a bunch of ants running on the railway that are killing each other but ultimately have high unit costs and cannot attack the large base of lorry drivers.*[16]

The government did not seek to deny that there were high fixed costs and economies of scale in rail transport but argued that, with Railtrack in charge of the infrastructure and instructed to charge on a flow-by-flow basis, a large proportion of the fixed cost became variable to the rail haulier. Road transport, while effective competition for much rail freight business, especially prospective new business, is not effective for some "captive" customers for whom road is logistically unattractive, who are moving enormous volumes of material, who have planning restrictions on road movements or who have substantial sunk investment in fixed rail facilities. Competing operators, as well as bringing downward pressure on prices and upward pressure on quality of service, also bring welcome product differentiation and innovation reducing the possibility that certain sectors of demand will remain unsatisfied because a single rail company is unenthusiastic about addressing certain markets. Burkhardt counters that such a view is completely unrealistic, the brainchild of "a bunch of ideologue consultants, economists, public servants of various types, all very intelligent and capable people, but no one with a true knowledge of what it meant to run a railway."

Mawhinney secured an appointment with Burkhardt after intervention from the British Consul General in Chicago who knew the Wisconsin Central President fairly well. The Consul General had suggested to Burkhardt that it might be useful for him to meet Mawhinney if only to discuss the government's proposals and Burkhardt agreed on the condition that "he [Mawhinney] is going to have to listen to a lecture from me." When the two met, Burkhardt told the Secretary of State: "No one in North America is going to read past page 1 [of the proposals]. I said 'this structure is crazy.'" It was true that no other American rail firm had been willing to involve itself in the freight sell-off. Mawhinney's reaction was uncharacteristically contrite (he was renowned for his combative style – see Chapter 6) and revealed an air of desperation. Burkhardt recalls:

He said, "Let's grant for a moment that we've made mistakes. The fact is that this will be subject to an open bidding and the bidder will take the structure into account in their bidding, won't they?" And I said, "That's true ... and the big loser will be the taxpayer in Britain because you are going to get less for these properties than you should." So he said, "You ought to get involved, you might get a bargain. I see you people as being pretty good at buying operations that have problems and then solving those problems."[17]

Burkhardt was not aware at this point that there were no other bidders except management-buyout teams – "bidders of last resort," as Burkhardt puts it – but agreed to get involved if Mawhinney would accept bids to buy the three Trainload Freight companies as one unit. This Mawhinney agreed to do – the lack of outside interest was rather forcing his hand – and Loadhaul, Mainline and Transrail were reunited and sold for £225 million to a Burkhardt-led consortium comprised of Wisconsin Central, Berkshire Partners (a Boston based investment firm which had been involved with Burkhardt in Wisconsin and New Zealand) and Fay-Richwhite (a venture-capital firm which had also participated in the New Zealand railway privatisation).

Being forced to offer the freight businesses for sale as a reunified concern was disappointing to ministers but reflected a growing realisation that consolidation either at the point of sale or afterwards was likely to occur. At the same time the reality that a consolidated sale would generate a higher price than the sale of separate companies began to focus ministerial minds. Nevertheless, the DoT justified its decision in a statement released in December 1995:

Privatisation offers the best prospects for the rail freight industry. The Government and BR structured the Trainload Freight competition so that bidders had the flexibility to make offers for the three companies singly or in any combination. This would enable us to judge which bids were likely to offer the best combination of competition, proceeds to the Exchequer and speed of sale. In the light of the final bids which were received earlier this month negotiations are being taken forward on the basis that the three companies will be sold to one bidder. It was clear from the bids that the market's strong preference is for a combined sale of the three companies. Bidders judge that a unified trainload freight business will be in the best position to increase rail's share of the freight market by offering customers an attractive alternative to road freight. The bids also reflect the prospect of increasing competition in the rail freight market from own-account operators. The enthusiasm which bidders have shown for acquiring these businesses demonstrates a strong and welcome commitment to the future of freight on rail.

An alternative analysis is offered by academics Andy Cumbers and John Farrington, who suggest that:

In a desperate attempt not to lose face by having to halt the privatisation programme, the government was prepared to sell to the first party it could interest in its proposals without any semblance of a competitive bidding process. Clearly, it was a case of ideological dogma and political necessity dominating the process rather than a more systematic and measured approach.[18]

The sale of the other freight businesses was generally less fraught, although some difficult subsidy issues needed to be resolved. The most straightforward sale was that of RES, the business based on the servicing of the Royal Mail contract, which was sold in December 1995 for £24.2 million. RfD followed in 1997. Both companies were sold to the Wisconsin Central consortium (which now operates its UK businesses under the EWS name), meaning that Burkhardt had acquired five of the six freight businesses and effectively destroyed any hope of large-scale competition in the industry. The RfD deal was particularly generous as it involved the government underwriting Channel Tunnel access charges until 2005 and a substantial one-off "restructuring grant". The EWS Board still argued long and hard over the wisdom of taking on a business losing "a million pounds a week" but Burkhardt persuaded them with the argument that the real prize for rail freight lay in the long-distance trans-European movements.

Freightliner was the only freight business not sold to EWS. Offered for sale in May 1994 as a going concern, it was finally sold to a management-buyout team in May 1996 for £5.4 million. The delay was in part due to the fact that the company was unable to support even minimal track-access charges and was eventually sold with a £75 million track-access grant providing diminishing support levels over a 5-year period.[19]

Open Access and Barriers to Entry

Despite the sale of much of the freight business to EWS, a renewed interest in open access was expressed by existing rail freight customers who felt they could make savings of between 25 and 50 per cent by running their own operations, terminal operators seeking to reduce the high cost of feeder services to their premises and others looking to establish general-haulage operations to fill the gap left by the closure of Speedlink and BR's withdrawal from the wagonload-network service.

As we have seen, attempts to promote open-access entry in the BR era were unsuccessful. Following legislation, interested parties now had a legal right to initiate new services, although potential problems remained for would-be open-access operators in the form of high barriers to market entry. In 1994 the RFG published a paper, *Entering the Rail Freight Market as an Open Access Train Operator*, which set out the extent of these barriers. Key among these was the non-availability of second-hand locomotives – despite a large number being surplus to requirements following a substantial retrenchment in BR's freight business during the previous 5 years. In January 1995, it was reported that private-sector companies were being prevented from launching rail freight services because BR was refusing to make second-hand rolling stock available.[20] BR denied that it was attempting to stifle rival operators saying it had not received any "serious requests" from organisations wanting to buy its rolling stock, but the RFG countered that a number of companies interested in acquiring ex-BR locomotives and rolling stock had had their interest formally registered with the vendor unit for up to 12 months and still heard nothing. Despite a protocol being agreed between the government and the BRB in early 1994 that genuinely surplus equipment would be made available for sale, little or no equipment was sold and, on privatisation, all locomotives were divided among the BR successor companies. This issue continues to the present day with EWS in 1999 being required by the Regulator to make surplus equipment available for sale rather than be sold for scrap.

Other barriers to entry included the cost of putting together a safety case, difficulties in recruiting drivers with appropriate "route knowledge", training new drivers and the prohibitively high cost of insurance based on the minimum of £155 million third-party-liability insurance which was a condition of licence. Insurance premiums to cover the minimum third-party-liability insurance limit of £155 million could be as high as £500,000 for a small operation where turnover could be only £1–2 million. One operator had been quoted a premium of £130,000 to cover an operation involving one train a day in each direction along a freight-only line.

Two open-access operators did emerge relatively quickly notwithstanding these issues. National Power, an electricity-generating company, had decided early on that running its own rail services would have substantial cost benefits. Speaking in May 1994 at the annual Rail Freight Conference, Keith McNair, Director of Fuel Management at National Power, said:

> With rail cost accounting today for as much as 20 per cent of the delivered cost of coal at the margin, the price of rail [transport] disadvantages coal-fired generation. Make no mistake, [the] cost ... of rail today makes quite a difference to the relative competitiveness of gas and coal-fired power stations.

National Power had already acquired a new Class 59 locomotive (Figure 8.5) and twenty-one wagons based at Ferrybridge and these were used to haul limestone from the Peak District to Drax Power Station for use in the flue-gas desulphurisation process. This operation was essentially similar to that established several years previously by Foster Yeoman and subsequently ARC to use their own equipment – but using BR drivers – to transport stone from their Mendip quarries. Following its decision to go for open-access operation, National Power went on to acquire a further five locomotives and eighty-five coal wagons and obtained its own operators' licence. On 29 November 1995, the first open-access freight train since the Railways Act ran from the Selby coalfield to National Power's Eggborough power station. In March 1998 the operation was sold back to EWS as part of a haulage contract but National Power was thus able to retain the transportation-cost benefits which had accrued as a result of its initiative. The company hadn't anticipated developing its freight business into a company offering third-party haulage.

A second open-access operation was established by Direct Rail Services (DRS), a subsidiary of British Nuclear Fuels Limited (BNFL), and this remains as a stand-alone operation today (Figure 8.6). The motivation to establish DRS was set out

Figure 8.5   National Power Class 59/2 locomotive on coal duties. Source: EWS.

by the late Max Joule, then International Business Development Manager of BNFL's Transport Division, at the same conference. He identified numerous threats posed to BNFL's use of rail transport by the Railways Act and the impending sale of BR's freight businesses. These included price escalation, a reduction in standards, the closure of branch lines and ongoing instability. Conversely, the opportunities presented through establishing open-access operations were price reduction, the possibility of strategic control, improved levels of service and the introduction of a new culture. Joule explained that BNFL's emphasis was on strategic control of an essential transport mode rather than cost savings.

Post-Privatisation: Coping with Growth

Once the privatisation of the freight railway had been completed, the government felt that it had fully discharged its duties in respect of the industry and behaved accordingly. In response to continuing demands from freight operators, customers and the RFG to address key issues such as promoting competition and levelling the playing field with road transport, ministers made clear that these were now up to the industry to sort out on its own. As John Watts, Freeman's successor, pointed out:

> *What we have done is to create a framework to encourage more competitive and responsive rail freight services. It is now up to industry to take advantage of the*

Figure 8.6   Direct Rail Services Class 20 locomotive. Source: Milepost $92\frac{1}{2}$.

opportunities ... For the future, therefore, the provision of rail freight and associated services will be a matter for the private sector.

Of course, ministers were still involved in some areas of the freight industry – such as dealing with grant applications – but the need to sustain a further element of intervention became apparent very quickly. On-rail competition has been slow to develop after the initial entries mentioned above, although there is evidence that the *threat* of competition is beginning to drive prices down. Burkhardt reckons that up to £80 million per year is shaved off EWS's revenues because of existing or threatened open-access operation. At the time of writing, only one application to commence open-access operation – a joint venture by quarry operators Hanson and Foster Yeoman – is being prepared. Having sold much of the freight industry to one company, it might have been expected that the Conservatives would have sought to encourage more open-access competition in the freight sector.

Growth has come much faster. We have already seen that ministers and officials saw little prospect of major growth occurring in the freight sector after privatisation – at best, the sell-off was viewed as a means of arresting the decline in traffic which had been going on for over 40 years – but the new private-sector operators were quick to reverse the fortunes of rail freight through a combination of reduced prices, better customer service and increased investment. EWS has procured, through the Rosco Angel Train Contracts (see Chapter 5), 250 new

Class 66 locomotives and a further thirty Class 67s; it has also acquired a fleet of new wagons. Freightliner has ordered new and refurbished locomotives. Aided by a general economic upturn, both companies have reported double-digit annual-growth rates and EWS's has been achieved against a background of continuing structural decline in the power-station coal business, although tonne kilometres have been bolstered by some longer distance movements of imported coal, notably from Hunterston to Yorkshire. The operators are optimistic about their future prospects: EWS is aiming to triple tonne kilometres in 10 years and Freightliner is planning for 50 per-cent growth over the same period. Unfortunately, however, EWS and Freightliner are becoming victims of their own success in that the recent and projected growth in freight traffic is, when combined with the increase in passenger-train movements (see Chapter 7), begin-ning to put pressure on network capacity. The feeling is that, once again, the development of the passenger railway is being prioritised at the expense of the freight sector.

Freight interests in track capacity and other infrastructure investment are frequently given short shrift by Railtrack and this is clearly demonstrated in the upgrade of the West Coast Main Line (WCML) it has agreed with Virgin Trains. As noted in Chapter 4, these two companies have put together a deal to upgrade passenger facilities to allow the introduction of 140-mph tilting trains on the route but the consequences for freight operators are adverse because, travelling at only 60–75 mph, their trains would seriously reduce capacity and are impractical for – and therefore discouraged from – the line for that reason. The Regulator approved the deal between Railtrack and Virgin on the understanding that the former would provide extra capacity for freight but no exact targets were set. Railtrack has so far failed to make clear how it plans to accommodate the freight operators' path requirements and, at the time of writing, the issue has still not been resolved.

A further proposal to enhance the loading gauge on the WCML to allow the carriage of lorry semi-trailers on rail wagons – the Piggyback Project – also foundered as a result of the potentially limited freight capacity on the West Coast Main Line. The consortium of interests backing the project (the "Piggyback Consortium") has been unable to convince potential investors – including Railtrack – that the project is viable and operators such as EWS have not viewed the proposal as a top priority. Piggyback could deliver considerable growth in rail freight volumes because of its potential to attract custom from those currently deterred from using rail freight on the basis that they would need to invest in specialised equipment for transferring cargoes to rail wagons. As long as the project is stifled, the prospects for winning such business remain slim.

It is now widely recognised that as well as track-capacity increases, sustained rail freight growth will necessitate substantial numbers of new terminals of various types. Of course, the RFG and others argued at the time of privatisation that the proposals failed to anticipate that land would be needed for reinstating or expanding the network and that, in the absence of regulation, much of this would be sold. This has indeed turned out to be the case. Although some 90 sites are designated Strategic Freight Sites and cannot be disposed of without the agreement of the major freight operators, some property has been sold for non-rail use and pressure is growing for Railtrack's property activity to fall within the scope of its licence. Graham Smith, now of EWS, explained that at the time of privatisation:

> *There was a fundamental misunderstanding of how important land would become for building up a freight business bearing in mind that at this time there was absolutely no perception within government — both politicians and civil servants — that the freight business would ever grow. It would at best continue its slow decline focusing on trainload business. The need for land for new sites and new terminals just didn't register with anybody.*

It was not until the Transport Subcommittee of the House of Commons Select Committee on Environment and Transport, under the chairmanship of Gwyneth Dunwoody, MP, called for a moratorium on further sales that a review was announced and sales suspended. In another positive development, the government has recently issued new planning guidance for both regional and local authorities requiring them to take the transfer of freight from road to rail into account in their land-use planning policies and specifically in the Regional Transport Strategies and Local Transport Plans.

A further current issue concerns the cost of freight access to the infrastructure. Railtrack argues that the cost of freight is higher than previously thought and that, in particular, the marginal cost of freight access — the cost of running each additional freight train — is substantially higher. This has implications for the growth of freight on the railway and will fall to the Regulator to tackle as part of his periodic review of Railtrack's access charges (see Chapter 4). The Regulator will have to take a view on the charges for freight in terms of both their total level and the balance between fixed and variable elements. The result will have implications for the affordability of access, particularly with respect to "marginal" freight movements such as intermodal and less-than-trainload which are unlikely to be able to afford much more than the current low-marginal rate. The decision will also affect the incentives Railtrack has to allocate capacity to freight and to invest in additional network capacity and enhancement projects. The resolution of these conflicting issues is likely to involve regulatory, as opposed to financial, incentives to accommodate freight and a certain amount of investment to support freight growth from the government. Key industry players will be watching Railtrack very closely as some are of the view that the company is inefficient and that, as a result, its track-access charges are higher than they ought to be. As Burkhardt points out, Wisconsin Central's track costs in North America are considerably less than the amount Railtrack charges EWS for a similar service.

A problem common to all the above issues is that the privatisation measures put in place by the Conservatives failed to put in place any one body capable of, or empowered to, provide long-term strategic guidance for the benefit of the rail industry as a whole. Without such a body, it is difficult for the industry to take an objective view of its priorities and plan for the future as a coherent whole. This state of affairs has been recognised by the new Labour government in its 1998

White Paper, *A New Deal for Transport: Better for Everyone.* The White Paper proposes a Strategic Rail Authority, currently operating in shadow form, to provide the long-term guidance which is currently lacking and, with specific reference to the freight sector, notes:

> *Through a new Strategic Rail Authority, we will bring vision to the privatised railway and we will ensure that it meets the needs of passengers and the freight customers it serves . . . The Strategic Rail Authority will ensure that freight is given proper consideration in the operation and planning of the network; and to the obstacles to growth . . . which include loading gauge, track-capacity constraints and access to additional land . . . It will support integrated transport initiatives and provide for the first time a clear focus for the promotion of rail freight . . . Local Authorities, in preparing development plans, will be expected to consider, and where appropriate protect, opportunities for rail connections to existing manufacturing, distribution and warehousing sites adjacent or close to the rail network and allocate sites for suitable new developments which can be served by rail.*[21]

The creation of an SRA is perhaps more important now than ever for rail freight. The departure of Ed Burkhardt as Chief Executive and Chairman of the EWS Board in July 1999 sent shock waves through the industry. A majority of Wisconsin Central board members appeared unhappy with Burkhardt's "speculate to accumulate" investment strategy because it appeared to be damaging the short-term share price. The company has also encountered an unexpected drop in business recently. Freightliner, too, is having difficulties as it has failed, despite efficiency improvements and growth, to achieve a sustainable business without a continuation of the track-access grant assistance which was agreed at privatisation. The prospects for international rail freight are even more problematic. The quality of service provided by trains between the UK and the rest of Europe via the Channel Tunnel is very poor and volumes are only half the levels envisaged prior to the opening of the Tunnel and on a number of routes are declining. Despite a number of vigorous initiatives by the European Commission including the Trans European Rail Freight Freeway (TERFF) concept and other liberalisation measures no breakthrough has yet been made. It is too early to say whether these are temporary hiccups or portents of more serious long-term decline, but it is likely that strategic issues facing freight operators – such as those outlined above – have played a part. What is clear is that the prospects for long-term growth in the freight sector will be severely constrained unless the SRA is able to break the current mould.

Conclusion

Rail freight had languished both in absolute terms and relative to road haulage for four decades before its privatisation in the mid-1990s. While many in the rail freight industry, including the RFG, viewed privatisation as the only way to reverse this trend, the government was less optimistic, hoping that the policy would at best arrest the decline in rail freight traffic rather than stimulate significant growth. Privatisation clearly has delivered growth and in this sense the policy must be viewed as a success. Equally, however, the rail freight industry is now in real danger of becoming a victim of its own success and for this the architects of privatisation must accept at least some responsibility as rail freight policy was rather ill-thought-out in places. In one respect, this was almost inevitable because officials and consultants were operating to very tight timescales as a result of the government's inability to decide upon the structure of privatisation until after the 1992 general election (see Chapter 1). But matters were compounded because the freight sector was of relatively limited importance to ministers whose political priorities lay in making privatisation work for the passenger railway.

Various mistakes were made; a notable example is the Trainload Freight debacle, although industry lobbyists supported ministers' attempts to promote competition within the industry. The RFG still believes market liberalisation is important. Of more significance from the freight operators' perspective was the Conservatives' failure to put in place a body to form a strategic, long-term view of the rail industry as a whole and take decisions on that basis. The substantial post-privatisation growth is in danger of being unsustainable for a whole range of reasons. Some of these, especially issues of track capacity, affect passenger as well as freight operators but it does seem that the passenger railway remains a higher priority for key decision makers in Railtrack, the Office of the Rail Regulator and elsewhere.

Some solutions can and must come from within the rail industry itself. It may be possible, for example, for Railtrack to increase capacity by rescheduling some maintenance work to free up track through the night and at weekends. All parties have an obligation to reduce remaining inefficiencies and further raise performance standards. Yet a significant responsibility for the development of the rail industry as a whole still lies with the government. Enhanced rail freight grants are a welcome result of privatisation and a sign that Conservative ministers were aware of the environmental arguments underpinning modal shift in freight transport. But the urgent need now is for strategic guidance and the present Labour administration's proposed SRA is an important development indeed. The SRA must consider the role of freight in the context of the rail industry as a whole and in turn liaise with government to establish the role of rail as a part of ministers' wider transport, environmental, social and economic agendas. Speaking with the benefit of hindsight, Freeman now suggests:

> *We never said it would bring full benefits in the short run. In the long run it will work out, there are good signs that it will. So I think everyone has suspended judgement ... they have simply said "OK, we have now got a 1993 Railways Act, let's revisit it in 2003 and see what has happened."*

In 1999 we stand part way through the process of change with some way yet to go.

Notes

1. In one celebrated case, taken up by the Rail Freight Group on behalf of a member, BR claimed – and the Department of Transport believed – that a flow of steel amounting to close to 100,000 tonnes per year from an east-coast port to a Midlands terminal and generating gross revenue of the order of £250,000, was actually cash negative – i.e. it did not even cover its direct avoidable costs. The traffic was lost to rail although has recently been won back.
2. Burkhardt's letter is contained in the Rail Freight Group archive, along with letters to/from Julia Clarke, Roger Freeman, Malcolm Rifkind and Bob Reid mentioned in this chapter.
3. Wadsworth, B. "British railways case study" in R. Kopicki and L. Thompson (eds), *Best Methods of Railway Restructuring and Privatisation*, World Bank.
4. Ibid.
5. Cmnd 2012. *New Opportunities for the Railways*, 1992.
6. Rail Freight Group. *Policy Statement on Open Access*, RFG, 1992.
7. Gibb, R., Lowndes, T. and Charlton, C. "The privatisation of British Rail" in *Applied Geography* **16**, 1996.
8. The Group contended that road hauliers should be made to pay their *true* costs which take account of environmental and safety considerations.
9. House of Commons. *Railways Bill 1993*, HMSO, 1993.
10. House of Commons. *Railways Act 1993*, HMSO, 1993.
11. *Hansard*, **218**, Cols 156–255, 2 February 1993.
12. Lorries carrying goods in containers or swapbodies, to and from railheads only, would be allowed to operate at up to 44 tonnes gross weight on six axles provided they are specially equipped with road-friendly suspension and axle layout. The latter ensures lorries are no more damaging to roads than 38-tonners on five axles.
13. *Hansard*, op. cit.
14. Department of Transport. *Rail Freight Privatisation: The Government's Proposals*, DoT, 1993.
15. *Newsline*. "Transrail 'invades' territory" March 1995.
16. Quoted in Cumbers, A. and Farrington, J. "Keeping privatisation on track: the active state, the unwilling investor and the case of rail freight in the UK", *Area*, Forthcoming.
17. Ibid.
18. Ibid.
19. *Rail Privatisation News*, 13 June 1996.
20. *Financial Times*, 18 January 1995.
21. Cmnd 3950. *A New Deal for Transport: Better for Everyone*, The Stationery Office.

9. The Role of the Rail Regulator

John Swift

The decision to establish a system of regulation specific to the railway industry was taken for the principal reason that the government was worried about "market failure"; that is to say, that the commercial interests of the privatised companies, even when paid by the state to provide socially necessary services, would not coincide with the public interest and, in particular, would not deliver all of the network benefits (such as through-ticketing and railcards – see Chapter 1) perceived to flow from the single, vertically integrated enterprise of British Rail (BR). In order to sell privatisation of the railways to a generally sceptical, even downright hostile, public, political guarantees had to be made which would be delivered by the new companies under "regulation": for instance, it was decided that the level and quality of train services should be maintained after privatisation regardless of whether they were profitable or loss-making.

Interactions within the "new" fragmented industry would also need policing, especially where the monopolist Railtrack was involved. A clear distinction was therefore drawn between BR's successor companies and some of the previously privatised firms such as British Airways and British Steel. Despite occupying significant positions within their respective parts of the economy, the government was satisfied that their activities could be appropriately controlled by a mixture of competition and the existing regulatory authorities. The railways were instead categorised with the privatised utilities – telecommunications, gas, electricity and water – as requiring their own regulatory arrangements.

Uniquely, there were to be two bodies responsible for the exercise of regulatory functions in the new railway. The Office of Passenger Rail Franchising (OPRAF) has been discussed in detail in Chapters 6 and 7. This chapter examines the role of the Rail Regulator. It reviews the main considerations which influenced the creation of the Office of the Rail Regulator (ORR) and its functions within a system of "dual" regulation. It is not intended that what follows should provide an exhaustive account of the policies adopted and administered by the ORR (some of these, such as the approval of the West Coast Main Line upgrade, have already been discussed elsewhere in the book). Rather, the chapter provides a broad overview of the context in which the Office took its decisions and presents three main case studies – the policies used to review Railtrack's access charges, to ensure consumer protection, and to restrict "on rail" competition between train operators – to give an indication of how the ORR worked in practice. The chapter concludes by outlining some key policy lessons which have been learnt as a result of establishing the ORR.

Dual Regulation

The traditional role of a utility regulator is to ensure that prices paid by dependent users of a utility are fair and reasonable, whilst being set at levels that provide substantial incentives for the utility to invest and improve its efficiency. A central plank of utility regulation is that the regulator is independent from the government in order to ensure that the regulated industries are not subject to ministerial interference – usually undertaken for political, rather than industrial, gain – as they would be in the public sector. The government was keen to extend these principles to the rail industry, but there were complicating factors in that the railway industry lost money – around £1 billion per year – and that the shortfall was covered by state subsidy. This very much influenced the thinking of ministers and officials as they developed a policy of rail regulation.

The nub of the problem was that it would not be possible to have a regulator handing out government subsidy on the one hand and acting as an independent arbitrator within the industry on the other. Wherever the train operators were receiving state support, controls over how that money was spent would have to remain in ministers' hands – the government clearly has a right to ensure that it is receiving good value in respect of monies it spends – so any such "Regulator" would have to allocate and administer franchise contracts in accordance with government policy. But he would also, for example, need to make sure that track-access agreements between the Train Operating Companies (TOCs) and Railtrack were fair and this function would bring him into tension with the government because it would affect the level of subsidy being paid at any given time. If Railtrack were unable to fund network enhancement because track-access charges were too low, the Regulator might decide that, in the interests of consumers who want a better railway, they should go up. Such an increase would have to be passed on to the government because TOCs' existing subsidies and revenues would be insufficient to cover the new levy. This might be against the interest of ministers preoccupied with minimising the subsidy bill and, accordingly, they would exert pressure on the Regulator to leave the charges alone and instead seek additional efficiency gains from Railtrack. A sole Regulator would simply not be independent if one of his primary functions was to protect the interests of the government.

Chapter 1 established that, when the White Paper *New Opportunities for the Railways* was published in July 1992, the government had only a basic framework within which the new industry would function. There was minimal detail beyond this in almost all areas of rail policy and regulation was no exception. In fairness, the concept of "dual regulation" – a system whereby not one but two regulators would have theoretically complementary powers to police different aspects of the rail industry – was outlined in the White Paper, although this had been decided in the short time between the 1992 general election and the publication of *New Opportunities for the Railways* and there was very little understanding of how the system would work in practice. As one observer put it:

> *It's extraordinary if you put the manifesto alongside the White Paper, which comes out three months later. At the time of the manifesto they hadn't even thought of the Franchising Director, but he's there three months later because they suddenly realised, "hang on a second, we've got this competition model and we've got subsidy. Who's going to hand out the subsidy? God, it's going to be the same person who's going to do competition and sort out the charges; we'd better have another one." They were inventing dimensions almost every week.*

The White Paper pointed out that while one of the regulators would be independent, the other, who would head up a "Franchising Authority", would act on behalf of ministers to oversee the allocation of subsidy. Crucially, the Franchising Authority would regulate by contract – a train operator would be required to fulfil certain obligations in respect of the subsidy it received – whereas independent regulation would be by licence. TOCs would need an Operating Licence, and Railtrack a Network Licence, in order to trade in the privatised railway (Station and Depot licences were also issued to relevant users of these facilities).

The two regulatory bodies were, of course, named the Office of Passenger Rail Franchising and the Office of the Rail Regulator, with the latter being the independent entity. The first Franchising Director was Roger Salmon (see Chapter 6) and I became the first Rail Regulator. Both Salmon and I were appointed in January 1993 although, because the Railways Bill had not yet received Royal Assent, we could act only as "special advisers" to the Secretary of State. Neither of us was appointed in our official capacities until after the Bill became law. The "Franchising Director designate" and the "Regulator designate" were given newly refurbished offices facing each other and we were very aware, as were industry observers and press commentators, that the task facing us was enormous. The concept of dual regulation – never mind the potential difficulties in sorting out how it would work – was proving difficult for the press to comprehend; references to John Salmon and Roger Swift were not unheard of and were rarely corrected throughout 1993.

New Opportunities for the Railways had envisaged the Rail Regulator as a "champion of the consumer". The White Paper suggested that not only would he ensure fair play between industry actors but he would also control fares and demand high quality of service in areas where TOCs "enjoyed monopoly power." The Regulator would also "have a role in ensuring that network benefits are maintained," seek to promote competition and prevent anti-competitive practices. These last functions were at the time seen as particularly important by the government given that a key argument for the track-authority model of privatisation it had adopted was that it would liberalise the rail service market.

The notion of the Regulator being the consumer's champion seemed sensible. After all, it was consistent with the role of the independent utility regulators which had been carved out in the 1980s and early 1990s. The Office of Telecommunications, for example, would oblige British Telecom (BT), as the de facto monopoly provider of telecommunications services, to keep its prices below a certain level. The company's licence also contained conditions requiring it to serve customers indiscriminately, to protect the well-being of its workers and to fulfil certain environmental responsibilities where appropriate. The gas, water and electricity regulators all performed similar roles, although the obligations imposed upon the industries tended to become more onerous as the government gained experience of how to regulate privatised monopolies.[1]

Throughout 1993 I attended frequent meetings with Salmon, ministers and officials with the aim of establishing the basic regulatory ground rules. I was particularly keen that, as the White Paper had proposed, the ORR should have jurisdiction over basic consumer-protection measures. The logic underpinning my position was that if, once the regulatory matrix had been established, it appeared the Regulator had no control over fares, punctuality, reliability, overcrowding and all the other aspects of railway performance which passengers regard as critical, then the credibility of the whole rail-privatisation exercise – and certainly that of the independent Regulator – would be damaged; the sale would be seen as achieving little more than formalising by contract the government's existing control over BR.

It was quickly evident, however, that ministers were having second thoughts. This was for two main reasons. First, the government was keen to avoid over-complicating the regulatory system. As mentioned above, ministers were entitled to demand certain levels of service quality in respect of the subsidy they were paying the train operators and these would be enshrined in the contracts between the TOCs and OPRAF. If the ORR were then to have additional consumer-protection measures, set out as licence conditions, there would be potential confusion regarding the responsibility of each regulator. But this argument holds only if the split between the two regulators is messy and there was no reason why that should have been the case. It would have been straightforward to determine a relatively comprehensive suite of measures – e.g. fares, service quality (including punctuality and reliability) and network benefits – to be administered by the ORR, with only the *amount* of services and, perhaps, investment commitments being negotiated by the Franchising Director.

The second, and more than likely decisive, reason for ministers' change of heart was that making the Regulator solely responsible for ensuring consumer protection would have substantially increased the "regulatory risk" faced by private-sector train operators. Unlike other privatisations, which had been generally popular and conducted in a relatively relaxed timescale, the sale of BR was surrounded by uncertainty and subject to intense public and media criticism (see Chapter 6). With potential bidders already assumed to be suspicious about rail privatisation, ministers simply did not want to create further obstacles for themselves.

A compromise position, whereby the regulators would have operated with some form of shared jurisdiction was opposed by ministers on the grounds that this could have propagated a situation of "dual jeopardy" for TOCs, in which I might have intervened on an issue to require different rules or standards to those regarded as acceptable by the Franchising Director. It was, in fairness, crucial that Salmon and I were not seen to be engaging in "turf wars", although that would have been unlikely as we had quickly established a good working relationship (see Chapter 6).

The outcome was that OPRAF was given most of the consumer-protection duties, whereas the principal jobs of the ORR would be: to issue, modify and enforce licences for Railtrack and the train, station and light-maintenance depot operators – the so-called facility owners; to regulate the infrastructure owner, Railtrack; and to oversee the relationships between Railtrack and its customers, that is, the TOCs, open access and freight operators, who would be bound to each other by contracts agreed by them and approved by the Regulator. This third aspect of the powers – the arbitral role – is essential to an understanding of the purposes of the privatisation programme. The idea was that commercial operators should make the kind of agreements they wanted and change them when they wanted subject only to the overall *supervision* of the Regulator. This arrangement, which carried with it the risk that commercial operators would not press Railtrack as hard as they might, in order to get a deal they could live with, was to sit uneasily with the Labour administration, elected in 1997, which had a much greater preference for direct controls over a railway which was in receipt of substantial state funding.

Whilst exercising my powers, I was also bound by a number of duties – which are outlined in more detail in Chapter 2 – designed to ensure that I promoted the use of the railway network, encouraged competition and efficiency and enabled railway businesses to plan their future with a reasonable degree of security. Despite the concern of ministers outlined above, the ORR was given *some* jurisdiction over consumer-protection issues, such as the preservation of network benefits, protecting the rights of disabled people and facilitating the activities of the Rail Users' Consultative Committees (RUCCs). Table 6.1 shows the jurisdiction of the Rail Regulator and the Franchising Director regarding consumer protection and Table 9.1 summarises the functions and duties of the Rail Regulator.

The division of functions between Franchising Director and Regulator tended to disguise the critically important role of the government in the new railway: the Franchising Director could only act in accordance with Objectives, Instructions and Guidance from the Secretary of State which left ministers in the driving seat so far as policy, finance and railway development were concerned. I was therefore determined to exercise fully my remaining powers of consumer protection; to my mind the economic regulation of the railways, and the control of monopoly, still had as its primary justification the more efficient use of resources for the benefit of the public. I was aware that in so doing I might tread on the toes of the Franchising Director (the division of jurisdiction between the two regulators was rather blurred in places – see Chapter 6) but that was, in my view, a necessary risk. My stance was bound to give rise to concern among those who considered that independent regulation and the pursuit of the public interest had no place in a state-subsidised railway.

> **Table 9.1** Functions and duties of the Rail Regulator. Source: Office of the Rail Regulator. *Regulating the Railway in the Public Interest: Annual Report 1996/97,* ORR, 1997. Reproduced with permission from the Office of the Rail Regulator.
>
> The main areas of the Regulator's statutory functions are:
>
> − the issue, modification and enforcement of licences to operate trains, networks, stations and light-maintenance depots;
> − the approval of agreements for access by operators of railway assets to track, stations and light-maintenance depots;
> − the enforcement of domestic competition law;
> − consumer protection.
>
> The Regulator has duties under Section 4 of the Railways Act 1993 which include:
>
> − the protection of the interests of users of railway services, including disabled people;
> − the promotion of the use and development of the national railway network for freight and passengers;
> − the promotion of competition;
> − through-ticketing;
> − minimisation of regulatory burden;
> − commercial certainty and security;
> − the protection of persons from dangers arising from operation of railways, with the advice of the HSE;
> − the environmental effect of railway services;
> − certain statutory guidance from the Secretary of State for Transport;
> − the financial position of the Franchising Director and holders of network licences (including Railtrack).

Creating the Office of the Rail Regulator

The business of putting the ORR together started in January 1993. Supporting me at that time was a small team which included a handful of civil servants and a secretary. It was clearly important, given the size of the task in hand, to strengthen this team but no staff could be taken on officially until the Railways Bill had become law. The first recruits were secondees from BR. I said to the officials, "how do I build up my team? I have no railway background." We obtained a list of BR employees who had shown some interest in joining either the Rail Regulator's office or the Franchising Director's office or both. I then asked the officials for their views on the quality of these people, they marked them on a list and Roger Salmon and I carried out a series of interviews. Chris Stokes went to OPRAF to become Salmon's Deputy whereas Charles Brown and John Rhodes came to the incipient ORR. Brown, Rhodes and I worked closely together to thrash out a basic policy framework throughout 1993, although our role was very much advisory until the Bill became law. Ministers made it very clear that they would rely first and foremost on advice from civil servants at this early stage and so it was crucial that we forged a constructive working relationship with Sir Patrick Brown, the Permanent Secretary at the Department of Transport (DoT), and other key players such as Nick Montagu and Philip Wood if policy making was to progress smoothly.

Later in the process the Office was expanded considerably. We, like OPRAF, were keen to establish a competent team in order to work through policy questions and provide checks and balances for our decision-making processes. Three directorates were established – Personnel, Finance and Administration; Network Regulation (to be responsible for the approval of track-access agreements); and Passenger Services Regulation (to be responsible for licensing, promoting competition and protecting passengers) – and a group of specialists was brought in. Chris Bolt became Chief Economic Adviser (and was later to become Acting Rail Regulator after the expiry of my contract in 1998); Tom Winsor, seconded from Denton Hall, was the first full-time legal adviser, in place for 2 years from July 1993 (he is the current Regulator); and a Technical Advisory Services unit was also established. Finally, three consultants, including the distinguished transport economist Professor Stephen Glaister, were seconded to the ORR's Committee in a non-executive capacity.

Although, as Chapter 6 explains, OPRAF was frequently at loggerheads with officials, the ORR got on well with the DoT. For the most part, this was because both parties appreciated from the outset that the key objective was to ensure the speedy privatisation of the railways and recognised, accordingly, that creating unnecessary obstacles may preclude this. That is not to say, however, that I did not intervene in proceedings where I felt the public interest was being compromised, such as in the review of Railtrack's access charges described below. Key to establishing this relationship was an early undertaking on the part of the DoT to accept and respect the Office's independence.

Independent Regulation

Although the concept of independent regulation had been outlined in the White Paper, it was important to make clear to everybody concerned with rail privatisation – not only within government but also potential investors – precisely what it would mean in practice. We have already seen that one reason underlying ministers' decision to place responsibility for consumer protection in OPRAF's hands was to reduce the potential for regulatory risk. There were also the statutory duties to consider. I was anxious to ensure that the ORR's remaining jurisdiction would not be compromised or further eroded as the regulatory "matrix" developed. This view was shared by others in the process:

Throughout 1993 the government started to get very windy about the whole concept of independent regulation of the railways. It wasn't just the fact there was subsidy, there was also the fact that if they gave all these powers to the Regulator and he actually used them to frustrate the whole object of the exercise [it could] render privatisation so difficult it wouldn't take place ... I sensed these concerns, that [the ORR] were welcome as a concept of independent regulation but that they might use their independent powers to frustrate the objective.

A real danger for the ORR was that, even though the concept of an independent regulator had been included in the Railways Bill, the Secretary of State would retain the right to determine which sections of the legislation would come into effect and when. There was the possibility that, having established the post of Regulator and used my advice during 1993, the government would postpone the exercise of the ORR's powers over access charges and licence enforcement until some or all of the railway had been privatised. Such a move was a distinct possibility and could have been justified on the grounds that it was following the precedents of other utility sell-offs where the regulators only took "possession" of the industries once they had been privatised on terms set by the government.[2] In the event, ministers backed away from this option because, at least in my view, it would have been a U-turn too far, showing a complete lack of confidence in the new institutional structure which they had defended and justified for the whole of the Parliamentary year. They did impose, however, through a "General Authority", restrictions on the obligations which I could include in licences to train operators. The General Authority forbade the ORR to impose on TOCs certain consumer-protection measures such as those which had been transferred to OPRAF and effectively gave the operators legal protection against dual jeopardy in those reserved areas.

Ministers were also keen to subject the Office to certain principles designed to "guide" its policy decisions. Although these were not included in the Bill (they had not been formally worded in time), it was clear that the general thrust would be that I should exercise my functions so as to facilitate the early privatisation of the railway industry. The guidance would apply only until 1 January 1996 – just long enough to ensure that most major policy decisions would have been taken by the time it ran out. I was quite ready to agree to time-limited guidance but only on the understanding that I would be required to "take account of", as opposed to "act in accordance with", the wishes of the Secretary of State. The semantics are critically important – by committing only to take account of any guidance, I was ensuring the ORR's independence by giving no guarantee that I would follow it.

Perhaps surprisingly, given ministers' "windy" approach to independent regulation, the government agreed to my demands. In 1994 senior officials offered me the chance to see a draft version of the guidance, but I declined on the grounds that it was their guidance to me, not mine to them; although the wording turned out to be very prescriptive (see Table 9.2), I knew that I would only have to "take account of" the government's views in my decision-making processes even if the end result was at variance with that suggested in the guidance. I should add that the government and civil servants were scrupulous in their observance of the "independence" line.

In September 1993, when it began to look likely that the Railways Bill would receive Royal Assent, the ORR moved away from Whitehall. The shift away from the government machine was a further, if largely symbolic, expression of the

Table 9.2 The Regulator's guidance. Source: Office of the Rail Regulator. *Annual Report 1994–95*, ORR, 1995. Reproduced with permission from the Office of the Rail Regulator.

- The Regulator should exercise his functions so as to facilitate the privatisation of railway services;
- the Regulator should facilitate the objective of franchising passenger services as soon as reasonably practicable;
- the Regulator should discuss with the Franchising Director proposals put forward by him for the moderation of competition. He should also discuss with Railtrack, and consult the Franchising Director on, proposals put to him by Railtrack relating to access contracts negotiated with open-access operators. He should, so far as he considers consistent with his other duties, exercise his powers relating to access agreements in accordance with such proposals;
- the terms of any access agreements required or approved by the Regulator should be based on the agreed templates. The Regulator should adopt the principles of the access charging structure established for 1994–95. Payments under access agreements should be sufficient for Railtrack to recover its reasonable costs and to meet its rate of return under the Government's financing regime;
- the Regulator should not require or approve any access agreements which may prejudice or significantly interfere with the franchising programme. Before approving access agreements for an open-access operator, the Regulator should consult the Franchising Director and have regard to representations he makes as to the likely effect of the grant of such access on his franchising programme;
- The Regulator should not require or approve any access agreements relating to British Rail's freight-only depots in such a way as to prevent the transfer of those depots to the private sector or closure where there is insufficient market demand;
- the Regulator should exercise his functions in a way that does not prejudice or significantly interfere with Railtrack's achievement of its financial regime or any financial controls or targets set by the Government; and
- in granting licences, the Regulator should only depart from the models annexed to the Guidance where to do so would help him to conform to other parts of the

ORR's independence, and it moved into Waterhouse Square in High Holborn. A 25-year lease was secured at under £14 per foot which well satisfied the government's rules on value for money. Policy making now began in earnest.

Policy Making

The first "stage" of policy making was between November 1993 and 31 March 1994. At this time not only were the railways within the public sector, they were also still vertically integrated as the Railways Act would not effect the split intended for privatisation until 1 April 1994. Ministers did not allow the Office to exercise any powers until the reorganisation had taken place and it effectively acted as a consultee to the government in respect of the licences to be issued and the rest of the regulatory matrix, which included the vast and complex set of interlocking agreements known as the "access agreements" – for track, station and light-maintenance depots. The Office was also consulted in respect of the government's plans to transfer BR's freight interests to the private sector.

My principal concern throughout this period was to ensure that the structure and content of the regulatory matrix would establish public-interest criteria against which the new companies' commercial aspirations should be set. Within the licences we ensured that operators in dominant positions could not abuse them – well in advance of similar provisions in the Competition Act 1998, which took effect in March 2000. Within the Access Conditions we ensured that changes to contracts we had approved had to meet the statutory objectives of the Act, in effect the public-interest criteria such as improvement of the railway to the benefit of passengers and users.

The government was keen to exercise its discretion and its judgement in determining the broad structure of the licences as it wanted to be clear that the "ground rules" it had established through the statutory duties and the division of regulatory responsibility were adhered to. Ministers were aware, however, that I would assume jurisdiction over the licences in 1994 and they were careful to act in consultation with the ORR as they did not want to instigate a situation where I would seek to overturn the system when I became empowered to monitor and enforce it.

There were lively but constructive debates between the Office and officials regarding the substance of the licence conditions, including the powers of the Regulator to call for information from the licensees. The ORR had wanted all information required for the exercise of the Regulator's functions to monitor and enforce licences but BR and the nascent Railtrack were wary of regulatory interference in what they and the government wanted to be, and to be seen to be, liberalised and competitive markets. In the event compromise was reached on most issues when the line was finally drawn on 1 April 1994.

Disagreements of substance as to what should be within the regulatory matrix became known in the Office as "flagpole" issues. The government and the Franchising Director would remind me of the urgent need to privatise by "raising their flags": "if you insist on that condition or this obligation we cannot sell the franchises, or Railtrack or the freight companies." The flags became somewhat tattered as they were hoisted many times, but it was made clear by me that *objective* justification and not a *subjective* "feel" should be presented to satisfy me that some favoured policy option would really halt proceedings. The aim of insisting on objective justification was not to be awkward; rather it was to encourage careful analysis, within the time available, and prevent corner cutting.

When the ORR assumed its powers, it set about satisfying itself that matters were proceeding according to plan. No changes of substance were needed to the licences to be granted by the Office after 1 April 1994 because of the Office's active involvement in establishing their character during 1993 and early 1994. It was very quickly established, however, that the regulation of Railtrack through its relationship with train operators would be prime policy concerns. Railtrack was to be the only true natural monopoly in the new railway industry. TOCs and freight operators would be rivalled by other transport modes even in areas where there was no on-rail competition; Roscos, maintenance and "central" group companies would, over time at least, be forced to compete for contracts; but there was only one infrastructure provider. Train operators could not buy track access from anyone else, so it was crucial to ensure that the price they paid for, and the terms and conditions upon which they were granted, that access were fair and met their reasonable requirements.

The Review of Railtrack's Track-Access Charges

As Chapter 3 explains, a track-access charging regime had been put in place before April 1994 by the Charging Implementation Group. Although a considerable amount of work had gone into developing the charging regime, the Office suspected that the system as proposed would be far too lenient towards Railtrack. It believed that the regime would provide virtually no incentive for Railtrack to improve its efficiency and that the company would quickly find itself in a position to abuse its monopoly. I therefore concluded, after lengthy consultation with Railtrack, BR, OPRAF, the DoT and other interested parties, that, while there was little that could practically be achieved with the *structure* of the charges, their *level* was too high and could practically be reduced.

I announced that the charges were to be reduced by 8 per cent in 1995–96 and then by a further 2 per cent in real terms in each of the 5 subsequent years.[3] The reason for imposing a 6-year regime was to afford Railtrack a degree of certainty in planning its future activities. This was exactly in line with one of my statutory duties and was regarded by the industry as essential to break away from the short-term financial regimes traditionally set by the government. Although a shorter period would have allowed an earlier review if it had been found that the reductions were insufficient, I decided that this would have introduced an unacceptably high element of regulatory risk to the company. The changes as they stood would in any case save the train operators (and thus the government through reduced subsidy) an estimated £1.5 billion.

A senior member of the ORR team who was heavily involved with the access-charge review explains that initially the government did not want the Office to change the regime which had already been created:

> *There had been a great debate in 1993–94 about what should be the basis of Railtrack's charges. It had been decided that all the emerging units in the privatised railway should be profitable in their own right [although the TOCs would, of course, be supported by subsidy]. Back in 1994, the government was very keen that we [the ORR] should not disturb the original model. [Ministers] were also considering the use of government powers effectively to require the Regulator to set access charges for Railtrack in line with the proposals that had already been laid out.*

Ministers had become concerned that a review of the access charges might delay the privatisation process in general and/or reduce Railtrack's market value in a potential future sale (it had not yet been decided to divest Railtrack before the next general election) and were effectively "raising a flag". Nevertheless, the ORR, as a constitutionally independent body, was equally worried that the charges as they stood would severely disadvantage the train operators and therefore act against the public interest:

> We [the ORR] rebelled. It was an indication of the government getting pretty upset about what an independent regulator might do to upset the position carefully constructed by the government. Once they realised that they had given the [constitutional] powers to the Regulator, they just had to accept it.

Learning from experience gained by other utility regulators, I was keen to introduce an RPI minus x regime in respect of the passenger track-access charges. Such a scheme, first suggested by economist Stephen Littlechild, was designed to limit the amount a monopolist could raise its charges to inflation (as measured by the Retail Price Index) minus a predetermined figure.[4] The idea is that RPI minus x prevents a monopolist from abusing its position whilst at the same time giving it an incentive to increase its efficiency as it gets to keep any profits it does make within the cap. The problem for the ORR was determining an appropriate level for x, as it had to act in accordance with its statutory duty to ensure that Railtrack would not find financing its activities unduly difficult. The Office had to move quickly with very little information to get the regime in place but most commentators would agree that the regime introduced as a result of the review considerably improved that which it replaced.[5]

Railtrack insisted all along that my proposals represented a huge risk to its financial prospects and, when ministers revealed that the company was to be sold sooner rather than later, argued strongly that it simply could not be privatised if the regime were imposed as its post-privatisation profits would be imperilled. The government, now concerned that Railtrack's flotation could be delayed, agreed to resolve the dilemma by paying an access charge "supplement" to the company over a finite period. Ironically, however, the supplement had to be set by the ORR, as it was able to act as an independent arbitrator between Railtrack and ministers. This was a strange situation as no regulator had previously been put in the position of determining the amount of money the State must pay a nationalised company in order to secure its privatisation.

Deciding the level of the access-charge supplement proved to be a tortuous process. I was forced to take account of wildly conflicting views with Railtrack demanding considerable sums while the British Railways Board (BRB) — who would make the payment to Railtrack on behalf of the government — argued that the company should receive only a minimal amount as it was bound to make significant efficiency gains. The judgement of Railtrack's directors seemed to be based on little more than questionable statistical techniques and some historical experience and was extraordinarily difficult to test in practice. The sums claimed were exceptionally high and did not follow the steep downward curve which might have been expected from an efficient concern. The BRB dismissed Railtrack's position as completely unreasonable and expected that, at the very least, the access supplements must in the course of the review period fall to zero.

The consultation procedure helped determine a figure which seemed appropriate – this fell somewhere in between the demands of Railtrack and the BRB – and both parties and the DoT were informed. The BRB was of the opinion that the figure was too high, although its chairman, John Welsby, accepted my judgement. The DoT commented simply that it would accept the decision on the basis that it would take whatever steps were necessary in order to effect the speedy sale of Railtrack. I then told Railtrack's chairman, Sir Robert Horton ("Have you a pen? Have you got a piece of paper? Will you write down the following numbers?") who also, after only a brief delay, agreed, but he later sent the ORR a letter noting, in general terms, that "this is an extraordinarily difficult and challenging prospect and could well affect our prospect of privatisation. We hope you understand this." In the event, the level of the access-charge supplement did not prevent the sale of Railtrack, which took place in May 1996, although there is some evidence that its market value was affected.[6]

Following the imposition of the RPI minus x regime on Railtrack's track-access charges, it was made clear to the company that the ORR would monitor the company's investment to ensure that it was not being compromised by profit demands. In actual fact, Railtrack has invested more year on year than the Office's initial expectations (see Chapter 3), but it quickly became obvious that both the amount being invested and our original requirements were too low and both parties have had something of a stormy relationship since Railtrack's privatisation. The Office has been forced to modify Railtrack's licence and I, Bolt and Winsor – my successors in Office – have all frequently castigated the company for failing to secure necessary improvements to its network. The key policies adopted by the ORR with regard to the regulation of Railtrack are discussed in detail in Chapter 4 and some reflections on my actions in this area follow towards the end of this chapter.

Consumer Protection

As we have seen, the ORR was given relatively little jurisdiction over those consumer-protection measures such as punctuality, reliability and overcrowding which passengers identify with most closely. Nevertheless, the Office was given the responsibility for ensuring certain safeguards including the maintenance of network benefits (although their administration would be undertaken by the Association of Train Operating Companies (ATOC) – see Chapter 6), the protection of disabled passengers and the facilitation of the RUCCs. Some network benefits, such as railcards, were legally protected by the Railways Act although other consumer-protection measures would have to be enforced by regulation. Examples of these are the National Rail Enquiry Service (NRES) (again adminstered by ATOC) and the provision of accurate and impartial retailing. I wanted to ensure that high standards were attained after privatisation but, in one case, came to the opinion that they were not. The licence conditions concerning NRES specified that 90 per cent of calls should be answered within 30 seconds, but when this target was consistently missed I imposed fines and the response times improved dramatically.

The key problem was that the ORR shared its responsibility for certain network benefits – such as interavailable ticketing – with OPRAF and indeed it was the latter who developed the Compulsory Interavailability requirement designed to restrict the amount of dedicated ticketing around the network (see Chapter 6). I became increasingly frustrated that the ORR's powers in terms of the TOCs were restricted, especially since I was having to field many complaints from passengers – who were unaware of the ORR's impotence in this area – about their journey experiences. I thought that to be "passing the buck" at a time when the public was expecting rail privatisation to deliver results did little to encourage confidence in the new industry and decided that I should become more proactive in setting regulatory objectives for TOCs. In early 1997, the Office published a document, *Regulatory Objectives for Passenger Train and Station Operators*, which called upon TOCs to go "beyond the letter of [their] franchise contract or licence" to bring about improvements for the benefit of passengers.[7] The document encompassed sections on the operators' relationships with Railtrack, passengers' access to the rail network, ticket retailing services and systems, passenger-information provision, access to the railway for disabled passengers and the development of the network.

The publication of *Regulatory Objectives for Passenger Train and Station Operators* caused a considerable degree of friction between OPRAF and the ORR. Although I was attempting to approach the issue from the perspective of my own jurisdiction, there were overspills and the Franchising Director was of the view that the regulation of TOCs was primarily the responsibility of OPRAF. As I have already noted, the prospect of possible "turf wars" between the regulators would do little to bring about a better railway and John O'Brien, Salmon's replacement, and I embarked on a series of meetings aimed at using our respective powers in furtherance of similar objectives. I should, on reflection, have consulted OPRAF more *before* I published the document, although the good working relations between John O'Brien and myself assisted our search for common ground on the subject. Nevertheless, I was convinced that the message for improvement had to be communicated and that the regulatory matrix put in place at the time of privatisation should 3 years on be tested and adjusted where appropriate to facilitate and require such improvements to be paid for by the shareholders.

In terms of disabled persons, the Railways Act made important and positive contributions to improving accessibility to the railway. The ORR was placed under a duty to produce a Code of Conduct which railway operators were required to take into account when producing Disabled Persons' Protection Policies. Regular meetings were held with representatives of disabled persons and most ORR staff were given basic training in understanding their needs. A major conference in July 1998, aimed at identifying problems faced by disabled persons and potential solutions, was sponsored by the ORR and no invited speaker within government or industry declined to attend. Indeed they responded with enthusiasm. There is no doubt that major improvements have been made in response to the statutory requirements and regulatory policies in terms of facilities on trains and stations and in information systems.

The statutory consultative committees, established in 1947 to protect the interests of passengers, found their position greatly enhanced under the Railways Act but their organisation was in need of improvement. Part-time members, sponsored by a division of the Department of Trade and Industry in its consumer-protection role and assisted by secretaries who were with few exceptions employees of the BRB, could not be expected to be the most efficient and co-ordinated set of bodies at a time of radical change in the railway industry. Working closely with the Chairman of the Central Rail Users' Consultative Committee (CRUCC), the ORR instigated several changes to the existing system while respecting the statutory autonomy of the committees. Efficient IT systems were installed, new criteria for appointment of members were established, ORR presence at Committee meetings enabled us to respond more quickly to their concerns and they began to fulfil a much more effective role as guardians of the consumers' interests. Public assurances by the present government should ensure their continued presence and enable the newly constituted committees to prosper and contribute to a better railway.

Moderating Competition

One of the most significant policy decisions which fell to the ORR concerned the moderation of open-access competition. We have seen in Chapter 1 that facilitating on-rail competition was, for some within the government, the *raison d'être* of the track-authority model of rail privatisation and one means of doing this was to allow train operators, both incumbents and new entrants, to initiate new subsidy-free services between origin/destination pairs where a market for them existed. As Chapter 6 explains, however, ministers were forced to concede that their original plans for open access were flawed and a "free-for-all" would not be viable as it would destroy the financial base of many TOCs. John MacGregor announced in early 1993 that some franchisees would be granted "exclusivity" where necessary.[8]

Whilst MacGregor had accepted that the scope for open-access competition would need restricting, he had not yet worked out how it would be done. Giving evidence to the Transport Select Committee in 1993, he suggested that responsibility for ensuring exclusivity might be the remit of the Franchising Director or the Regulator and, in response to persistent questions fired by Committee member Andrew MacKinlay, he admitted that "there is still, at this stage, quite a lot of detailed information . . . to be filled out."[9] This task of "filling out" was quickly devolved to the ORR which devised the Moderation of Competition (MoC) regime to regulate open-access new entry.[10]

The decision to grant exclusivity around part or all of the network introduced an obvious tension into the Conservatives' rail-privatisation policy which John Prescott, then Labour's transport spokesman (and now Deputy Prime Minister), was quick to point out:

> If the [government's] proposals will not lead to competition in the provision of services, . . . instead of the public monopoly about which the government are so

concerned, we shall have what the Secretary of State called "exclusive service" – in other words, a private monopoly. We shall be replacing the public monopoly with a private one.[11]

I raised this point in my first meeting with senior DoT officials:

I said that, as I understood it, one of my duties was to promote competition in the supply of railway services. I addressed the question to the Permanent Secretary. He said: "Yes, that's perfectly correct." I said that, as I understood it, "you are setting up Railtrack as a monopoly and you are proposing to moderate competition in respect of the first set of franchises, so Railtrack will be supplying track-access services to the franchisees who will themselves be protected from competition." I asked: "how, in these circumstances, am I to promote competition?" There was a pause, and the Permanent Secretary said: "that is a perfectly good question, I will ask the Deputy Secretary to answer that." So the Deputy Secretary looked at the Permanent Secretary and said: "John has identified a possible tension in the development of our policies, but I will ask the Under Secretary to give the full answer." He turned to the Under Secretary, who then sought to explain that it was all really a question of time and that one might engage in a process of moderation of competition in the short term in order to develop competitive structures on a sound basis in the longer term.[12]

The decision to devolve responsibility for the policy's formulation to the ORR was logical since the independent regulator was primarily responsible for promoting competition and requiring the government to justify their possibly short-term deviation from the open-access policy. In practical terms only the Regulator could effect exclusivity by requiring Railtrack to grant it through the access contracts with the train operators. Thus the government would now have to accept that decisions about how much, and where, competition should be modified would be made independently. Provided I operated in accordance with my statutory duties, ministers would have to accept the mechanism I proposed.

There were numerous factors to take into account when policy formulation began. Key among these was the consideration that, although ministers wanted to restrict competition because of its potential to harm the franchising process, there were instances where it might prove beneficial. After all, certain TOCs would enjoy not only a rail monopoly but also a modal monopoly – it is simply not the case, for example, that many London commuters can travel to work by alternative means – and should not the patrons of these franchisees enjoy a choice?

A consultation document, soliciting views from interested parties, was published in mid-1994 stressing the need for the policy both to moderate open-access competition in the short term – to facilitate franchising – and to permit its development in the longer term should this become necessary or desirable. The paper suggested four policy options, three of which, "negotiated charges", "equalised access charges" and "access deficit charges" were financial mechanisms based upon different means of charging operators for access to the rail network. These methods were ultimately regarded as unsuitable by both the ORR and the majority of those who responded to the consultation exercise either (a) because they were not capable of moderating competition at all, or (b) because they created barriers to entry, some artificial, which would have been difficult to remove in the future. The fourth option, "Controlled Competition in Contestable Markets" – which became known as Moderation of Competition – was predominantly administrative in nature and was perceived as being the most likely to achieve the ORR's stated policy goals.

MoC operates in stages. Stage 1 accorded TOCs effective exclusivity until 1999, whilst Stage 2 – which is currently in operation – imposes fewer restrictions on competitive new entry and runs until at least 2002. A further relaxation of restrictions is possible after 2002. In essence, MoC works by defining TOCs' markets as a series of point-to-point "flows" and then by protecting those flows nominated by the TOCs from open-access entry.[14] Point-to-point flows comprise services operated by a TOC between any two points on its network. For example, a First Great Western service between London and Plymouth will serve a number of flows – Plymouth to Exeter St David's, Exeter St David's to Taunton, Taunton to London Paddington and so on – not just Plymouth to London Paddington. The ORR protects nominated flows by controlling Railtrack's ability to sell access rights to other operators. Under Stage 1, all nominated flows received full protection, whereas Stage 2 allows competition for up to 20 per cent of an incumbent's revenue on any given flow. After 2002, the incumbent Regulator may relax this ceiling to 50 per cent.

The regime has, to date, been largely successful in terms of its aims. It provided almost total protection for incumbents during Stage 1 and gave bidders sufficient confidence that their revenues would not be plundered by a "cherry-picker" as soon as the ink on the franchise contract was dry. It also allowed some service innovation, as it it did not prevent the introduction of new services where none existed previously. Central Trains' services into Manchester and Stansted airports are examples.

The decision to impose this relatively strict regime until 1999 was, in common with all my other activities, made entirely independently of the government. At no time were there any express or implied threats from the government regarding the characteristics of the competition policy they wanted to see. I insisted that the Franchising Director would have to provide objective justification wherever he deemed that protection from competition was necessary to enable franchising to go ahead; it was not sufficient for him to argue, on a subjective basis, that "I don't believe I can sell the franchises unless I have exclusivity." Objective justification was forthcoming in a study undertaken by Mercer Management Consulting Limited. The study showed that, although open access would produce some short-term benefits for passengers, it would be wholly outweighed by the cost to the taxpayer. Subsidy levels, the report contended, would need to be very high – far higher than the government was willing to pay – in order to offset the risk potential franchisees would face from un-fettered open-access competition. It is probably true to say that ministers would have been happy if I had ruled out competition altogether, but an official at the

DoT admits that he and his colleagues were "very relieved with what the Regulator came up with."

The decision to move into Stage 2 was taken after further consultation with the industry. Some TOCs were clear that there was no need for Stage 1 to be relaxed on the grounds that on-rail competition was simply a distraction and would undermine operators' efforts to attract motorists out of their cars and on to the railways:

> *Of course, on-rail competition misses the real point, which is that rail has a pathetically small market share in most markets … The idea of competition between rail companies is a bit of a distraction if you're trying to encourage more people to use trains generally. It potentially dissipates the effort if the rail operators are competing against themselves when they should be competing against other forms of transport.*

My own view, which was influenced by the consultation procedure, was that many TOCs were being unnecessarily constrained from developing new services by MoC Stage 1 and that the introduction of an element of competition would be a shot in the arm for the rail industry. Some price competition, such as that between WAGN and GNER between Peterborough and London (see Chapter 7), had been a virtually unqualified success and it was hoped that this may be extended around the network.[15] A few operators had publicly announced plans to introduce new services if the rules were relaxed (more had done so privately).

The problem, however, was to decide how much competition to allow. An overly liberal regime might have bankrupted some incumbents, whereas an overly strict one would have continued to stifle innovation. In the event, there was very little relevant experience on which the ORR could draw and the 20 per cent figure was chosen not as the result of any mechanistic economic analysis; it was a qualitative judgement of what would be fair. Put simply, 10 per cent seemed too low and 30 per cent too high. The simple, and I believe correct, message to the TOCs is the obligation to improve the quantity and quality of service through greater innovation and greater intensity of use – including, where appropriate, new agreements with Railtrack – and not to assume some superior right of service provision which denies other and more innovative operators the right to challenge and compete.

Under MoC Stage 2, the ORR reserves the right to overrule applications from TOCs to introduce new services if it feels they will act against the public interest (perhaps by producing a "bunched" rather than an even-interval timetable) or if they are overtly abstractive (i.e. they are designed principally to plunder another operator's revenues rather than to grow the market overall). Some new services have already been approved, such as Northern Spirit's services to Glasgow, and it remains to be seen how quickly open-access competition will develop around the network before 2002. What is clear, however, is that the system in place, developed through consultation to promote flexibility and accountability, should enable the current Regulator to ensure the outcome is in the best interests of the public.

Some Points for Discussion

This chapter has outlined the role of the Rail Regulator and presented an overview of the context in which the ORR took its policy decisions. There are several points implicit in the discussion which are worth raising in conclusion. The first of these is the importance of independent regulation. The concept of independent regulation is well established in the British privatisation programme, although the sale of BR provided fresh challenges to ministers. Not only did the railways lose money, but the Regulator assumed authority over a newly fragmented industry when it was still wholly in the public sector. Although an independent regulator in these circumstances might have introduced a considerable regulatory risk for potential investors, it was in my view essential that the ORR was able to act without the interference of ministers in order to produce a workable contractual and regulatory matrix which would promote, and would be seen to promote, the public interest. I did not see it as my job to unnecessarily frustrate the key objective of the Railways Act – i.e. to privatise BR – but instead to ensure that this was done in a manner consistent with my statutory duties set out in the Act. On occasion, such as the review of Railtrack's access charges, I was of the opinion that the government's own actions ran contrary to those duties and remedial steps were taken accordingly.

A second point to make concerns the "split" of jurisdiction between the two regulatory bodies, the ORR and OPRAF. Despite my having pressed for the role of "consumers' champion" – as fulfilled by other independent utility regulators – responsibility for many basic consumer-protection measures (punctuality, reliability and so on) were allocated to the Franchising Director to be regulated under contract. The split was messy and led to confusion among customers regarding which regulatory body their concerns should be addressed to. My attempt to set regulatory objectives for TOCs irritated OPRAF which viewed the ORR's efforts as an incursion on its territory.

There are two conflicting views about how the existing system of dual regulation could be improved. On the one hand, it can be argued that OPRAF's consumer-protection measures should be transferred to the ORR to bring the rail industry's regulatory arrangements more in line with those of other industries. This option, which was my preference, should instil confidence in rail passengers as their well-being would be placed in the care of an independent authority legally required to promote the public interest rather than an agent of government. Alternatively, it would be possible to strip the Regulator of his remaining consumer-protection powers and transfer them all to the Franchising Director. This view is endorsed by some of the TOCs. As Christopher Garnett, Chief Executive of GNER, points out:

> *There has been an inconsistency in that things which have been with the*

Regulator really belong with OPRAF ... For example, why were the RUCCs and things like that with the Regulator? The Regulator should be there to regulate the Railtrack/TOC interface.

This approach is the one adopted by the current Labour government in its transport legislation. OPRAF is being merged with the remnants of the BRB to create the Strategic Rail Authority (SRA) – a recommendation of the Transport Select Committee, reconstituted after the May 1997 election – which will have wide-ranging powers over the private-sector railway companies. While this policy has been adopted with the best interests of the passenger at heart, it is in my view potentially dangerous as it may call into question the future role and value of independent regulation. It remains to be seen whether this "renationalisation", as Simon Jenkins has described it, will bring about a long-term improvement in the regulation of the railways.[16]

Third, it was very important to me that strong elements of transparency and accountability were introduced into all aspects of the policy-making process. Government departments are all too often seen as ivory towers behind which officials can hide away from the public gaze. Consultation with interested parties, including the public, preceded all major policy decisions and assisted the ORR greatly by exposing policy makers to a wide range of opinions and enabling them to make well-informed recommendations. It should be noted that I was careful to ensure that my decision making was influenced no more by interest groups than it was by the government; this would also have posed a threat to the ORR's independence. Although the majority view for any given policy option may have been *x*, I reserved the right to select *y* if I considered it was in the better public interest. For example, many train operators were critical of the fines levied on them for the poor performance of NRES, but not to have imposed a harsh penalty would have been tantamount to condoning that performance and it is doubtful whether recent improvements would have occurred.

In terms of specific policies, the ORR's approach to regulating Railtrack continually received most public and media attention. My policies require some justification, particularly in the light of current political and regulatory messages that they were not "tough enough". It was generally agreed that the most urgent issue facing the new railway at the time of privatisation was the need for investment, not only in new trains but also in the infrastructure. The ORR produced, through its review of Railtrack's access charges, a financial framework for that programme of renewal and also the regulatory rules which imposed some controls over the manner in which Railtrack deployed its funds. The structure we created was in my opinion right for the first phase of the privatisation process and produced clarity and transparency. The prospect of regulatory micro-management of investment – with each proposal being submitted to the Regulator for approval – would have introduced such a high regulatory risk as to have prevented the industry from providing its own solutions to passenger and freight demand. This, save where the State has a genuine interest in intervening (such as guaranteeing service levels), is the main purpose of privatisation and to have had the market almost entirely controlled by the State or the Regulator would have run contrary to that objective. In times of change it is often best to allow the new businesses, operating under the terms of engagement which their shareholders approved and bought into, to use their freedoms within the regulatory rules to manage their businesses independently. The precise role of the State in relation to the supply of passenger and freight rail services is still to be determined; although the creation of the SRA changes the institutional furniture, it does not necessarily resolve issues of policy or finance.

The regulatory system was effective. At the outset, it forced Railtrack to concentrate on reducing delays attributable to the company for the obvious reason that if it failed to do so it would pay large sums of money to operators. There was no reason to intervene further so long as the system was working. But Railtrack, in my view, "got greedy" sometime in 1997. It was being feted as a growth stock but its investment programme was still largely determined by renewal rather than enhancement: the company seemed reluctant to take new capital on to its balance sheet without absolute certainty of full return. Despite the existing programme of regulatory objectives, Railtrack became the cause of too many complaints regarding what I would call its lack of accountability. The existing system of regulation was put under strain and change – in the form of Condition 7 (see Chapter 3) – was needed to make Railtrack more accountable. Had the company behaved differently to its customers, had it been prepared to develop innovative programmes with the government and train operators with short franchises, then the imposition of Condition 7 might not have been necessary. The prevailing, and to my mind incorrect, view among officials at the time was that the existing regulatory matrix was sufficient and that Condition 7 was a retrograde step as it might undo the structure of the incentives to invest put in place at the time of privatisation.

The Labour government elected in May 1997 made clear its dissatisfaction with both the structure and, rightly, the performance of the new railway. I sought an early meeting with the new Deputy Prime Minister and Secretary of State for Transport, John Prescott, to explain the need to tighten the regulatory matrix through the introduction of the new Condition 7. The government was supportive on that issue but it was clear that it was looking for much greater institutional changes to reassert control and direction over what was perceived to be a disaggregated and leaderless railway. Those institutional changes could only be introduced through new legislation and it was not clear what priority would be given to the reform of the structure. In the meantime, in a period of serious political lack of focus on what could be achieved through the existing machinery, we had to work out how the new change to the regulatory matrix could be made to work. We formed the view that the train operators were not going to use the new licence condition to prosecute their serious if confidential complaints against Railtrack and that the government was lacking in any strategic view as to the future railway infrastructure it was prepared to finance beyond the period covered by the first financial settlement. Given that lack of pressure, we decided that we had to regulate for key performance indicators by enforcing Railtrack's obligations under Condition 7. That was the background to the decision to require Railtrack to improve its performance in respect of delays attributable and then to move to other key indicators such as track quality.

Railtrack reacted first with opposition but then realised, sensibly, that it was failing its customers in certain areas and also that it would have been difficult for those customers to have used the rights under the access contracts to achieve what they wanted. The requirement described in Chapter 4, that delays attributable to Railtrack must be reduced by 7.5 per cent a year, was agreed in this context. The new licence condition was also the means through which the Office could assist the Health and Safety Executive (HSE) in tightening up Railtrack's safety responsibilities in the event that it formed the view that its own sanctions needed reinforcing. However, the division of responsibilities as between the ORR and the HSE remained as before: the ORR complied with its duties under the relevant section of the Railways Act through the procedure agreed with the HSE at the beginning of the operation of the regulatory matrix. Condition 7 was seen to have teeth and I had no hesitation in using it.

A final point to make with regard to my policies on regulating Railtrack is that from 1997 until the time I left office, the company was in no doubt that the outcome of the current review of track-access charges (see Chapter 4) – which will affect the vast bulk of its revenues – would be critically dependent on its performance during the period following privatisation in which it had enjoyed relative freedom from governmental control. We put Railtrack on notice that we would be setting charges on a basis conventionally used for other regulated authorities – which included an assessment of the cost of capital and the regulatory asset base – and reminded the company that, as a monopoly, it had duties to serve its customers well and meet their requirements at a time of growth. Railtrack was made very aware that the review's outcome would only be favourable from its own perspective if it took heed of our reminder.

In making these points I have sought to avoid passing the buck. It fell to me to decide how, if at all, the regulatory regime should be changed after 1994, when the ORR first assumed its powers. I held the view that between 1994 and 1997, when the last of the TOCs, ScotRail, passed into private ownership, the new rail industry did not need the regulatory matrix re-examining save where a serious gap became apparent. To that extent the Office held back, reserved its position, declined to make waves, sought to clarify relations with former and new governments and enforced cases of actual and prospective breach of licence. It is my view that, by November 1998, at the end of my 5-year term, the rail industry displayed a far greater degree of maturity than was evident at the beginning of the privatisation process; that new, well-financed companies were committed to the provision of passenger and freight services; that the prospects for profitable expansion were far greater than before; and that the regulatory system had made a positive contribution to facilitating that situation.

The actions of the ORR – and, indeed, of all involved in the rail-privatisation process – have to be seen in the context of the circumstances in which our work was conducted. The method of rail privatisation adopted created enormous uncertainty and the job of OPRAF, the ORR and government officials was to ensure the system would function well enough to enable its transfer to the private sector. The intense pressures of time (there were less than 3 years in which to establish the entire regulatory and contractual matrix) and resources (all departments and offices were understaffed) meant that planning for the long term was, in many cases, difficult. That the restructured BR could be sold within the lifetime of one Parliament, with the required regulatory systems in place, is a remarkable achievement by all involved. But it is not in the least surprising that the current government has identified faults which need rectifying now that the dust has settled.

Acknowledgements

I am very grateful to Robert Pettigrew and Jon Shaw for their assistance during the writing of this chapter.

Notes

1. Explicit provisions to regulate service quality were not included in the plans to privatise BT and British Gas but, following complaints about standards, quality-of-service regulation including a financial liability scheme was formally established prior to the sale of the water and electricity industries.
2. The Regulator was keen to avoid a situation like this as it had led Nicholas Ridley to famously boast that the utilities are more easily controlled by government when they are in the private sector.
3. Office of the Rail Regulator. *Railtrack's Access Charges for Franchised Passenger Services: The Future Level of Charges*, ORR, 1995.
4. Littlechild, S. *The Regulation of British Telecommunications' Profitability*, Department of Industry, 1983.
5. Working with limited information from industry is a common problem for regulators.
6. Kleinwort Benson valued Railtrack at £3.3–£4.3 billion but, after the Regulator's policy statement, the market value was revised downwards to £2 billion.
7. Office of the Rail Regulator. *Regulatory Objectives for Passenger Train and Station Operators*, ORR, 1997.
8. *The Guardian*, 20 January 1993.
9. *House of Commons Papers*. Session 1992–93, 246i, 20 April.
10. The Franchising Director was given the responsibility for developing the policy of Compulsory Interavailability (see Chapter 6).
11. *Hansard*, **225**, Cols 156–255, 2 February 1993.
12. Swift, J. "Chairman's comments" in M. Beesley (ed.), *Regulating Utilities: A Time for Change?* Institute of Economic Affairs, 1996.
13. Office of the Rail Regulator. *Competition for Railway Passenger Services: A Consultation Document*, ORR, 1994.
14. MoC Stage 1 did not permit the nomination of "non-material" flows. These occur when a flow represents less than 0.2 per cent of a TOC's total farebox revenue. New entry on such flows was unlikely but, if it were to take place, it could not significantly affect the incumbent's overall income.

15. WAGN's action were taken as a result of a clause of the Compulsory Interavailability regulations rather than MoC. However, it was hoped that similar conditions might be created on other routes following the introduction of new services under a relaxation of MoC.

16. *The Times*, 9 July 1999.

10. New Directions for Britain's Railways

Bill Bradshaw

Railwaymen have a long history of making things work. The enormous contribution of the railways to the war effort in 1939–45, the way in which the industry fought its way through the fuel crisis and investment famine of the post-war years and the almost constant succession of reorganisations of the industry during the years of state ownership are testament to the adaptability of railway managers and staff. This ability to cope with change and still keep the trains running was perhaps put to its greatest test during the years of the Major government when, during a period of great financial stringency, managers in the industry were obliged to put in place the mechanisms for privatisation which would result in many of them losing their jobs. Privatisation has worked and will work principally because of the dedication and professionalism of these managers and staff. In this chapter I offer some personal thoughts about potential new directions in British railway policy. I will address three key questions: Was privatisation a necessary step in the development of our railways? Was the best method of privatisation adopted? And how should the industry now develop?

Was Rail Privatisation Necessary?

This question is easily disposed of. It would have been difficult to argue, especially following the privatisation of nearly all the other transport related industries, as well as the public utilities, that the railways should have remained in the public sector. There are two main reasons for this. First, the government could not but continually interfere in what were essentially managerial decisions, often in a way that was invisible to the public but was enormously inhibiting to efficient management. Fare rises, industrial-relations disputes, changes in services and orders for new trains and equipment were all examples of subjects upon which a constant stream of phone calls passed between government and the British Railways Board (BRB) and these were usually designed to protect or enhance political reputations rather than promote commercial or operational logic. Secondly, no government, at least in the current financial climate, would ever provide finance on the scale needed to reinvigorate the railway. There are always more politically important targets for public investment – e.g. schools and hospitals – which push railways towards the back of the queue. As other industries escaped these cloying influences it became more and more obvious that privatisation offered a better alternative than continued public ownership. But with the rail industry in need of continuing subsidy, the question was whether a mechanism could be devised to transfer both the management of the industry and the responsibility for raising the necessary investment to the private sector.

Was the Best Method of Privatisation Adopted?

The method of privatisation chosen by the Conservatives was certainly complex and the key reason for this was the decision to move from a vertically integrated organisation where operations, rolling stock and infrastructure are the responsibility of one company to the disintegrated solution of separate ownership of the various components of production. A primary reason for the break-up of the system was the desire to see competition in train operation but ministers also wanted to liberalise the rolling stock (including maintenance and major overhaul) and infrastructure services markets. This meant splitting many of the former BR activities into smaller parts and offering them for sale separately. In train operation, franchises were let, mostly for short periods of time and in defined regions, although frequently services with different speed and marketing characteristics on a particular line were divided between different operators. Emphasis was placed upon the fact that relatively short contracts would keep the franchisees on their toes. On-rail competition was advanced as another way of securing passenger benefits and, of course, as a main justification for the decision to create an infrastructure authority as the independent manager of the timetable and of day-to-day management of signalling and operational control.

There has been some competition in the supply of rolling stock which now often includes maintenance deals. But rolling-stock supply would probably have followed its present course whatever model of privatisation had been followed because the government was already seeking private-sector financing initiatives in public-sector organisations. However, it is unlikely that rolling-stock supplies would have worked efficiently in a state-owned industry as John Prideaux describes in his references to the Network Express saga (see Chapter 5). The current Deputy Prime Minister, John Prescott, had argued in opposition in favour of more leasing deals for the supply of rolling stock, particularly in the debate leading up to the closure of the rolling-stock works at York, but the government regarded these as financing deals and therefore within the scope of the Public Sector Borrowing Requirement (PSBR) (see Chapter 1).

In the field of engineering the initial number of companies offering services such as track maintenance and renewal has declined with the mergers and takeovers which have taken place since privatisation. Nine different companies bought the thirteen infrastructure and maintenance companies offered for sale at the time of privatisation. Through takeover and buyouts there are now five. There is still competition but a couple more mergers may blunt this and, as in the British bus industry, it is impossible to make big players compete if they show no inclination to do so because tacit collusion, except at the margins, is financially a more attractive policy (see Chapter 1).

True, there was competition in the bidding for passenger rail franchises, especially the later ones, but if these bids prove to have been optimistic in terms of the potential for revenue growth or for cost reduction, it remains to be seen who will actually suffer most as a result and whether the then Franchising Director and his well-paid advisers, admittedly under enormous political pressure, were foolish to have allowed this optimism to win the day. At least some of the franchises are now being renegotiated but it is difficult as yet to see how any genuine element of competition will be introduced into the franchise renegotiation process.

The whole concept of on-rail competition looks like being a damp squib. It was always difficult to accept the free marketeers' dream of the traveller turning up at Waterloo having a choice of a red, blue or green train to Woking with a choice of fares. But with franchisees understandably not keen to let in competitors and Railtrack not enthusiastic about squeezing more paths into the timetable, partly through fear of the possible effects on punctuality, there will only be few genuine opportunities to add services of value to the user. There will also be a temptation for operators to play games if the income sharing arrangements continue automatically to give a share of the revenue on a route to a new operator. It is to be hoped this distortion which arises from the computer system ORCATS, which allocates revenue between operators using a formula, will be removed as ticketing systems develop.

In the freight industry, ministers were forced to reintegrate the Trainload Freight companies after they found that a market for them as separate entities did not exist. Almost all of BR's freight business was sold to the consortium headed by Wisconsin Central Transportation and now operates as English, Welsh and Scottish Railway (EWS). However, as Julia Clarke explains in Chapter 8, there is some evidence that the threat of open-access operations is keeping EWS's prices considerably lower than they might otherwise be and this is to be welcomed from a freight customer's point of view.

So was all the tearing apart necessary? It cost huge amounts – some estimate around £600 million – just to set up the new railway and its running costs are still higher than they were under British Rail (BR). Privatisation should bring a net financial gain to the government before too long, but this is dependent on franchisees being able to fulfil their current contracts. It also takes no account of any efficiency gains BR or a different successor might have achieved. There has been only limited success in promoting competition. The myriad contractual relationships mean that any meeting between industry parties is likely to include lawyers and financiers where none would previously have been needed and railway professionals are not blind to the huge salary differentials between themselves and these professionals whom they have had to teach to do the job. The process of privatisation was drawn out over a long period, led to great uncertainty and created a hiatus in investment, especially in infrastructure and in new rolling stock.

But has the tearing apart benefited the user? In terms of coherence and accountability, it is unlikely. With BR it was clear who was responsible. The buck could not be passed and even after disasters such as the Clapham crash

BR quickly accepted the blame. By contrast 2 years after the Southall rail crash victims still await compensation. Many users are simply confused about with whom they are doing business and the record number of passenger complaints is probably much to do with frustration resulting from this. Train performance is still patchy with punctuality and reliability levels barely improved since the BR days (see Chapter 7). In part this is because of mistakes made by the TOCs such as shedding too many staff, but it is also to do with the considerable increase in services since privatisation. More trains has meant more congestion which in turn has resulted in more delays. The current access-charging regime gives Railtrack little incentive to alleviate the bottlenecks but, as the company has gained a reputation for underinvesting in its assets, there is no guarantee that it would spend more if its revenue increased.

Perhaps the most telling commentary on the tearing apart is the strong desire in many parts of the industry to reverse the process. This is evident in a wide range of examples, from the agreement between Virgin and Railtrack on the West Coast Main Line, where the infrastructure company has an equity interest in the success of the line's upgrading (see Chapter 4), to Railtrack seeking to train TOCs' staff to deal with minor incidents like lorries hitting bridges (as they always used to) rather than waiting for Railtrack staff to arrive from some distant centre to declare the line safe. The acquisition by Stagecoach, the owner of the South West Trains franchise, of the rolling-stock company Porterbrook, also introduced a degree of vertical reintegration (see Chapter 5).

Running an efficient railway is an immense team game where the user will only benefit if all the players work together to provide a satisfactory experience. Many of the discontinuities imported into the system during the dismembering process may make sense to those theorists seeking to introduce competition and to the professionals who advise them. But not only do they fail to produce effective competition, they are also contrary to the desire of the user who wants the seamless service which springs from co-operation.

In my opinion, the track-authority model chosen by the Conservatives was wrong for all these reasons. While some service improvements have undoubtedly been made, there would almost certainly have been more – at a significantly lower cost – had a different method of privatisation been used.

How the Industry Should Develop

Although there are problems with the track-authority model, future policy emphasis must be placed on working within the constraints of the present system rather than a full-scale reorganisation of the rail industry. Primarily this is because there has been too much reorganisation over recent decades. British railway managers have, in the words of Chris Green, Chief Executive of Virgin Trains, become world leaders at restructuring, but it is about time they were able to concentrate solely on running the trains. A key reason for the present system's weaknesses is that Railtrack has failed to take a strategic role in the development of the industry through its Network Management Statement which has to be prepared each year. The task of providing coherent leadership, embracing the whole industry, will pass to the Strategic Rail Authority, currently operating in shadow form, when the government's present Transport Bill receives Royal Assent. The SRA, under the chairmanship of Sir Alistair Morton, will replace the Office of Passenger Rail Franchising (OPRAF) and the BRB and assume some consumer-protection duties from the Rail Regulator. It will also have a role in the future development of rail freight. The track-authority model of rail privatisation can be made to work under the leadership of the Strategic Rail Authority (SRA) provided several key improvements are made in the areas of co-operation and competition, regulation and investment.

Co-operation and Competition

The emphasis on competition in the rail industry should be reduced. Although competition has a limited role to play, privatisation will work better if regulators, politicians and others continue to allow the industry to reintegrate those parts of the business where it can clearly be demonstrated that users will benefit. Companies should be allowed to seek economies of scale in their operations and reintegration might be vertical, horizontal or both. In terms of on-rail competition, it must be remembered that most railway users, apart from commuters travelling to London, do have the choice of other modes. One of the tasks of the Regulator is to protect captive customers from abusive behaviour and it may be better to rely on this mechanism rather than contrived competition which may or may not arise from the possibility of open access. The travellers to London must be protected from exploitation by the regulation of quality and fares. But rather than encouraging open-access competition it may well be more worthwhile to encourage, where the opportunity presents itself, the development of alternative competitive routes such as between Birmingham and London, and London and Scotland. These will also have the advantage of providing alternative routes when the most direct is unavailable. It will enable yardstick comparisons to be made and encourage the railway companies to focus on their real competitors, namely other transport modes.

Regulation

If competition is to take a back seat, then it is essential that tougher regulatory regimes are in place to protect consumers. One way of ensuring this might be for regulation to focus more upon the *outputs* which are desired rather than simply expenditure totals. Consideration would be given to targets such as the generation of passenger miles and freight tonne-miles with appropriate weightings being attached to those which are generated when busiest and most congested roads are under the greatest pressure. Existing output targets should also be clear and honest so that everyone understands what is being produced, even if this means that standards appear to fall in the short run. For example, punctuality should mean "on time" – rather than the current 5 or 10 minutes late – for all trains. In setting targets and indeed in such matters as revenue allocation between operators perverse incentives should be identified and rooted out.

Performance regimes are an area where perverse incentives are created. If large fines are imposed for unpunctuality then it is likely that Railtrack and Train Operating Companies (TOCs) will adopt defensive timetabling strategies with slower than achievable point-to-point running times and deliberate timing to miss connections at junctions. Neither of these outcomes are what the customer wants and it is likely that existing timetables actually waste track capacity by reducing the amount of paths which are available for alternative operators or for freight trains. It is important that performance measures address and encourage better outcomes for users, not simply measure what it is most simple to measure.

Decisions about safety, disabled access and other features which have significant cost implications should be taken more transparently with organisations such as the Health and Safety Executive (HSE) being required to justify both their own levels of expenditure and the cost and potential benefits of the recommendations which they make. It would also be informative if they were to show intermodal comparisons of safety standards and costs. In the end the consumer will pay for these decisions and people have a right to know all the implications of recommendations.

One of the features of rail privatisation which is the least satisfactory is the monopoly status of Railtrack. While Railtrack may hold competitions between suppliers of infrastructure equipment and services it is very difficult for an external agent such as the Regulator to know whether the expenditure levels quoted in its Network Management Statement represent value for money. It would be ideal to reach a situation where instead of telling Railtrack how much money it should spend it was possible to specify outputs in terms of infrastructure quality and capability which it should achieve. This might mean that the Regulator would require average journey times to fall by, say, 5 per cent over the coming 5 years.

The Regulator has employed the consultants Booz Allen & Hamilton to investigate the efficiency of Railtrack's spending but it is difficult to be as satisfied as one might be if Railtrack were divided, with comparisons available between different organisations in the same field of business activity.[1] Whether in the end this conundrum can be solved without breaking up Railtrack is uncertain, although any break-up of the company might herald the regrouping of the railway into vertically integrated entities. There is also the charge levied by former EWS Chief Ed Burkhart that the cost of maintaining the freight railway in Britain is far higher than in the United States. Bearing in mind the fact that similar comments about the costs of domestic wagon building proved to be well founded, the issue deserves consideration and maybe some thought should be given to the possibility of transferring the responsibility for maintaining some "freight only" lines to the operator.

The Need for Investment

The increasing use being made of the railways in the last few years is being cited both as a measure of the success of privatisation and as a reason for the overcrowding, infrastructure failure and other shortcomings in the standard of service being provided. It is important to see the increased use in an historical context and in relation to movements in the economy more generally as there is a close correlation between GDP and the use of the railways.[2] Yet other factors which have a bearing on railway use are the relative costs of train travel and motoring and the worsening congestion on the road network. One of the by-products of the privatisation process was, of course, the imposition of caps on some rail fares and, as Christian Wolmar showed in Chapter 7, these will probably have an increasing impact over the years if they remain in place. It is also likely, given the drastic scaling down of the road-building programme, that the road network will become more congested for longer periods and over greater distances and this may be having an effect on rail use. All TOCs require growth in passenger numbers – some more than others – if they are to remain profitable and increased investment in both infrastructure and rolling stock will be of paramount importance if their aspirations are to be met.

In the freight business it is reported that there is significant overcapacity in road haulage. Considerable pressure to reduce haulage costs is being exerted on government by lobby groups such as the Road Haulage Association to seek cuts in Vehicle Excise Duty and diesel-fuel taxes so that they are nearer to European levels and also to allow lorry weights to increase to 44 tonnes (see Chapter 8). Both EWS and Freightliner have seen growth since privatisation and the companies have invested heavily. However, the likelihood of these businesses winning substantial traffic from road will depend upon their only being called upon to pay very low track-access charges. It will require incentives to be offered to customers and terminal operators, many of whom have never used rail, to adapt to using trains. What privatisation has achieved is a much more positive attitude towards freight as well as the substantial investment in new locomotives and wagons. But there still remains the problem of fitting freight trains into an increasingly congested network at times when the freight needs to be moved and to find the money necessary to meet the costs of new freight infrastructure both on the track and at terminals. Much of this spending will need to come from public funds and will require justification in social cost-benefit terms. Freight is not out of intensive care yet but the resuscitation team are hard at work and the undertaker has been sent back home.

Sir Alastair Morton, Chairman-to-be of the SRA, recently described his priorities as investment, investment and investment. Whilst many users might have hoped to see the word "quality" included, Morton's message was basically sound. But before the SRA even thinks about where this money will come from, it needs to address two prickly administrative problems. The first is that investing in the railways takes so long. There are monstrous delays which now face any scheme as it trundles through the seemingly interminable process of consultation, planning, more consultation, public inquiry, appeal, judicial review, tendering, protest and implementation. Hopefully the new Transport and Works Act procedures will shorten this process and every effort should be made to see that they do, otherwise the delays in dealing with the bottlenecks on the railway will lead to high levels of dissatisfaction and renewed demands for further road building.[3]

Secondly, a distinction needs to be made between investment – which in most people's definition means the acquisition of new assets – and more routine expenditure on the repair, maintenance and replacement in up-to-date form of existing assets. This distinction applies particularly to track, signalling, structures (such as bridges and tunnels) and stations. Even in BR days the distinction between investment and maintenance was blurred with, for example, the replacement of jointed track with continuous welded rail being treated in some years as a capital item and in others as revenue expenditure. In the case of rolling stock, new trains would always count as investment but overhaul counts as revenue expenditure with major refurbishment being in the contentious area. The new railway urgently needs investment in the sense of expenditure which adds to the capability and capacity of the network, and both Morton and the Rail Regulator, Tom Winsor, are keen to see this.

Sources of Investment

Finance for new investment in the railways is likely to come from four main sources. These are Railtrack, TOCs and Roscos, public funds and the farebox. There has been some discussion of the limit of such finance and the answer is that there is no limit other than that the market should be satisfied that the railway can generate sufficient revenue to meet the cost of the capital. This financial capacity is one of the potential gains of privatisation because even in good times in the past it was rarely possible for the railway to persuade the Treasury to meet its investment needs.

It is important that the cost of borrowing capital to improve the railway should be kept as low as reasonably possible, a fact very recently acknowledged by the Rail Regulator. The cost of capital can be driven up by regulatory uncertainty, by political risks and by the imposition of unreasonable cost burdens on the railways in respect of issues such as safety and disabled access where very marginal improvements can be extremely expensive to achieve. It would be possible for Railtrack to borrow extensively on the strength of its balance sheet provided investors are satisfied that future revenue streams are strong and certain enough to support this debt. The necessary funds will come from existing track-access charges (much of this source is, of course, underwritten by the Treasury), revenue-sharing deals with operators or public/private partnerships with the SRA (see below).

The second source of investment funds is the TOCs and Roscos. Whilst there has been considerable investment in rolling stock and some other improvements in security and information systems, many of the passenger companies have short franchises and are already coming to the end of the initial expenditure programmes to which they committed themselves. Rolling-stock manufacturers now talk about the potential for another hiatus in orders like that between 1993 and 1996.[4] In spite of the fact that one of the reasons advanced for establishing the Roscos was that they could take a long-term view of investment (see Chapter 5), it is claimed by some franchisees, notably GNER, that it is not possible in the remaining years of their contracts to order and take delivery of new trains to supplement their overstretched fleets. This argument is proving particularly strong where a franchisee needs rolling stock which is not readily transferable to another franchise area because it has a higher residual-value risk. The same problems apply to any infrastructure works with long payback periods, such as new stations or major car-park extensions, to which franchisees were expected to contribute.

The potential for such investment pauses was always a weakness of the franchises as they were let and now it is necessary to address the subject of premature franchise renewal to keep investment flowing. There is no doubt that some franchisees are willing to commit themselves to significant programmes if they are allowed extensions. The difficulty is that some operators will not surrender a franchise early and allow open competitive bidding for renewal. In the absence of such competition any negotiator, acting in the public interest, will find it difficult to satisfy critics that the best bargain has been obtained for the user and the taxpayer.

In this latter context it is also important to be clear about what constitutes a good deal for the taxpayer. While in very simple terms this can be defined as the lowest subsidy or highest premium which meets the specification set out by the Franchising Director, there is no doubt that many interest groups will be seeking higher quality standards as opposed to best bids judged in purely financial terms. The government, with its commitments in the 1998 White Paper, is proposing alternative transport options to reduce dependence on the motor car such as road pricing, congestion charging, pollution controls, taxation of private non-residential parking and green commuter plans. It is most unlikely that any of these policies will prove politically acceptable without a sea change in the quality of public transport. The Franchising Director has already published criteria for evaluation of bids but many quality features are not easily amenable to economic assessment and a degree of pragmatism will be required in assessment. This is difficult territory for public officials and requires a clear statement of objectives and decision criteria.

The renegotiation of some franchises offers the possibility of new rolling stock, improved levels of service, new stations and, through revenue-sharing deals with Railtrack such as that agreed to fund the West Coast Main Line upgrade, new lines, better line speeds and a range of other amenities. It will also be an opportunity to include within the contract a number of features which were ignored in the first franchise round such as station staffing and security, cleanliness and adequacy of car and cycle parking. It was believed at the time of franchising that the new private-sector companies would, as a matter of course, keep trains and stations clean, employ sufficient staff to sell tickets and staff stations and would be concerned about providing secure storage of cars and bicycles. This assumption has proved to be wrong and renegotiation will almost certainly seek to impose minimum standards in these areas. It is clear that what is not in the contract cannot be demanded and that cost reduction still ranks very high in the priorities of some franchisees despite evidence from others that such investments are worthwhile. However, renegotiation does offer a real opportunity to draw in more investment funds and while it may be difficult to rank bids in purely financial terms it will be possible to compare best practice and set benchmarks of quality and attempt to secure commitments to ratchet up standards. Thus strong pressure can be brought upon management, companies and shareholders who fail to deliver in a form of yardstick competition.

Some other franchisees may have to admit they have committed themselves to impossible targets and, while it may be tempting to squeeze these companies until the pips squeak, it will be difficult to do this and not hurt the customers and potential customers of these companies. So some franchises may be available for reallocation, possibly being broken up into more sensible businesses in the process. The original division of the railway into twenty-five franchises should not be regarded as immutable and it is most unlikely that decisions taken in such haste when the original franchises were let, represent the best that can be achieved. It is probably not wise, now that the industry has been privatised, to allow the state to step in to run TOCs as this would introduce a climate of some uncertainty and distort the franchising market, although some small and remote parts of the railway would be better operated as local units. Some form of micro-franchising should be given a chance to prove whether better value can be achieved.

The third main source of investment is public funds. The SRA will have some money to spend on passenger rail partnerships and freight. In addition, it is proposed to give the SRA some borrowing power as well as accommodation for taking over outstanding liabilities of the BRB. This covers such items as obligations under the Channel Tunnel agreement and claims for injuries from former employees. There are in addition other funds which the SRA may seek to acquire. Many franchisees will soon be paying a premium for their franchises. Under the Railways Act 1993 this money flows directly to the Treasury while a completely separate flow of funds is paid by the Treasury to the Franchising Director with which to fund the unprofitable franchises. This has the effect of exacting a "tax" paid by the users of profitable franchises. This has been reported as amounting to £20 per journey on first-class passengers travelling between Manchester and London by the new Virgin Trains services when these are established. Such "taxes" will reduce the use of rail and seem to sit ill with policies to discourage people from using their cars. A fairly strong case can be argued for investing the income from franchise premia in the network, especially in the development of diversionary routes and additional capacity to make the network more robust against inevitable interruptions. Strengthening the dependability of the railway will certainly make it more attractive.

Another source of public funds is the replacement for the fuel-tax escalator. Although the new levy is to be more ad hoc than its predecessor, any real increase will be hypothecated to transport. Thinking railway people will have ready a programme of improvements which will appeal particularly to motorists in respect of that part of the proceeds which are to be hypothecated to improving public transport.

Local authorities, the Scottish Parliament and the Welsh Assembly may also provide some funding although this is likely to be marginal unless local authorities are able to raise substantial amounts of money from local road pricing. There have been suggestions that some schemes like Crossrail could be funded by capital raised in the City of London.[5] The improvement of the rail network around Edinburgh is likely to be funded from grant paid through the Scottish Executive and the local authorities. A positive attitude to planning matters by local authorities can be very helpful in moving schemes ahead.

The public funds which are available will need to be used to lever in the maximum amount of private money and great skill will be needed to ensure that the leverage is used to greatest effect. This is the essence of negotiation of public/private partnerships. One danger which arises when public money is committed to investment is that the schemes become subject to the same scrutiny and second guessing by government officials as was the case with BR and before long it would be easy to see the proxy management from Whitehall being re-established. The rules for the proposed private-funding partnerships will have to be written to ensure that this does not happen. It will be important that risk sharing is properly defined and that the focus is upon responsibility for delivering measurable outputs.

Finally, in the search for additional investment funds, one area which may need to be revisited is fares regulation, which places a strict limit on the extent to which ticket prices can be raised to pay for service improvements. In BR days the Treasury always insisted that fares should be raised following modernisation and some steep rises in real terms were recorded. If fares cannot be raised then the extra revenue needed to fund investment must be raised from carrying more passengers or from higher levels of efficiency. The government must be clear about fares policy. Does it want a large proportion of fares to remain capped so that rail becomes a more attractive alternative to other modes? What will its attitude be to cases where significant investment delivers upgrades in quality? Obviously such decisions are vital in evaluating future investment.

Whatever the source of investment funds, the future of the railway needs planning in a coherent and strategic way and the role of the SRA will be central here. The capability of the core network and diversionary routes needs to be specified in terms of intensity of use, train speeds, axle weights, connectional patterns, train lengths and so on in order that developments and investment proceed towards a coherent target. One possible use of public funds is to pay the extra cost of creating capacity for future use, the payment for which may be deferred until traffic levels rise. Many railway schemes in the past have been engineered and equipped for present rather than potential levels of activity. The Treasury used to work from the principle that excess levels of demand could be priced off, but such a policy would be inconsistent with the new direction of transport policy outlined in the 1998 White Paper.

New Directions for the Railways

Privatisation of the railways will work because it has to. There is now no realistic prospect of renationalisation and even if the money were available it would be difficult to argue a case for such a reversion.

Britain has no National Transport Plan. There is no plan to increase road capacity, no airports plan, no ports plan and no plan to develop railway capacity. In the latter respect Britain is at the opposite end of the spectrum from, say, Switzerland, where for the last 15 years the country has been working, with popular support expressed through referenda, towards its Rail 2000 plan. This has produced investment in new infrastructure and new trains providing a network of connecting rail and bus services covering the whole country. These services run at hourly intervals throughout the country and are half-hourly between the main centres. Three times as many journeys per head of population are made by rail in Switzerland as in Britain. The challenge facing the SRA is to produce the coherence evident in Switzerland's rail policy in a perilously short timescale. This requires a vision of a public-transport strategy and a mechanism for delivery to be incorporated into the current refranchising process.

The Labour Party is on the horns of a dilemma. It recognises that it is necessary to provide decent modern public services whether it involves the London Underground, National Air Traffic Services, the railways or the National Health Service. The Treasury wants to maintain a very tight control over current public spending and is willing to look to the private sector to finance as much capital expenditure as possible even where the cost of capital exceeds, as it invariably must, the cost of public borrowing. Part of the justification for this policy is that the private sector will deliver the investment more efficiently and will bear the risk of failure. But the policy will be undeliverable unless politicians avoid constantly revisiting and changing the parameters of schemes (such as fare levels, safety conditions or the scope of plans). If such discipline can be achieved after one review – of the the kind suggested in this chapter – has taken place, this will be advantageous and may result in investment being delivered more quickly and cheaply. Labour's biggest problem is convincing its own supporters of the merits of a "hands off" policy.

In respect of the railways, we have moved from a Conservative Party approach in the mid-1990s which saw the industry as a problem which needed to be contained within a decreasing subsidy level and no significant expansion was foreseen. An almost unprecedented rise in demand for rail services has led to a revision of the industry's prospects and the change of government has created a more favourable climate for railway expansion even though, as yet, there has been no extra public expenditure on the industry over and above the plans inherited from the Conservatives. The refranchising process will determine the contribution needed from public funds over the next 10–20 years to meet public aspirations and it is likely that this money will be found either within existing funds or from the supplement on the fuel duty which will replace the "escalator". The key task for the franchise renegotiators is to use these funds to lever in several times as much from the private sector as comes from the public purse. Freight will continue to need support both to pay for realistic track-access charges and to offset the high cost of transhipment of goods between road and rail. This financial support will be justified by pointing to savings in lorry miles on the increasingly congested road network.

The lack of willpower on the part of governments to impose any effective form of road pricing on the motorway and trunk-road network will lead to such bad traffic conditions by 2010, with congestion rising by over 250 per cent above 1996 levels, that more passengers and freight will be obliged to look as an alternative to the railways. Expanding rail capacity will in many cases prove cheaper and more acceptable than road building and will allow the government to spend money on railways without risking unpopularity. The recent propaganda of the roads lobby about the "persecuted motorist" may well have discouraged politicians from adopting congestion charging, which is the only policy capable of providing a rational use of road space. Instead, it is likely that no traffic management policies will be adopted and the problems on the road will continue to worsen. We have reached the position of paralysis in roads policy, with every attempt to manage capacity efficiently being condemned, usually illogically, by the roads lobby. The populist press is encouraging this tendency. Perhaps ironically, such an approach will strengthen the competitive position of rail, particularly if train operators have the sense to provide adequate car parking and standards of service acceptable to the motorist.

It will greatly assist the competitive position of the railways if the Strategic Rail Authority and the Rail Regulator try to ensure that the incentive structures of the participants in the industry are aligned to produce attractive standards of service. There will continue to be a need to keep a tight watch on the providers of rail services abusing monopolistic positions and the opportunity should be taken both to set enforceable quality parameters within franchises and to encourage competition on parallel routes. This will become possible as some closed or downgraded routes are reinstated.

Almost by accident the railways stand on the verge of an era of opportunity. The industry is fractured, it lacks a coherent business strategy and its assets are in poor shape. Yet the market prospects look as strong as they have been in living memory. Some restructuring and a partnership between the SRA and the private sector has a better than even chance of revitalising the industry.

Notes

1. *Railtrack's Performance in the Control Period 1995–2001*. A confidential report for the Office of the Rail Regulator, parts of which were quoted in the media.
2. Nash, C. and Preston, J. "Franchising rail services" in A. Harrison (ed.), *From Hierarchy to Contract*, Transaction Books, 1993; Owen, A. and Phillips, G. "The characteristics of railway passenger demand" in *Journal of Transport of Economics and Policy*, **21**, 1987.
3. The procedures brought into force under the Transport and Works Act 1992 aim to simplify the procedures relating to infrastructure development, particularly enabling Parliament to vote on schemes of national significance at an early stage and avoid the costs and delays associated with the private-bill process.
4. *Rail*, No. 370, 17–30 November 1999.
5. The Crossrail scheme proposes to build an underground, heavy rail link from London Liverpool Street to Paddington to enable mainline through services between Essex/East Anglia and the Home Counties and vice versa.

Bibliography

The lists below detail numerous books, academic articles, policy documents and other sources of information about rail privatisation. The lists are by no means exhaustive, but they do provide a useful starting point for researchers and interested readers.

Adam Smith Institute (1983) *The Omega Report: Transport Policy*, Adam Smith Institute, London.

Adamson, M., Jones, W. and Pratt, R. (1991) 'Competition issues in privatisation: Lessons for the railways', in D. Banister and K. Button (eds), *Transport in a Free Market Economy*, Macmillan, London.

Bradshaw, W. (1991) 'A review of policies for the future of Britain's railways', paper presented to the Railways Study Association, 13 November, London.

Bradshaw, W. (1996) 'The privatization of railways in Britain', *Japan Railway and Transport Review* September 1996, 15–21.

Bradshaw, W. (1996) 'The real costs of rail privatisation', *Public Transport Information* September/October 1996, 8–9.

Bradshaw, W. (1997) 'Competition in the rail industry', *Oxford Review of Economic Policy* 13(1), 93–102.

Bristow, A., Preston, J. and Nash, C. (1998) 'Investment planning and appraisal issues in the privatised railway – the British experience', *Transport Reviews* 18(4), 353–362.

Campbell Bannerman, D. (1993) *Levelling the Tracks – Using Rail Privatisation to Right an Historical Imbalance*, The Bow Group, London.

Charlton, C., Gibb, R. and Lowndes, T. (1995) 'Rail privatization and local authority reorganization', *Journal of Transport Geography* 3(3), 221–226.

Charlton, C., Gibb, R. and Shaw, J. (1997) 'Regulation and continuing monopoly on Britain's railways', *Journal of Transport Geography* 5(2), 147–153.

Cumbers, A. and Farrington, J. (2000) 'Keeping privatisation on track: The active state, the unwilling investor and the case of railfreight in the UK', *Area*, forthcoming.

Curwen, P. (1997) 'The end of the line for British Rail', *Public Money and Management* 17(4), 55–67.

Department of the Environment, Transport and the Regions (1998) *Developing an Integrated Transport Policy: Factual Background*, DETR, London.

Department of the Environment, Transport and the Regions (1998) *A New Deal for Transport: Better for Everyone*, DETR, London.

Department of Transport (1992) *New opportunities for Britain's Railways*, Cmnd 2012, HMSO, London.

Department of Transport (1992) *The Franchising of Passenger Rail Services: A Consulation Document*, Department of Transport, London.

Department of Transport (1992) *Railway Privatisation: A Voice for the Passenger*, Department of Transport, London.

Department of Transport (1993) *Railway Privatisation: Passenger Rolling Stock*, Department of Transport, London.

Department of Transport (1993) *Gaining Access to the Railway Network: The Government's Proposals*, Department of Transport, London.

Department of Transport (1993) *Railway Pensions after Privatisation: The Government's proposals*, Department of Transport, London.

Department of Transport (1993) *Rail Freight Privatisation: The Government's Proposals*, Department of Transport, London.

Department of Transport (1994) *Britain's Railways: A New Era*, Department of Transport, London.

Department of Transport (1996) *Transport. The Way Forward*, Department of Transport, London.

Dnes, A. (1993) 'Franchising passenger rail', *Scottish Journal of Political Economy* 40(4), 420–433.

Dodgson, J. (1989) 'Privatising Britain's railways: Lessons from the past?, *Discussion Papers in Economics* Number 59, University of Liverpool.

Dodgson, J. (1994) 'Railway privatization', in M. Bishop, J. Kay and C. Mayer (eds), *Privatization and Economic Performance*, Oxford University Press, London.

Else, P. (1996) 'Subsidy requirements in a restructured rail network: with particular reference to British Rail', *Transport Policy* 3(1/2), 13–15.

Economic Research Centre (1993) *Report of the Ninetieth Round Table of Transport Economics*, held in Paris on 4–5 February 1993 on the following topic: Privatisation of railways, European Conference of Ministers of Transport, Paris.

Fawcett, P. (1997) *The Railways Act in Practice: A Guide to the Provisions and Definitions of the Railway Privatisation Legislation*, TR&IN, Huddersfield.

Foster, C (1994) *The Economics of Rail Privatisation*, Centre for the Study of Regulated Industries, London.

Freeman, R. (1993) 'Opportunities for the private sector', speech given to *Financial Times* Conference on the economics of rail privatisation', London, 22 November.

Gibb, R., Lowndes, T. and Charlton, C. (1996) 'The privatization of British Rail', *Applied Geography* 16(1), 35–51.

Gibb, R., Shaw, J. and Charlton, C. (1998) 'Competition, regulation and the privatisation of British Rail', *Environment and Planning C: Government and Policy* 16(6), 757–768.

Glaister, S. and Travers, T. (1993) *New Directions for British Railways? The Political Economy of Privatisation and Regulation*, Institute of Economic Affairs, London.

Grantham, A. (1998) 'Privatisation and reorganisation: Case studies in rail policy implementation', unpublished PhD thesis, University of East Anglia.

Gritten, A (1998) *Reviving the railways: A Victorian future?*, Centre for Policy Studies, London.

Harman, R. (1993) 'Railway privatization: Does it bring new opportunities?', *Public Money and Management* January–March, 19–25.

Harris, N. (1999) 'Competitive strategies for railways in the UK: A corporate perspective', *Transport Reviews* 19(2), 191–202.

Harris, N. and Godward, E. (1997) *The Privatisation of British Rail*, The Railway Consultancy, London.

Helm, D. (1996) 'Putting the railways back together again: Rail privatisation, franchising and regulation', in M. Beesley (ed.), *Regulating Utilities: A Time for Change?*, Institute of Economic Affairs, London.

Helm, D. and Thompson, D. (1991) 'Privatised transport infrastructure and incentives to invest', *Journal of Transport Economics and Policy* 25(3), 231–246.

Henshaw, D. (1991) *The Great Railway Conspiracy*, Leading Edge, North Yorkshire.

House of Commons (1993) *Railways Act 1993*, HMSO, London.

Irvine, K (1987) *The Right Lines*, Adam Smith Institute, London.

Jenkins, S. (1995) *Accountable to None: The Tory Nationalization of Britain*, Penguin, London.

Jones, I., Marks, P. and Willis, C. (1993) *Franchising Passenger Rail Services*, National Economic Research Associates, London.

Joy, S. (1998) 'Public and private railways', *Journal of Transport Economics and Policy* 32(1), 27–49.

Kennedy, D. (1995) *Competition in the British Rail Industry*, Regulatory Brief 6, Chartered Institute of Public Finance and Accountancy, London.

Knill, C. and Lehmkuhl, D. (1998) 'An alternative route of legal integration: The Community's railways policy', *European Integration Online Papers* 2(3), 1–18. Online at: http://eiop.or.at/eiop/texte/1998-003a.htm

Knowles, R. (1998) 'Passenger rail privatization in Great Britain and its implications, especially for urban areas', *Journal of Transport Geography* 6(2), 117–133.

Knowles, R. and Farrington, J. (1998) 'Why has the market not been created for Channel Tunnel regioanl passenger services?', *Area* 30(4), 359–366.

Lowndes, T. (1997) 'Privatisation, rural railways and community development', unpublished PhD thesis, University of Plymouth.

Mountford, R. (1996) 'Roscos: Private sale of the year', *Privatisation Yearbook, 1996*, HMSO, London.

Nash, C. (1990) *Role of Rail in Future Transport Policy*, Transport and Society Discussion Paper No. 12, Rees Jefferys Road Fund, Oxford.

Nash, C. (1993) 'Rail privatisation in Britain', *Journal of Transport Economics and Policy* 27(3), 317–322.

Nash, C. and Preston, J. (1992) *Barriers to Entry in the Railway Industry*, Working Paper 354, Institute for Transport Studies, University of Leeds.

Nash, C. and Preston, J. (1993) 'Franchising rail services', in A. Harrison (ed.), *From Hierarchy to Contract*, Transaction Books, Oxford.

Nash, C. and Preston, J. (1994) 'Railway performance – How does Britain compare?', *Public Money and Management* 14(4), 47–53.

National Audit Office (1996) *The Award of the First Three Passenger Rail Franchises*, The Stationery Office, London.

National Audit Office (1998) *The Flotation of Railtrack*, The Stationery Office, London.

National Audit Office (1998) *Privatisation of the Rolling Stock Leasing Companies*, The Stationery Office, London.

Powell, T. (1997) *The Prospects for the Franchised Railway*, Save Our Railways, London.

Preston, J. (1996) 'The economics of British Rail privatization: An assessment', *Transport Reviews* 16(1), 1–21.

Preston, J. (1997) *The Privatisation of Passenger Rail Services: Analysis and Monitoring*, Transport Studies Unit, University of Oxford.

Preston, J., Whelan, G. and Wardman, M. (1999) 'An analysis of the potential for on-track competition in the British passenger rail industry', *Journal of Transport Economics and Policy* 33(1), 77–94.

Redwood, J. (1988) *Signals from a Railway Conference*, Centre for Policy Studies, London.

Salveson, P. (1996) *Out of the Sidings: A Radical Approach to Rail Policy*, TR&IN, Huddersfield.

Shaw, J. (1999) 'Privatising Britain's passenger railway: Expectations and outcomes of the 'free' market approach', unpublished PhD thesis, University of Plymouth.

Shaw, J., Charlton, C. and Gibb, R. (1998) 'The competitive spirit re-awakens the ghost of railway monopoly', *Transport Policy* 5(1), 37–49.

Shaw, J. (2000) 'Competition in the British passenger rail industry: Prospects and problems', *Transport Reviews*, forthcoming.

Shires, J., Preston, J., Nash, C. and Wardman, M. (1994) *Rail Privatisation: The Economic Theory*, Working Paper 419, Institute for Transport Studies, Leeds.

Shires, J., Preston, J., Nash, J. and Wardman, M. (1994) *Rail Privatisation: The Practice. An Analysis of Seven Case Studies*, Working Paper 420, Institute for Transport Studies, Leeds.

Snowdon, P. (1993) 'Privatising British Rail', *Public Money and Management* October–December, 4–5.

Starkie, D. (1984) 'BR – Privatisation without tears', *Economic Affairs* October–December, 16–17.

Starkie, D. (1993) 'Train service co-ordination in a competitive market', *Fiscal Studies* 14(2), 53–64.

Steer Davies Gleave (1993) *Rail Privatisation: A Way Forward*, Railway Industry Association, London.

Stittle, J. (1996) 'The use of modern equivalent asset values in UK rail privatization', *Public Money and Management* January–March, 59–64.

Transport 2000 (1989) *Rails for Sale? The Privatisation of British Rail*, Transport 2000, London.

Truelove, P. (1991) 'Movement towards the privatisation of British Rail', in K. Button and D. Pitfield (eds), *Transport Deregulation: An International Movement*, Macmillan, London.

van de Velde, D. (1999) *Changing Trains. Railway Reform and the Role of Competition: The Experience of Six Countries*, Ashgate, Aldershot.

Wadsworth, B. (1994) 'British railways case study', in R. Kopicki and L. Thompson (eds), *Best Methods of Railway Restructuring and Privatisation*, CFS Discussion Paper Series No. 111, World Bank, Washington, DC.

Welsby, J. and Nicholls, A. (1999) 'Rail privatisation: An insider's view', *Journal of Transport Economics and Policy* **33**(1), 55–76.

White, P. (1998) 'Rail privatization in Britain', *Transport Reviews* **18**(2), 109–130.

Williams, C. (1992) *Can Competition Come to the Railways?*, Centre for the Study of Regulated Industries, London.

Wolmar, C. (1996) *The Great British Railway Disaster*, Ian Allen Publishing, Shepperton.

Wolmar, C. (1998) *Stagecoach: A Classic Rags to Riches Tale at the Frontiers of Capitalism*, Orion Books, London.

Zahariadis, N. (1996) 'Selling British Rail: An idea whose time has come?', *Comparative Political Studies* **29**(4), 400–422.

Other Useful References

Debates in the House of Commons relating to rail privatisation are found in *Hansard*. Some key dates are:

1992
- Vol. 211, Cols 971–986, 14 July
- Vol. 213, Cols 1,160–1,233, 29 October

1993
- Vol. 216, Cols 771–889, 12 January
- Vol. 218, Cols 156–255, 2 February
- Vol. 225, Cols 585–727, 24 May
- Vol. 231, Cols 38–125, 156–316, 419–451 and 625, 1, 2, 3 and 5 November

The Transport Select Committee's two reports on *The Future of the Railways in the Light of the Government's White Paper Proposals*, along with the Government's response, are published as *House of Commons Papers*. The Second Report is a huge document, containing a formidable amount of gathered evidence:
- First Report: Session 1992–1993, 375, 13 January
- Second Report: Session 1992–1993, 246-I, 20 April

The Government's response to the Second Report is:
- Session 1992–1993, 685, 19 May

The Transport Select Committee's report on *Railway Finances* is also relevant:
- Session 1994–1995, 206, 5 July

The tortuous progress of the Railways Bill through its Committee stages in 1993 is also published in the *House of Commons Papers* collection.

A quarterly *Bulletin of Rail Statistics* is available from the DETR. OPRAF (currently the SSRA) and the ORR publish many documents between them relating to all aspects of their work.

Trade journals such as *Rail, Modern Railways, The Railway Magazine, Railway Gazette, International and Rail Privatisation News/Rail Business Intelligence*, along with broadsheet newspapers such as *The Times, The Daily Telegraph, The Guardian, The Financial Times, The Independent, The Economist* and *The New Statesman* are also excellent sources information. Refer to the above titles from Autumn 1988 for the majority of articles regarding the progress of the rail privatisation project.

Index